PREPARING EFFECTIVE BUSINESS PLANS

AN ENTREPRENEURIAL APPROACH

Bruce R. Barringer, Ph.D.

Department of Management
University of Central Florida

PEARSON
Prentice
Hall

UPPER SADDLE RIVER, NEW JERSEY 07458

Library of Congress Cataloging-in-Publication Data

Barringer, Bruce R.
   Preparing effective business plans : an entrepreneurial approach / Bruce R. Barringer.
      p. cm.
   Includes index.
   ISBN 0-13-231832-6
   1. Business planning.   2. Entrepreneurship.   3. New business enterprises—
Planning.   4. Small business—Planning.   I. Title.

   HD30.28.B36837 2009
   658.4'01—dc22

                                                                            2007047120

Editor-in-Chief: *David Parker*
Acquisitions Editor: *Jennifer M. Collins*
Product Development Manager: *Ashley Santora*
Editorial Assistant: *Elizabeth Davis*
Marketing Assistant: *Ian Gold*
Associate Managing Editor: *Suzanne Grappi*
Project Manager, Production: *Ann Pulido*
Permissions Project Manager: *Charles Morris*
Senior Operations Supervisor: *Arnold Vila*
Operations Specialist: *Carol O'Rourke*
Senior Art Director: *Janet Slowik*
Cover Design: *Karen Quigley*
Cover Photo: *Angelo Cavalli/Digital Vision/Getty Images*
Composition: *ICC Macmillan Inc.*
Full-Service Project Management: *Leo Kelly/ICC Macmillan Inc.*
Printer/Binder: *STP/RR Donnelley/Harrisonburg*
Typeface: *10/12 Times Ten Roman*

Credits and acknowledgments borrowed from other sources and reproduced, with
permission, in this textbook appear on appropriate page within text.

Pearson Education Ltd., London   Pearson Education Australia PTY, Limited
Pearson Education Singapore, Pte. Ltd.   Pearson Education North Asia Ltd.
Pearson Education, Canada, Ltd.   Pearson Educación de Mexico, S.A. de C.V.
Pearson Education–Japan   Pearson Education Malaysia, Pte. Ltd.

10 9 8 7 6 5 4 3 2 1
ISBN-13: 978-0-13-231832-7
ISBN-10: 0-13-231832-6

Dedication

To my wife Jan, my best friend

BRIEF CONTENTS

CONTENTS

PREFACE

THE SURGE IN INTEREST IN ENTREPRENEURSHIP ON COLLEGE CAMPUSES AND BEYOND

There is tremendous interest in entrepreneurship on college campuses and around the world. In academia, some 2,100 colleges and universities now offer coursework in entrepreneurship, up from just 380 in 1990. As a result of these programs, about 400,000 undergraduate and graduate students took at least one entrepreneurship course in 2005. The numbers for 2006 and 2007 are thought to be even higher.

Ordinary citizens are equally interested in starting entrepreneurial careers. According to a recent study completed by Yahoo! and Harris Interactive, three in four American adults (72%) have considered starting their own business.

THE IMPORTANCE OF BUSINESS PLANS

An important tool that helps people who intend to start a new business is a business plan. A business plan is a written document that carefully explains every aspect of a new venture. Although many entrepreneurs and small business people do not write a business plan before they start their business, it's highly recommended. For most businesses, a business plan serves two functions. Inside the firm, the plan helps a company develop a "blueprint" to follow in executing its strategies and plan. Outside the firm, it introduces potential investors and other stakeholders to the business opportunity the firm is pursuing and how it plans to pursue it.

OBJECTIVES OF THE BOOK

The objectives of this book are twofold. The first objective is to help students and others learn how to write a business plan. This book provides step-by-step instructions for writing a plan. Second, the book immerses its reader in the process of thinking through the issues that are important in starting a business. This objective may be the most compelling advantage of the book. A full business plan is written, chapter-by-chapter, as an example through the course of the book. The issues that are considered in writing this plan provide a template for others to use as they consider their own business ventures and write their own business plan.

ORGANIZATION OF THE BOOK

The book is organized into four distinct parts:

Part	Topic	Chapters in the Book
1	Starting the Process	1
2	What to Do Before the Business Plan is Written	2–3
3	Preparing a Business Plan	4–10
4	Presenting the Business Plan	11

DISTINGUISHING FEATURES

A number of distinguishing features set this book apart from other business plan books that are available.

FOCUS ON THE ENTIRE "FRONT END" OF THE ENTREPRENEURIAL PROCESS

Although the primary purpose of the book is to describe how to write a business plan, the entire "front end" of the entrepreneurial process is discussed and defined. The most effective business plans are part of a comprehensive process that includes (1) identifying a business idea, (2) screening the idea (or ideas) to determine their preliminary feasibility, (3) conducting a full feasibility analysis to see if proceeding with a business plan is warranted, and (4) writing the plan. Each step in this process is explained in the book.

FEASIBILITY ANALYSIS WORKSHEETS

Two worksheets are included to help students and others work through the feasibility analysis process. The first worksheet is called the "First Screen," and helps determine the preliminary feasibility of a business idea. The second worksheet is a full feasibility analysis and is much more comprehensive. Combined, the worksheets represent a sequential way for students to determine the "feasibility" of their business ideas before they enter the business planning process.

SAMPLE BUSINESS PLAN

A business plan, for a fictitious company named Prime Adult Fitness, is built through the course of the book. Every aspect of the plan is described and discussed. This plan will give students and others a solid point of reference as they build their own business plans.

PRESENTING A BUSINESS PLAN

The final chapter in the book provides tips and suggestions for presenting a business plan with confidence and poise. Based on a 20- to 30-minute hypothetical presentation, a 12-slide PowerPoint presentation is provided with suggestions for what to include on each slide.

BUSINESS PLAN INSIGHT BOXED FEATURES

Each of the first ten chapters includes a boxed feature that provides special insights on writing a business plan or launching a new venture.

ABOUT THE AUTHOR

Bruce R. Barringer is an associate professor in the Department of Management at the University of Central Florida. He obtained his Ph.D. from the University of Missouri and his MBA from Iowa State University. His research interests include feasibility analysis, firm growth, corporate entrepreneurship, and the impact of interorganizational relationships on business organizations. He also works closely with the University of Central Florida technology incubator.

Bruce's work has been published in *Strategic Management Journal, Journal of Management, Journal of Business Venturing, Journal of Small Business Management, Journal of Developmental Entrepreneurship*, and *Quality Management Journal*. He is coauthor of the textbook *Entrepreneurship: Successfully Launching New Ventures*.

His outside interests include running, biking, and reading.

CHAPTER 1

WHY PLAN?

INTRODUCTION

On college campuses and around the world, entrepreneurship garners tremendous interest. In academia, some 2,100 colleges and universities now offer coursework in entrepreneurship, up from just 380 in 1990. As a result of these programs, about 400,000 undergraduate and graduate students took at least one entrepreneurship course in 2005.[1] Across the United States, interest in entrepreneurship is growing, among all demographic groups. According to a recent survey completed by Yahoo! and Harris Interactive, three in four American adults (72%) have considered starting a business.[2]

An important tool that helps people who intend to start a new business is a business plan. A **business plan** is a written document that carefully explains every aspect of a new business venture.[3] Although some entrepreneurs simply "wing it" and start a business without the benefits of formal planning, experts recommend preparing a business plan. For most new ventures, the business plan is a dual-purpose document used both inside and outside the firm. Inside the firm, the plan helps the company to develop a "road map" to follow in executing its strategies and plans. Outside the firm, it introduces potential investors and other stakeholders to the business opportunity the firm is pursuing and how it plans to pursue it. In many instances, having a business plan is a sheer necessity. Most bankers and investors, for example, won't consider financing a firm that doesn't have a formal business plan.

The most effective business plans are part of a comprehensive process that includes (1) identifying a business idea, (2) screening the idea (or ideas) to determine their preliminary feasibility, (3) conducting a full feasibility analysis to see if proceeding with a business plan is warranted, and (4) writing the plan. Many new businesses fail, not because the founders didn't work hard or weren't committed to the venture, but because the idea wasn't a good one to being with. This process sets forth a specific path for investigating the merits of a business idea. Although the primary purpose of this book is to describe how to write an effective business plan, the second section of the book, titled "What to Do Before You Prepare Your Business Plan," focuses on how to identify and screen business ideas (Chapter 2) and how to test their feasibility (Chapter 3). These topics are discussed in more detail later in the chapter.

Although writing a business plan may appear at first glance to be a tedious process, a properly prepared business plan can save an entrepreneur a tremendous amount of time, money, and heartache by working out the kinks in a business concept before rather than after the business is started. A large percentage of entrepreneurs do not write a business plan for their new ventures. In fact, only 31 percent of the 600 entrepreneurs that participated in a recent Wells Fargo/Gallup Small Business Study indicated that they had started their venture with a business plan.[4] Similarly, in 2002, *Inc.* magazine asked the founders of the firms that comprised the Inc. 500 that year whether they had written a formal business plan before they launched their companies. Only 40 percent said they had.[5] These statistics should not deter an entrepreneur from writing a business plan. Ample evidence supports the notion that writing a business plan is an extremely good investment of an entrepreneur's time and money.[6]

REASONS FOR WRITING A BUSINESS PLAN

There are two primary reasons for writing a business plan, as depicted in Figure 1-1. First, writing a business plan forces the founders of a firm to systematically think through each aspect of their new venture. This is not a trivial effort—it normally takes several days or weeks to complete a well-developed business plan—and the founders will usually meet regularly to work on the plan during this period. Writing a business plan is also an immersion experience—many founders work late nights and on weekends to get their plan completed. An example of how much work is sometimes involved, and how a well-planned new business unfolds, is provided by Gwen Whiting and Lindsey Wieber, the cofounders of The Laundress (http://www.thelaundress.com), a company that sells specially formulated laundry detergents and other fabric care products. Wieber and Whiting met at Cornell University while studying fabrics, and after graduating, the pair decided to start a business together. The following vignette comes from an interview they

FIGURE 1-1 Two Primary Reasons for Writing a Business Plan

Internal Reason	External Reason
Forces the founding team to work together to hammer out the details of a business venture	Communicates the merits of a new venture to outsiders, such as investors and bankers

gave to Ladies Who Launch (http://www.ladieswholaunch.com), a Web site that highlights the accomplishments of female entrepreneurs:

> *Gwen:* Lindsey and I went to college and studied textiles at Cornell together and always wanted to be in business together. We knew it was going to happen. We always talked about ideas. We were talking about this concept, and it was the right time for us. The first thing we did was the business plan and then a cash flow analysis. We wanted to do as much research as possible before developing the products.

> *Lindsey:* We spent Memorial Day weekend (2003) doing our business plan. We spent the Fourth of July weekend doing our cash flow. After we had our ideas on paper, we went back to Cornell, met with a professor there, and had a crash course in chemistry. She worked with us on the formulation of the products.

> *Gwen:* I found a manufacturer on Columbus Day. Every piece of free time we had, we dedicated to the business. We weren't at the beach with our friends anymore.[7]

The payoff for this level of dedication and hard work, which involved the preparation of a formal business plan, is that Whiting and Wieber now have a successful business. Their products are sold through their Web site and in many stores.

To provide another indication of the value of writing a business plan for the founders of a firm, Table 1-1 shows the contents of the business plan for a fictitious company named New Venture Fitness Equipment. This plan is probably similar to the plan that Gwen Whiting and Lindsey Wieber wrote for The Laundress.

TABLE 1-1   Business Plan Format for New Venture Fitness Equipment Inc.

Table of Contents

I.	Executive Summary	1
II.	Company Description	3
III.	Industry Analysis	6
IV.	Market Analysis	10
V.	Marketing Plan	14
VI.	Management Team and Company Structure	18
VII.	Operations Plan	22
VIII.	Product (or Service) Design and Development Plan	25
IX.	Financial Projections	30
	Appendices	
	Summary of Feasibility Analysis, Including Customer Reaction to the Product or Service	
	Supporting Industry Research	
	Resumes of Management Team Members	

New Venture Fitness Equipment plans to sell a new generation of fitness machines that will take the boredom out of exercising indoors by equipping its machines (treadmills, stationary bikes, and rowing machines) with flat-panel monitors that will allow exercisers to compete against virtual opponents, in a sort of video-game format, on a variety of simulated outdoor courses. Spend a few minutes looking at each of the topics included in Table 1-1, and then imagine the founders of New Venture Fitness Equipment talking through each of these topics. Imagine the debate that will inevitably ensue as the founders grapple with tough issues, such as projecting the size of their industry, specifying their target market, pricing their products, and determining how many machines they will have to sell to break even in each of their first three years. This process forces a team to not only work together, but to turn abstract ideas like "these machines are so great they should sell like hotcakes" into concrete realities like "we'll need to sell 9,850 machines each year during our first three years to break even." The benefit of this type of intense analysis before a business is started provides a compelling rationale for writing a business plan.[8] This sentiment is affirmed by Guy Kawasaki, a well-known Silicon Valley entrepreneur and venture capitalist, who wrote:

> All the late-night, back-o'-the envelope, romantic intentions to change the world become tangible and debatable once they're put on paper. Thus, the document itself is not nearly as important as the process that leads to the document. Even if you aren't trying to raise money, you should write one (a business plan) anyway.[9]

The second reason a business plan is important is because it is a selling document for a company. It provides a mechanism for a young company to present itself to potential investors, suppliers, key job candidates, and others. In fact, the number of organizations asking firms for copies of their business plans is growing. For example, most university- and community-sponsored business incubators, which are growing in number, require a business plan from their applicants. A **business incubator** is an organization that provides physical space and other resources to new firms in hopes of promoting economic development in a specific area.[10] An example of how incubators use business plans to screen applicants is provided by Mary Moslander, the founder of LiveHealthier.com, a subscription-based fitness oriented Web site for women:

> I attended a conference for women in business, which was sponsored by the local chamber of commerce, where I learned about the Maryland Technology Development Center, which is a physical "incubator" for biotech and IT startups. I had to write a business plan with financial projections and present it to a 15-person committee. They were looking for startup companies that show promise that will eventually be able to hire people in Montgomery County and become taxpaying corporate citizens. I was accepted and moved into the Maryland Technology Development Center Incubator on May 9, 2005. For a 200-square foot office, I pay $495 a month, which is unheard of in this market. I have

essential resources at my disposal, such as a centralized receptionist, conference rooms, a production and mail room, and through the Maryland Intellectual Property Legal Resource Center, I have access to free legal assistance on intellectual property matters.[11]

Ms. Moslander's willingness to write a business plan, which apparently cut muster with the incubator's 15-person selection committee, was the key to her admittance to the incubator and access to the resources the incubator provides.

Investors rely almost exclusively on business plans for their initial investment screening decisions, and research has shown that having a business plan is positively related to the acquisition of startup funding.[12] The type of information that investors initially ask for has changed some, as many investors now ask for an **executive summary,** which is a short overview of a business plan, or they ask for a set of PowerPoint slides describing the merits of a new venture first and only ask for a full business plan if their interest is sufficiently peaked. Still, a full business plan will ultimately be asked for, and it's almost inconceivable that a new venture could attract funding or financing without a complete business plan.[13]

As a selling document, a business plan also helps a new company build credibility. For example, imagine that you are an investor and have enough money to invest in one new business. You chat informally with several entrepreneurs at a university-sponsored event for startups and decide that there are two new ventures that you want to know more about. You contact the first entrepreneur and ask for a copy of his business plan. The entrepreneur hesitates a bit and says that he hasn't prepared a formal business plan but would love to buy you lunch to talk about his business idea. You contact the second entrepreneur and make the same request. This time, the entrepreneur says that she would be glad to forward you a copy of a 30-page business plan, along with a 12-slide PowerPoint presentation that provides an overview of the plan. Ten minutes later, the PowerPoint presentation is in your e-mail inbox with a note that the business plan will arrive by FedEx the next morning. You look through the slides, which are crisp and to the point and do an excellent job of outlining the business opportunity. The next day, the business plan arrives just as promised and is equally impressive.

Which entrepreneur is likely to get your attention? All other things being equal, the answer is obvious: the second entrepreneur. The fact that the second entrepreneur has a business plan not only provides you with detailed information about the venture but also suggests that the entrepreneur has thought through each element of the business and is committed enough to the new venture to invest the time and energy necessary to prepare the plan.

Another way that a business plan helps establish credibility for a firm is by winning or placing high in a university-, community-, or state-sponsored business plan competition or similar event. These competitions are becoming increasingly numerous, visible, and well attended, and the winners are typically featured in local newspapers and business publications. In addition, several national magazines, including *Fortune Small Business* and *Jungle,* sponsor business plan competitions, and the finalists are prominently featured in the publications. This type of positive recognition can be very helpful for a young firm and can even lead to funding. This scenario played out for Jim Poss, the founder of Seahorse Power (http://www.seahorsepower.com), a company that makes innovative solar-power trash containers. Poss said that winning a business plan competition while he was an MBA student at Babson College helped attract the attention of an angel investor, who ultimately funded his firm.[14]

Even if a student or group of students places high in a business plan competition and ultimately decides to not start the business, the connections and hands-on experiences gained through participating in the competition can lead to positive outcomes. For example, two University of Pennsylvania students, Dhaval Gosalia and Jonathan Goodspeed, won the 2005 Wharton Business Plan Competition for their company FibrinX. FibrinX's business plan was focused on licensing technology that would enable the company to produce a tissue sealant capable of preventing excessive bleeding after a traumatic injury or during surgery. The developer of the technology ultimately decided to license it to another company, so FibrinX never panned out. Still, Goodspeed says that the connections he gained through the competition are what landed him where he is today—heavily involved in an early-stage nanotechnology and advanced materials startup in Philadelphia. "A lot of the people I met (through the Wharton Business Plan Competition) are still people I keep in touch with and bounce ideas off," he says.[15]

WHO READS THE BUSINESS PLAN AND WHAT ARE THEY LOOKING FOR?

There are two primary audiences for a firm's business plan. Let's look at each of them.

A FIRM'S EMPLOYEES

A clearly written business plan, which articulates the vision and future plans of a firm, is important for both the management team and the rank-and-file employees. Some experts argue that it's a waste of time to write a business plan because the marketplace changes so rapidly that any plan will become quickly outdated.[16] Although it's true that marketplaces can and often do change rapidly, the process of writing a business plan is often as valuable as the plan itself, as illustrated through the New Venture Fitness Equipment example. Not only is it useful for a management team to hammer out the contents of a business plan together, but also the process of working together on such an important project can help develop a strong, cohesive team. The process can also uncover potential trouble spots in a team. If particular members of a team can't work together to produce a business plan, it is unlikely they will be successful working together after the business is launched.

A clearly written business plan also helps a firm's rank-and-file employees operate in sync and move forward in a consistent and purposeful manner. The existence of a business plan is particularly useful for a new business that has geographically dispersed employees. For example, say you live in Richmond, Virginia, and were just hired to be the primary sales rep for the eastern United States for an information technology startup headquartered in California. Imagine how helpful it would be for you to have a copy of your new firm's business plan, so that you could refer to the plan to make sure everything you do and say is consistent with the overall plans and direction of the company.

INVESTORS AND OTHER EXTERNAL STAKEHOLDERS

External stakeholders, such as investors, potential business partners, potential customers, private and government-funded grant awarding agencies, and key employees who are being recruited to join a firm, are the second audience for a business plan. To appeal to this group, the business plan must be realistic and not reflect overconfidence on the firm's part. A good rule-of-thumb is that a business plan should be written with extreme empathy for the readers, who are typically busy people who like to read plans that are clear, concise, and plainly explain the business. Overly optimistic statements or projections undermine a business plan's credibility, so it is foolish to include them. At the same time, the plan must clearly demonstrate that the business idea is viable and offers potential investors financial returns that are greater than lower-risk investment alternatives. The same is true for potential business partners, customers, grant awarding agencies, and key recruits. Unless the new business can show that it has impressive potential, there is little reason for anyone to become involved.

A firm must validate the feasibility of its business idea and have a good understanding of its competitive environment prior to presenting its business plan to others, as will be emphasized throughout this book. Sophisticated investors, potential business partners, and others will base their assessment of the future prospects of a business on facts, not guesswork or speculation. The most compelling facts a company can provide in its business plan are the results of its own feasibility analysis, particularly if the analysis includes feedback from industry experts and prospective customers. A business plan rings hollow if it is based strictly on entrepreneurs' predictions and estimates of what they "think" will happen.

Particularly when writing for an external audience, entrepreneurs must avoid appearing naïve or uninformed, especially about the industry a firm is about to enter or the amount of competition a firm may encounter. To make this point, William A. Sahlman, a Harvard professor and expert on business plans, says that "Business is like chess: To be successful, you must be able to anticipate several moves in advance."[17] What Sahlman means by this statement is that a business plan that is overly optimistic and doesn't seem to anticipate any problems or competitive challenges to its product or service is by definition naïve and stands to lose credibility quickly. All companies have problems and competitors. In addition, a cardinal rule in approaching an investor or a banker with a business plan is to get a personal introduction. Bankers and investors receive many business plans, and most of them end up in a pile on their credenzas. To have your business plan noticed, find someone who knows the banker or the investor, and ask for an introduction.

GUIDELINES FOR WRITING A BUSINESS PLAN

Several important guidelines should influence the writing of a business plan. It is important to remember that a firm's business plan is typically the first aspect of a proposed venture that will be seen by an investor or whomever the plan is presented to. If the plan is incomplete or looks sloppy, an investor may easily infer that the venture itself is incomplete or sloppy. It is important to be sensitive to the structure, style, and content of a plan before exposing it to a firm's employees or sending it to an outsider. It is also important for the individuals writing the plan to continually measure the type of company that they are envisioning against their personal goals and aspirations. One of the worst things that can happen to an entrepreneur is to write a business plan, raise money, launch the business, and then realize that the business is inconsistent with his or her personal aspirations or preferred lifestyle and wish that the firm hadn't come to fruition.

Finally, when writing a business plan, it is important to produce a plan that is a definitive document but remains open to revisions as the entrepreneurs involved learn more about the industry they plan to enter, get feedback from potential customers, and as circumstances in the external environment change. Most businesses plans go through several iterations before their business models and target markets are completely nailed down.[18] Changes are also frequently made after a business is launched, as the founders get more substantive feedback from customers and channel partners.

STRUCTURE AND STYLE OF THE BUSINESS PLAN

To make the best impression, a business plan should follow a conventional structure, such as in the plan outlined earlier in Table 1-1. Although some entrepreneurs are creative and don't want their plans to "look like everyone else's," departing from the basic structure of the conventional business plan is usually a mistake. Typically, investors are very busy people and want a plan that allows them to easily find critical information. If investors have to hunt for something because it is in an unusual place or just isn't there, they might simply give up and move on to the next plan.

One of the most common questions that the writers of business plans ask is, "How long and detailed should it be?" Experts vary on the optimal page length, but most recommendations fall in the 25–35 page range. Many software packages are available that employ an interactive, menu-driven approach to assist in the writing of a business plan. Some of these programs are very helpful; however, entrepreneurs should avoid a boilerplate plan that looks as though it came from a "canned" source. The software package may be helpful in providing structure and saving time, but the information in the plan should still be tailored to the individual business. Some businesses hire consultants or outside advisors to write their business plans. Although there is nothing wrong with getting advice or making sure that a plan looks as professional as possible, a consultant or outside advisor shouldn't be the author of the plan. Along with facts and figures, a business plan needs to project a sense of anticipation and excitement about the possibilities surrounding a new venture, which is a task best accomplished by the creators of the business. Plus, hiring someone to write the plan denies the entrepreneur or team of entrepreneurs the positive benefits of the writing experience, as explained earlier in the chapter.

The appearance of the plan must be carefully thought out. It should look sharp but not give the impression that a lot of money was spent to produce it.[19] Those who read plans know that entrepreneurs have limited resources and expect them to act accordingly. A plastic spiral binder, including a transparent cover sheet and a back sheet to support the plan, is a good choice. When writing the plan, avoid getting carried away with the design elements included in word-processing programs, such as boldfaced type, italics, different font sizes and colors, clip art, and so forth. Overuse of these tools makes a business plan look amateurish rather than professional. Some style-related things can be done that show the amount of care and attention that went into a plan and that aren't overly flashy or costly. For example, if a company has a well-designed logo, it should be placed on the cover sheet of the business plan and on the header for each page. A simple design element such as having the colors in the charts and graphs in the plan match the colors in the logo shows an attention to detail and an eye toward branding that is impressive to most readers.

One important criterion that all business plans should adhere to is to convey a clear, coherent story of what the business plans to accomplish and how it plans to get there. Many entrepreneurs aren't very good at this, which lessens the potential impact of their plans. Robert W. Price affirms this sentiment in a book titled *Roadmap to Entrepreneurial Success,* which reports the observations of two experts on business plans regarding this issue:

> According to David Berkus, a past-president of the Tech Coast Angels, one of the largest angel investment groups in the United States, the first step to writing a business plan is fleshing out your "talking points" and weaving them into a storyline. Storytelling is having the ability to communicate succinctly and precisely what you do, what you want to do, and what you need to do it. Bill Joos at Garage Technology Ventures, who has heard some 100,000 pitches from entrepreneurs, agrees that there is a "big problem with entrepreneurs who have the inability to talk about what they do."[20]

One thing that a new venture can do to help develop a concise description of their business is develop an elevator speech. An elevator speech is a brief, carefully constructed statement, usually 45 seconds to 2 minutes long that outlines the merits of a business venture. It is explained in more detail in the following Business Plan Insight box. A properly prepared elevator speech can assist in writing a business plan by helping the founders develop a sharp and concise description of their business.

In business plans, savvy investors and others will pick up on several potential "red flags" when certain aspects of a plan are insufficient or miss the mark. These red flags, which are depicted in Table 1-2, not only undermine the credibility of the business plan but of the individuals who wrote the plan. The writers of a plan should work hard to avoid these potential complications.

Develop an Elevator Speech

A very useful exercise for a new firm is to develop an elevator speech. An elevator speech (or pitch) is a brief, carefully constructed statement that outlines the merits of a business opportunity. Why is it called an elevator speech? If an entrepreneur stepped into an elevator on the 25th floor of a building and found that by a stroke of luck a potential investor was in the same elevator, the entrepreneur would have the time it takes to get from the 25th floor to the ground floor to try to get the investor interested in the business opportunity. Most elevator speeches are 45 seconds to 2 minutes long.

An elevator speech might come in handy on many occasions. For example, many university-sponsored centers for entrepreneurship hold events that bring investors and entrepreneurs together. Often these events include breaks designed specifically for the purpose of allowing entrepreneurs looking for funding to mingle with potential investors. The other thing an elevator speech does for a young firm is force the founders to develop a very concise, to-the-point description of the business idea.

An outline for a 60-second elevator speech is provided here. A new venture's elevator speech should be carefully prepared and practiced often.

STEPS IN AN ELEVATOR SPEECH

Step 1: Describe the opportunity or problem that needs to be solved.	20 seconds
Step 2: Describe how your product or service meets the opportunity or solves the problem.	20 seconds
Step 3: Describe your qualifications.	10 seconds
Step 4: Describe your market.	10 seconds
Total:	60 seconds

CONTENT OF THE BUSINESS PLAN

Most business plan are divided into sections that represent the major aspects of a new venture's business, as depicted in the business plan outline shown earlier in Table 1-1. The titles of the sections will vary from plan to plan, although most plans follow a fairly standard format. What varies, of course, from plan to plan, is the quality of the writing, the substance of the plan, and the degree to which the plan convinces the reader that the business opportunity is exciting, feasible, defensible, and within the capabilities of the people launching the firm. Writing a plan that includes all of these elements is not an easy task, but it is a very useful one, as illustrated throughout this book.

The essence of what should be included in each section of a business plan is described in Chapter 4 through Chapter 10 of this book. After the plan is completed, it should be reviewed for spelling and grammar and to make sure that no critical information has been omitted. There are numerous stories about business plans being sent to investors that left out important information. One investor even said that he once received a business plan that didn't include any contact

TABLE 1-2 Red Flags in Business Plans	
Red Flag	*Explanation*
Founders with none of their own money at risk	If the founders aren't willing to put their own money at risk, why should anyone else?
A poorly cited plan	A plan should be built on hard evidence and sound research, not guesswork or what an entrepreneur "thinks" will happen. The sources for all primary and secondary research should be cited.
Defining the market size too broadly	Defining the market for a new venture too broadly shows that the true target market is not well defined. For example, saying that a new venture will target the $550 billion per year pharmaceutical industry isn't helpful. The market opportunity needs to be better defined. Obviously, the new venture will target a segment or a specific market within the industry.
Overly aggressive financials	Many investors skip directly to this portion of the plan. Projections that are poorly reasoned or unrealistically optimistic lose credibility. In contrast, sober, well-reasoned statements backed by sound research and judgment gain credibility quickly.
Hiding or avoiding weaknesses	It is foolhardy for a new venture to try to downplay or hide its weaknesses. All firms have weaknesses, and often one of the most important things an investor or banker can do, beyond providing money, is to help a new venture shore up the weaknesses that it has.
Sloppiness in any area	It is never a good idea to make a reader wade through typos, balance sheets that don't balance, or sloppiness in any area. These types of mistakes are seen as inattention to detail and hurt the creditability of the entrepreneur.
Too long of a plan	Most experienced readers of business plans know exactly what they're looking for, and to make them wade through 50 pages of material just gets in the way. Don't include page after page of descriptive information about an industry, for example. Two pages of "to the point" information and analysis is much more valuable than 20 pages cut and pasted from the Internet.

information for the entrepreneur. Apparently, the entrepreneur was so focused on the content of the plan that he or she simply forgot to provide contact information on the business plan itself. This was a shame because the investor was interested in learning more about the business opportunity.[21]

Entrepreneurs vary in terms of how much feedback they solicit during the business planning process. Companies that formulate their business plans in secret, to avoid tipping off potential competitors as to what they're planning, refer to themselves as operating in **stealth mode.** For example, during the time that Dean Kamer was developing the Segway, the self-balancing, two-wheeled human transporter, the project was code-named "Ginger." Other entrepreneurs get as much advice as they can and distribute early drafts of their business plans widely to friends, acquaintances, and industry experts for feedback. This was the case with Mary Moslander, the entrepreneur quoted earlier who founded LiveHealthier.com. Moslander worked for the *Washington Post* prior to founding her firm. Commenting on her experience writing a business plan, Moslander wrote, "I must have brought my business plan to 50 different people . . . people from *The Post* days, from the financial sector, the Web world, and then I really refined it." [22]

MEASURING THE BUSINESS PLAN AGAINST YOUR PERSONAL GOALS AND ASPIRATIONS

Another guideline for writing a business plan is that as a plan is being written, the people involved should continually measure the type of company that they are hoping to start against their personal goals and aspirations. This consideration is important for two reasons.

First, the old adage "be careful what you wish for" is as true in business as it is in other areas of life. For instance, if an entrepreneur identifies an opportunity that has a large upside potential and decides to write a business plan to solicit funds from a venture capitalist or other investor, the entrepreneur should know what to expect if the business is funded. In the case of venture capital, most venture capitalists shoot for a 30 to 40 percent annual return on their investment and a total return over the life of the investment of 5 to 20 times their original investment. [23] This level of expectation forces a firm into a fast-growth model literally from the start, which typically implies a quick pace of activity, a rapidly raising overhead, and a total commitment in terms of time and attention from the founding entrepreneurs. Accepting venture capital also involves surrendering equity in the firm to outsiders (in exchange for their investment) and heavy scrutiny at all levels. The upside is that if the new company is successful, the founders will normally do very well financially.

The point of this description, within the context of this chapter, is that entrepreneurs crafting business plans to try to attract venture capital should know what they are getting into and should make sure that the lifestyle associated with owning and managing a venture capital-funded firm is something that is consistent with their personal goals and aspirations. Those who want to own their own firm but place a high value on leisure time or family time or doesn't want the pressures associated with a group of investors continually looking over their shoulder are poor choices to launch venture-backed firms. These types of individual are better suited to launch a firm in a target (or niche) market that flies slightly under the radar of large competitors, and they should write business plans that solicit funds from friends, family, or a lender. There are many successful firms, which include clothing boutiques, Web retailers, and service firms, just to name a few, that fit this profile. In contrast, some people thrive in a high-pressure environment and have a high desire to make a large amount of money. An entrepreneur who fits this profile is better suited to launch a venture-backed firm.

The second reason that it is important for an entrepreneur to continually measure a business plan against personal goals and aspirations is that as a business plan evolves, the entrepreneur may find that aspects to the business that are not as attractive as originally anticipated. A firm that is envisioned to be a non-profit, for example, may not be financially viable as a nonprofit when the numbers are crunched and feedback is solicited from potential donors and other stakeholders. The firm may only be viable as a for-profit firm, which may be less appealing to the potential founders of the firm. Similarly, someone may find, through the course of writing the business plan, that the business being contemplated can only be successful if run at a much larger scale than was originally anticipated. The additional risk associated with the larger operation may be more than the potential entrepreneur is willing to undertake. In both of these instances, the process of writing the business plan may result in the entrepreneur deciding to not launch the business. This outcome should be considered to be a successful outcome of the process if the resulting business would have been inconsistent with the entrepreneur's personal goals and aspirations.

Recognizing That Elements of the Plan May Change

A final guideline for writing a business plan, which was touched upon briefly in the preceding section, is to recognize that the plan will invariably change as it is being written. An academic principle called the **corridor principle** states that once an entrepreneur starts a business, the entrepreneur begins a journey down a path where "corridors" leading to new venture opportunities become apparent.[24] The same principle applies during the preparing of a business plan. As an entrepreneur or team of entrepreneurs starts testing the merits of a business idea and starts writing the plan, new insights will invariably emerge that weren't initially apparent. This process continues throughout the life of a company, and it behooves entrepreneurs to remain alert and open to new insights and ideas. As a result of this phenomenon, experts like to stress that a business plan is a living, breathing document, rather than something that is set in stone. In support of this notion, Guy Kawasaki, the Silicon Valley investor and entrepreneur quoted earlier in the chapter, recommends to the authors of business plans to "Write Deliberate, (but) Act Emergent."[25] What Kawasaki means by this statement is that it is necessary to write a "deliberate" plan that provides a specific blueprint for a new venture to follow, but at the same time, the individuals involved should be thinking "emergent," which is a mindset that is open to change and is influenced by the day-to-day realities of the marketplace.

Types of Businesses

There are four distinct types of business, as shown in Table 1-3. All of these types of businesses are acceptable — there is no value judgment here. This book, however, focuses primarily on lifestyle firms, managed growth firms, and aggressive growth firms. Not all businesses grow rapidly and make tons of money but may still provide their owners satisfying lives and financial security. This book equally targets this type of business along with more aggressive growth firms.

TABLE 1-3 Types of Businesses		
Type of Business	*Explanation*	*Examples*
Survival	A business that provides its owner just enough money to put food on the table and pay bills	Handyman, lawn service, part-time childcare
Lifestyle	A business that provides its owner the opportunity to pursue a certain lifestyle and make a living at it	Home-based eBay business, sub shop, single-unit franchise, clothing boutique, personal trainer
Managed Growth	A business that employs 10 or more people, may have several outlets, and may be introducing new products or services to the market	Multi-unit franchise, regional restaurant chain, Web retailer (modest scale)
Aggressive Growth	A business that is bringing new products and services to the market and has aggressive growth plans	Computer software, medical equipment, Web retailer (large scale), national restaurant chain

THE PLAN FOR THE BOOK

This book is divided into four sections as shown in Figure 1-2 and as listed here:

Section 1: Starting the Process
Section 2: What to Do Before the Business Plan Is Written
Section 3: Preparing a Business Plan
Section 4: Presenting the Business Plan to Investors and Others

STARTING THE PROCESS (CHAPTER 1)

As discussed earlier, there are two primary reasons for writing a business plan: The process of writing a business plan forces the founders to systematically think through each aspect of their new venture, and a business plan introduces potential investors and others to the firm and the business opportunity it is pursuing. Although all business plans vary depending on the nature of the new venture, there are certain guidelines, discussed in this chapter, which can increase the odds that a particular plan will be successful. A particularly important consideration, normally unseen to the reader of a plan, is that an individual's business plan should coincide with the individual's personal goals or aspirations.

Although writing a business plan can appear to be a tedious process, a well-developed plan can save an entrepreneur a tremendous amount of time and money by working out the flaws in a business idea before rather than after the business is launched. Having a business plan is also an essential document for a firm to have at its disposal, particularly if it plans to reach out to others to try to gain access to resources.

FIGURE 1-2   Steps Involved in Identifying a Business Opportunity, Assessing the Feasibility of the Opportunity, and Preparing an Effective Business Plan

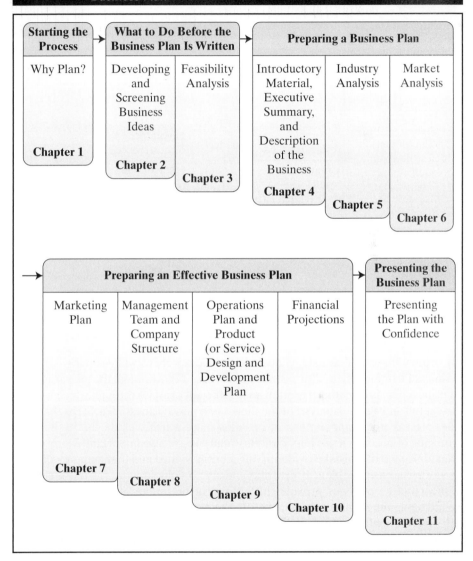

WHAT TO DO BEFORE THE BUSINESS PLAN IS WRITTEN (CHAPTERS 2 TO 3)

As mentioned in the introduction to the chapter, writing a business plan is part of a comprehensive process that includes (1) identifying a business idea, (2) screening the idea (or ideas) to determine their initial feasibility, (3) conducting a full feasibility analysis to determine if proceeding with a business plan is warranted, and

FIGURE 1-3 The Comprehensive Feasibility Analysis/Business Planning Process

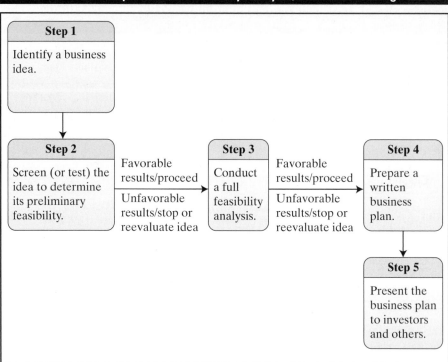

(4) writing the plan. These steps, labeled "The Comprehensive Feasibility Analysis/ Business Planning Process," are depicted in Figure 1-3. Although the preparation of a business plan is essential, it is often an insufficient exercise through which to complete a full and candid analysis of the merits of a new business idea. Steps that logically precede the completion of a business plan, which include the preliminary screening of business ideas and feasibility analysis, are also important. Many entrepreneurs make the mistake of identifying a business idea and then jumping directly to writing a business plan to describe and try to gain support for the idea. This sequence often omits or provides little time for the important steps of critically investigating the merits of the idea before the business plan is written.

The sequential nature of the steps shown in Figure 1-3 cleanly separates the investigative portion of thinking through the merits of a business idea from the planning and selling portion of the process. Steps 2-3 are investigative in nature and are designed to critique the merits of the business idea. Step 4, the business plan, is focused on planning and selling. The initial steps are important because there is no reason to write a business plan for a business idea that has little chance of succeeding. The reason it is so important to complete the entire process, according to John W. Mullins, the author of a highly regarded book titled *The New Business Road Test,* is to avoid falling into the "everything about my opportunity is wonderful" mode. In Mullin's view, failure to properly investigate the merits of a business idea (Steps 2-3) before the business plan is written runs

PEARSON | **PEARSON CANADA**

Packing List

Purchase Order Number: 4736933720
Packing List Number: 401731564
Order Type: Sample Customer SAN:

A division of /Une division de Pearson Canada Inc.
195 Harry Walker Parkway N., Newmarket, ON L3Y 7B3

Date: 8/01/08   Page: 1

Ship to Customer Number Expedier a client numero	Shipped Via Expedie par	Freight Terms Termes de fret	Carrier Expediteur	Waybill Number Numero Rexepisse
0000000000090	STD	PPD-ADD	PMB	

BOBBIE ROBERTSON
ASSINIBOINE COMMUNITY COLLE

BUSINESS EDUC. DEPT
BRANDON   MB R7A2A9
ATTN:

<table>
<tr><td rowspan="5">F
A
C
T
U
R
É</td><td>B
I
L
L

T
O</td></tr>
</table>

BOBBIE ROBERTSON
ASSINIBOINE COMMUNITY COLLE
BUSINESS EDUC. DEPT
1430 VICTORIA AVE EAST

BRANDON   MB R7A 2A9
ATTN:

<table>
<tr><td rowspan="5">E
X
P
É
D
I
T
O
R</td><td>S
H
P

T
O
À</td></tr>
</table>

ISBN ISBN	Quantity Quantite	Title Titre	Author Auteur	Unit Price Prix D Unite	Disc Disc $ Esc Prix Esc	Ext.$ Prix Et.	ST ST
9780132294386	1	ESSN ENTREPREN&SMLL BUSN 5/E (013229438 9)	ZIMMERER				IS
9780132318327	1	PREPARG EFFCT BUSN PLANS 1/E (013231832 6)	BARRINGER				IS

COMMENTS:

WE REGRET THAT THE FOLLOWING ITEMS ARE NOT AVAILABLE. AN ESTIMATED DUE
IN-STOCK DATE IS SHOWN, IF AVAILABLE. THANK YOU FOR YOUR PATIENCE.
013615457 3 REVW COPY EFF SMALL BUSN 9/E   SCARBOROU OS 08-08-2008
013224057 2 ENTREPRENEURSHIP: SUCC 2/E   BARRINGER OS WILL ADVISE
013206726 9 ENTREPRENEURSHIP:SUCCESSFULLY LANCHING BARRINGER NYP 02-01-2009
THIS MATERIAL WAS SENT TO YOU WITH THE   X
COMPLIMENTS OF YOUR SALES REPRESENTATIVE.   X
DENNIS GUEVARRA
1-877-243-4505
dennis.guevarra@pearsoned.com

We care about the rising cost of textbooks for your students and want to
do whatever we can to help. Please visit our website at
www.pearsoned.ca/samplereturn to print out a prepaid return label for
any unwanted samples. Or contact our customer service department at
1-800-567-3800 to arrange for pick up of any unwanted samples.

IP-In Print(Out of Stock)   OP-Out of Print
NYP-Not Yet Published   OSI-Out of Stock Indefinitely
PC-Publication Cancelled   PP-Publication Postponed
TU-Temporarily Unavailable   TOS-Temporarily out of stock
NLO-No Longer our Publication IS-In Stock

the risk of blinding an entrepreneur to inherent risks associated with the potential business and results in too positive of a plan. [26] A savvy reader is likely to pick up on this lack of awareness and overly positive slant, which undermines the credibility of the plan.

In fairness, some entrepreneurs are able to combine the steps depicted in Figure 1-3 and produce a very well-researched and well-documented plan. On some occasions, however, an entrepreneur might need to move quickly to capture a first-mover advantage or for another reason, so portions of the process depicted in Figure 1-3 need to be done in parallel rather than sequentially. Breaking the process down into the steps shown in Figure 1-3 is a more careful and prudent approach, however, unless this approach isn't practical for a compelling reason.

Chapter 2 in the book focuses on how entrepreneurs identify business opportunities and introduces the preliminary screen, which is a device for rapidly assessing the preliminary feasibility of a business idea (or ideas). Chapter 3 describes how to conduct a complete feasibility analysis.

PREPARING A BUSINESS PLAN (CHAPTERS 4 THROUGH 10)

Chapters 4 through 10 provide an explanation of how to complete each section of a business plan and describe (step-by-step) the business plan for a fictitious company named Prime Adult Fitness. Prime Adult Fitness is a fitness center for people 50 years old and older. The goal is to teach you to write a business plan that is complete, yet concise and to the point.

PRESENTING THE BUSINESS PLAN (CHAPTER 11)

If the business plan successfully elicits the interest of a potential banker or investor, or it is entered into a business plan competition, the next step will be to present the business plan to a small group or audience of individuals. The final chapter of the book provides suggestions and guidelines for presenting a business plan to investors and others. Concrete suggestions are given for how to make effective presentations using PowerPoint slides and how to field questions from an audience effectively.

Chapter Summary

1. A business plan is a written document that carefully explains every aspect of a new business venture.
2. The most effective business plans are part of a comprehensive process that includes (1) identifying a business idea, (2) screening the idea (or ideas) to determine their preliminary feasibility, (3) conducting a full feasibility analysis, and (4) writing the plan.
3. There are two primary reasons for writing a business plan: (1) It forces the founding team to work together to hammer out the details of the business venture, and (2) It communicates the merits of a new venture to outsiders, such as investors or bankers.
4. The process of writing a business plan forces a team to not only work together but to turn abstract ideas into concrete realities.

5. The two primary audiences for a firm's business plan are the firm's employees and investors/other external stakeholders.

6. A firm's business plan is typically the first aspect of a proposed venture that will be seen by an investor (or anyone else who reads the plan), and if the plan is incomplete or looks sloppy, it is easy for an investor to infer that the venture itself is incomplete or sloppy.

7. To make the best impression, a business plan should follow a conventional structure. Typically, the individuals who read business plans are very busy people and want a plan that allows them to easily find critical information.

8. As a business plan is written, the people involved should continually measure the type of company that they are hoping to start against their personal goals and aspirations.

9. There are four types of businesses: survival, lifestyle, managed growth, and aggressive growth. This book focuses on lifestyle, managed growth, and aggressive growth firms.

10. Although the preparation of a business plan is essential, it is often an insufficient exercise through which to complete a full and candid analysis of the merits of a new business venture. Steps that logically precede the completion of a business plan, which include the preliminary screening of business ideas and feasibility analysis, are also important.

Review Questions

1. What is a business plan? What are the advantages to preparing a business plan for a new venture?

2. What are the two most common reasons that entrepreneurs write business plans?

3. Who are the primary consumers of business plans? In what ways do the people who read business plans differ in the information they are looking for?

4. It is often argued that the process of writing a business plan is as important as the plan itself. How is this so?

5. Why is it important for the founders of a firm to continually measure whether the type of company they are envisioning, as described by their business plan, is consistent with their personal goals and aspirations?

6. What are the hazards involved with using a software package to help write a business plan or hiring consultants to write the business plan for you?

7. Describe the general rules-of-thumb for the length and appearance of a business plan.

8. Why is it important for a firm to test the feasibility of its business idea prior to writing a business plan?

9. What is the corridor principle, and how does an understanding of the principle help entrepreneurs remain open to change as their business plans are being written and after their businesses are launched?

10. What is an elevator speech? How can developing an elevator speech help a firm write a more effective business plan?

Application Questions

1. Sarah Peters is one of three founders of a medical products company. The founders have decided to write a business plan to try to obtain funding. In a meeting with her cofounders, Sarah said, "I know that we're all very busy, so I'd like to volunteer to write the business plan. I have a cabin on a lake about an hour from here, so if it's alright with the two of you, I'd like to take my laptop up to the cabin for a couple of days and hammer out the business plan. Any objections?" If you were one of Sarah's cofounders, what would you say? What alternative approach, if any, would you suggest to writing the plan?

2. Jim Bower, a friend of yours, has spent the past three years working on an innovative new type of car alarm. He was just awarded a U.S. patent on the device, and is thinking about leaving his job at General Motors to start a company to sell the alarm. Jim is planning to attend a new business conference in Chicago next month, which will feature a number of investors. You know Jim doesn't have a business plan. When you asked Jim what he'll do if he meets an investor at the conference and is asked for a copy of his business plan, Jim said, "If that happens, I'll tell the investor that I'd rather meet with him to talk about my ideas rather than go through all the work involved with writing a business plan. If he insists, I'll put together a plan as quickly as possible and get it in the mail." Describe what is wrong with Jim's thinking.

3. The founders of New Venture Fitness Machines have decided to send their business plan to a select group of investors who they know have funded fitness equipment companies in the past. The founders think that the group of investors they have identified represents their best shot at funding and don't want to blow the effort. They have decided to read through their plan one more time before sending it out. Make a list of the things that should be in the plan and the things that shouldn't be in the plan, based on the material in this chapter.

4. Lindsey Simpson is the founder of a company that plans to sell a new line of skin care products through high-end boutiques. Because her products will be priced at the high end of the market, Lindsey has decided to try to project an image of sophistication and class in everything she does. As a result, she plans to pay several thousand dollars to have her business plan professionally prepared, and each copy of the plan will be enclosed in a $59.00 leather binder. Do you agree with Lindsey's approach? If not, what advice would you give her?

5. Spend some time studying the Web site of LiveHealthier.com, the company started by Mary Moslander and referred to in this chapter. Search for additional information on the company. Write a 60-second elevator speech for LiveHealthier.com.

Endnotes

1. A. Barrett, "Hitting the Books," http://www.businessweek.com, Fall 2006 (January 8, 2007).
2. "Yahoo! Poll Shows Majority of American Adults Have Entrepreneurial Aspirations and the Internet Has Made Launching a Small Business Easier," (Yahoo Media Relations). http://docs.yahoo.com/docs/pr/release1230.html (January 18, 2007).
3. B. Honig and T. Karlsson, "Institutional Forces and the Written Business Plan," *Journal of Management* 30, no. 1 (2004): 29–48.
4. Wells Fargo/Gallup Small Business Index, "How Much Money Does It Take to Start a Small Business?" (Well Fargo Bank, August 15, 2006). http://www.wellsfargo.com (January 6, 2007).
5. S. Bartlett, "Seat of the Pants," *Inc.* October, 2002.
6. F. Delmar and S. Shane, "Does Business Planning Facilitate the Development of New Ventures?," *Strategic Management Journal* 24 (2003): 1,165–1,185.
7. "Meet Lindsey Wieber and Gwen Whiting," (Ladies Who Launch). http://www.ladieswholaunch.com (January 16, 2007).
8. G. Castrogiovanni, "Pre-Startup Planning and the Survival of New Businesses: Theoretical Linkages," *Journal of Management,* 22, no. 6 (1996): 801–822.
9. G. Kawasaki, *The Art of the Start* (New York: Portfolio, 2004)
10. "Business Incubator," (Wikipedia). http://www.wikipedia.com (January 6, 2007).
11. Ladies Who Launch homepage, http://www.ladieswholaunch.com (January 3, 2007).
12. H. Van Auken, "Pre-Launch Preparations and the Acquisition of Start-Up Capital by Small Firms," *Journal of Developmental Entrepreneurship,* 5, no. 2 (2000): 169–183.
13. S. Broring, L. M. Cloutier, and J. Leker, "The Front End of Innovation in an Era of Industry Convergence: Evidence from Nutraceuticals and Functional Foods," *R&D Management* 36, no. 5 (2006): 487–498.
14. Personal conversation with Jim Poss, May 12, 2006.
15. J. Gangemi, "The Afterlife of Business Plan Competition Winners," *Small Biz,* December 12, 2006.
16. A. Bhide, *The Origin and Evolution of New Businesses* (New York: Oxford University Press, 2000).
17. W. A. Sahlman, "How to Write a Great Business Plan," *Harvard Business Review,* July-August, 1997, 98–108.
18. K. Hindle and B. Mainprize, "A Systematic Approach to Writing and Rating Entrepreneurial Business Plans," *The Journal of Private Equity,* (Summer 2006): 7–22.
19. S. Rich and D. Gumpert, "How to Write a Winning Business Plan," *Harvard Business Review,* May-June, 1985, 1–5.
20. R. Price, *Roadmap to Entrepreneurial Success* (New York: American Management Association, 2004), 11.
21. Personal communication with Michael Heller, January 20, 2003.
22. Ladies Who Launch homepage, http://www.ladieswholaunch (January 3, 2007).
23. PricewaterhouseCooopers, *Three Keys to Obtaining Venture Capital* (New York: PricewaterhouseCoopers, 2001).
24. R. Ronstadt, "The Educated Entrepreneur: A New Era of Entrepreneurial Education Is Beginning," *American Journal of Small Business,* no. 10 (1985): 7–23.
25. G. Kawasaki, *The Art of the Start* (New York: Portfolio, 2004), 72.
26. J. W. Mullins, *The New Business Road Test* (London: Prentice Hall, 2003).

CHAPTER 2

DEVELOPING AND SCREENING BUSINESS IDEAS

INTRODUCTION

This chapter focuses on how to identify business ideas and how to determine if a specific idea is a good business opportunity. As mentioned in Chapter 1, many new businesses fail, not because the founders didn't work hard or weren't committed, but because the idea wasn't a good one to begin with. What's often missing in the ideas that fail is a lack of simple old-fashioned detective work. Detectives find clues by being curious and alert, by following leads, and by subjecting their ideas and evidence to scrutiny before they form judgments. Similarly, the best new businesses ideas occur to entrepreneurs who are curious and alert, know where to look for ideas, and are willing to subject their ideas to scrutiny and inspection.

To describe how to develop and screen business ideas, this chapter is divided into two parts. The first part focuses on the three most common sources of new business ideas and the techniques that entrepreneurs use to explore these sources and generate ideas. The second part of the chapter introduces a tool called the **First Screen,** which allows an entrepreneur to quickly determine whether an idea represents a potentially viable business opportunity. It's called the First Screen because after an idea is chosen, it should be subjected to a more thorough feasibility analysis (Chapter 3) to see if writing a full business plan is warranted. As mentioned in Chapter 1, these preliminary steps are important because there is no reason to write a business plan if an idea has little merit. The First Screen also provides an entrepreneur the flexibility to consider multiple business ideas,

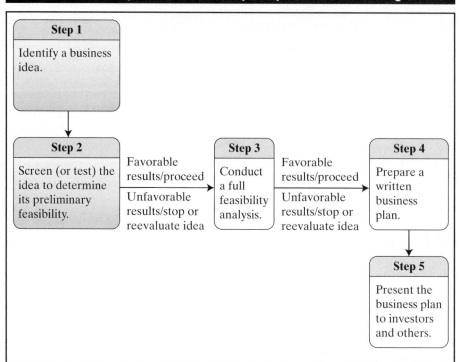

FIGURE 2-1 The Comprehensive Feasibility Analysis/Business Planning Process

rather than settling on a single idea from the outset. As will be explained later in the chapter, it shouldn't take more than an hour to run an idea through the First Screen worksheet. Hopefully, the expedient nature of this process will encourage a lot of idea generation, so the best possible idea ultimately emerges.

A reminder of the comprehensive feasibility analysis/business planning process introduced in Chapter 1 is provided in Figure 2-1. The highlighted areas show the stages of the process covered in this chapter. Recall that the comprehensive nature of this process is not meant to weigh it down or add extra work but instead to create a context in which only well-researched, well-thought out, and ultimately realistic and feasible ideas enter the business plan process.

Now let's look at the three most common sources of new business ideas and the specific techniques that entrepreneurs use to explore these sources and generate ideas.

THREE MOST COMMON SOURCES OF NEW BUSINESS IDEAS

The first step in creating an effective business plan is selecting an idea that fills a need and provides unique value to the customer. If a new business provides a product or service that's merely a different version of something that's already available, it has a tough road ahead. It's hard to get people to change their habits

FIGURE 2-2 Three Sources of New Business Ideas

| Changing Environmental Trends | Unsolved Problems | Gaps in the Marketplace |

or behaviors and switch from a product that they're currently using to a new one, even if the new product is better or less expensive. Instead, the most successful new business ideas add value in a unique or compelling way by capitalizing on one of the three sources of business ideas discussed here and shown in Figure 2-2.

CHANGING ENVIRONMENTAL TRENDS

The first source of new business ideas is changing environmental trends. The most important trends to follow are economic trends, social trends, technological advances, and political action and regulatory changes. Changes in these areas often provide the impetus for new business ideas. When looking at environmental trends to discern new business ideas, keep two caveats in mind. First, it's important to distinguish between trends and fads. Startups typically do not have the resources to ramp up quickly enough to take advantage of a fad. Second, even through we discuss each trend individually, they are interconnected and should be considered simultaneously when brainstorming new business ideas. For example, one reason the Apple iPod is so popular is because it benefits from several trends converging at the same time, including teenagers and young adults with increased disposable income (economic trend), an increasingly mobile population (social trend), and the continual miniaturization of electronics (technological trend). If any of these trends weren't present, the iPod wouldn't be as successful as it is.

Table 2-1 provides examples of how changes in environmental trends have provided the impetus for new business ideas. The following is a discussion of each trend and how changes in the trend provide openings for new business and product ideas.

ECONOMIC TRENDS

An understanding of economic trends is helpful in determining areas that are ripe for new business ideas and discerning areas to avoid. When the economy is strong, people are more willing to buy discretionary products and services that enhance their lives. Individual sectors of the economy have a direct impact on consumer buying patterns. For example, a drop in interest rates typically leads to an increase in new home construction, furniture sales, and appliance sales. Conversely, a string of corporate layoffs or a rapid decline in the stock market normally leads to a reduction in the demand for luxury goods.

When studying how economic forces affect opportunities, it is important to evaluate who has money to spend and what they spend it on. For example, an increase in the number of women in the workforce and their related increase in disposable income is largely responsible for the number of boutique clothing

TABLE 2-1 Companies Started to Take Advantage of Changes in Environmental Trends

Changing Environmental Trend	Resulting New Business Opportunities	Resulting Companies
Economic Trends		
Search for alternatives to traditional fossil fuels like gasoline and diesel fuel	Ethanol, biodiesel, solar power, wind-generated power	Altra Biofuels, SolFocus, Propel Biofuels, Miasole
Teenagers with more cash and disposable income	Designer clothes, CDs, MP3 players, game consoles	Hot Topic, Karma Loop, SanDisk, Alienware
Social Trends		
Increased interest in different, tastier, and healthier food	Healthy-fare restaurants, organic foods, healthy-focused grocery stores	Chipotle, Great Wraps, White Wave, Whole Foods
Increased interest in fitness as the results of new medical information warning of the hazards of being overweight	Fitness centers, in-house exercise equipment, health food stores	Curves, Stair Master Exercise Equipment, Espresso Fitness, GNC Nutrition Center
Technological Advances		
Development of the Internet	E-commerce, improved supply chain management, improved communication, social networking	Google, Amazon.com, Travelocity, MySpace.com, Facebook
Advances in biotechnology	Biotech-related pharmaceutical products, veterinary products, information services	Amgen, CardioDx, Orexigen, BioOnline
Political and Regulatory Changes		
Increased EPA and OSHA standards	Consulting companies, software to monitor compliance	ESS, PrimaTech, Compliance Consulting Services, Inc.
Sarbanes-Oxley Act of 2002	Software vendors, consulting companies	CEBOS, OiWare

stores targeting professional women that have opened in the past several years. Some of the boutiques, such as Ellen Tracey (http://www.ellentracy.com) and Tory Burch (http://www.toryburch.com), compete on a national scale, whereas others, such as Olivine (http://www.olivine.net), in Seattle, are single-store boutiques that have been opened by an individual entrepreneur. Similarly, as baby boomers reach retirement age, a sizable portion of their spending will be redirected to areas that facilitate their retirement. This trend will invariably spawn new businesses in many areas, largely because baby boomers have greater disposable income relative to previous generations. The most promising areas include finance, travel, housing, recreation, and health care.

An understanding of economic trends can also help identify areas to avoid. For example, this is not a good time to start a company that sells musical instruments, such as violins, trombones, and trumpets. Domestic production of musical instruments has declined 3 percent annually over the past four years, and U.S. imports of musical instruments were down 7 percent from 2005 to 2006.[1] A major reason for this decline is that middle schools and high schools, which have historically been major buyers of musical instruments, have reduced their purchases due to budget cuts. In addition, the advent of online auction sites, such as eBay (http://www.ebay.com), has made it easy for people to sell used musical instruments, which has cut into the market for new musical instrument sales.

SOCIAL TRENDS

An understanding of the impact of social trends on the way people live their lives and the products and services they need provides fertile ground for new business ideas and opportunities. Often, the reason that a product or service exists has more to do with satisfying a social need than the more transparent need the product fills. For example, the proliferation of fast-food restaurants isn't due primarily to people's love for fast food but rather to the fact that people are busy and often don't have time to cook their own meals. Similarly, social networking sites such as MySpace (http://www.myspace.com) and Facebook (http://www.facebook.com) aren't popular because they can be used to post music and pictures on a Web site. They're popular because they allow people to connect and communicate with each other, which is a natural human tendency.

Changes in social trends alter how people and businesses behave and how they set their priorities. These changes affect how products and services are built and sold. The following list provides a sample of the social trends that are currently affecting how individuals behave and set their priorities:

- Retirement of baby boomers
- The increasing diversity of the workforce
- Increasing interest in healthy foods and "green" products
- New forms of music and other types of entertainment
- The increasing focus on health care and fitness
- Emphasis on alternative forms of energy
- Increasing globalization of business
- Increased purchasing power of women

Each of these trends is providing the impetus for new business ideas and will continue to do so. For example, the increasing emphasis on alternative forms of energy is spawning business ideas ranging from solar power to wind-generated electricity to alternatives for fossil fuels. One new company, Greasecar Vegetable Fuel Systems (http://www.greasecar.com), makes conversion kits that allow diesel engines to run on vegetable oil. Justin Carvan, the company's founder, got interested in alternative fuels while at Hampshire College. The company is now growing at a rate of more than 200 percent per year and is projected to reach $2.5 million in annual sales shortly. [2] The increasing emphasis on green products is another social trend that is spawning interesting new business ideas. An example of a recent startup in this area is South West Trading Co. (http://www.soysilk.com), a business that specializes in earth-friendly, alternative fibers and textiles such as yarns made from bamboo, corn, and even recycled crab shells.

TECHNOLOGICAL ADVANCES

Technological advances provide an ongoing source of new business ideas. In most cases, the technology itself isn't the key to recognizing business opportunities. Instead, the key is to recognize how technologies can be used and harnessed to help satisfy basic or changing human needs. For example, the creation of the cell phone is a technological achievement, but it was motivated by an increasingly mobile population that finds many advantages to having the ability to communicate with coworkers, customers, friends, and family from anywhere and everywhere.

Technological advancements also provide opportunities to help people perform everyday tasks in a better or more convenient way. For example, OpenTable.com is a Web site that allows users to make restaurant reservations online and now covers most of the United States. If you're planning a trip to Boston, for example, you can access OpenTable.com, select the area of the city you'll be visiting, and view descriptions, reviews, customer ratings, and, in most cases, the menus of the restaurants in the area. You can then make a reservation at the restaurant of your choice and print a map of directions to the restaurant. The basic tasks that OpenTable.com helps people perform have always been done—looking for a restaurant, comparing prices and menus, soliciting feedback from people who are familiar with competing restaurants, and getting directions. What OpenTable.com does is help people perform these takes in a more convenient and expedient manner.

Another aspect of technological advances is that after a technology is created, products often emerge to advance it. For example, the creation of the Apple iPod has created an entire industry that produces iPod accessories. H2O Audio (http://www.H2OAudio.com), a company that was started by four former San Diego State University students, makes waterproof housings for the iPod and the iPod nano. The waterproof housing permits iPod users to listen to their iPod while swimming, surfing, snowboarding, or engaging in any activity where the iPod is likely to get wet. A wide variety of other accessories are also available for the iPod, from designer cases to car rechargers. It is now estimated that for every $3 spent on an iPod at, least $1 is spent on an accessory.[3]

POLITICAL ACTION AND REGULATORY CHANGES

Political and regulatory changes also provide the basis for new business ideas. For example, new laws create opportunities for entrepreneurs to start firms to help companies and individuals comply with these laws. Many firms have benefited by helping others comply with the Sarbanes-Oxley Act of 2002. Since the act was put on the books, publicly held companies have spent millions meeting new compliance regulations. The act requires companies to retain all business records, including electronic documents and messages, for at least five years. The beneficiaries of the act have been software and hardware companies, which help companies store and manage this data.[4]

On some occassions, changes in government regulations motivate entrepreneurs to start firms that differentiate themselves by "exceeding" the regulation. For example, several years ago, the Federal Trade Commission (FTC) changed the regulation about how far apart the wood or metal bars in an infant crib can be. If the bars are too far apart, a baby can get an arm or leg caught between the bars, causing an injury. An obvious business idea that might be spawned by this type of change is to produce a crib that is advertised and positioned as "exceeding" the new standard for width between bars and is "extra safe" for babies and young children. The change in regulation brings attention to the issue and provides ideal timing for a new company to reassure parents by providing a product that not only meets but exceeds the new regulation.

Political change also engenders new business and product opportunities. For example, global political instability and the threat of terrorism have resulted in many firms becoming more security conscious. These companies need new products and services to protect their physical assets and intellectual property as well as protect their customers and employees.

UNSOLVED PROBLEMS

The second approach to new business ideas is unsolved problems. Problems can be experienced or recognized by people through their jobs, hobbies, or everyday activities. Commenting on this issue and how noticing problems can lead to the recognition of business ideas, Philip Kotler, a marketing expert, said:

> Look for problems. People complain about it being hard to sleep
> through the night, get rid of clutter in their homes, find an affordable
> vacation, trace their family origins, get rid of garden weeds, and so on.
> As the late John Gardner, founder of Common Cause, observed:
> "Every problem is a brilliantly disguised opportunity."[5]

Consistent with this observation, many companies have been started by people who have experienced a problem in their own lives, and in the process of solving the problem, realized that they were on to a business idea. For example, in 2006, Christine Ingemi, a mother of 4 children under 11, became concerned by how loud her children were playing their MP3 players. She said she could hear music coming through her children's' MP3 players' earphones when she was driving her van with the music on. To prevent her children from playing their MP3 players too loud, she and her husband, Rick, did some research, interviewed several audiologists, and invented a set of earbuds that limit the volume entering the user's ears. After her kids started using the earbuds, Ingemi began getting inquiries from other parents asking where they could get a similar device. To make the device available to others, Ingemi started a business called Ingemi Corp. (http://ingemicorp.com) to sell her iHearSafe earbuds.[6] Similarly, Laura Udall, another mother, invented an alternative to traditional backpacks when her fourth-grade daughter complained daily that her back hurt from carrying her backpack. After conducting research, obtaining feedback from student focus groups, and building several prototypes, Udall invented the ZUCA, a backpack on rollers that strikes the ideal balance between functionality and "cool" for kids. ZUCA (http://www.zuca.com) is now a successful company, and its rolling backpacks can be purchased online or through a number of retailers.

Advances in technology often result in problems for people who can't use the technology in the way it is sold to the masses. For example, some older people find traditional cell phones hard to use—the buttons are small, the text is hard to read, and it's often hard to hear someone on a cell phone in a noisy room. To solve these problems, GreatCall Inc. (http://www.greatcall.com), a recent startup, is producing a cell phone called the Jitterbug, which is designed specifically for older users. The Jitterbug features large buttons, easy-to-read text, and a cushion that cups around the ear to improve sound quality. The phone also includes a button that connects the user directly with an operator, who can assist in completing a call. Another company, Firefly Mobile (http://www.fireflymobile.com), is now creating a cell phone designed specifically for tweens, ages 8 to 12. The phone only weighs two ounces and is designed to fit a kid's hand. The phone includes appropriate limitations for a young child and speed-dial keys for Mom and Dad.

If you're having difficulty solving a particular problem, one technique that is useful is to find an instance where a similar problem was solved and then apply that solution to your problem. An example is provided by Susan Nichols, the founder of Yogitoes (http://www.yogitoes.com), a company that makes nonslip rugs for yoga enthusiasts. Several yoga positions require participants to strike poses where they balance their weight on their feet at an angle. In this position, it is easy to fall or slip when using a regular rug or mat. Nichols looked for a yoga mat that would prevent her from slipping but found out that no one knew how to make one. So she started looking for an example of a product that was designed specifically to prevent it from slipping on a hard floor, to study how it functioned. Eventually, she stumbled upon a dog bowl with rubber nubs on the bottom to prevent it from sliding when a large dog ate or drank from it. Using the dog bowl (of all things) as a model, Nichols found a manufacturer who helped her develop a rug with small PVC nubs that prevents yoga participants from slipping when they perform yoga moves. Nichols started Yogitoes to sell the rugs, and sales were on track to hit $3 million in 2006.[7]

Many other colorful examples of people who launched businesses to solve problems are included in Table 2-2.

GAPS IN THE MARKETPLACE

The third source of business ideas are gaps in the marketplace. There are many examples of products that consumers need or want that aren't available in a particular

TABLE 2-2 Companies Started to Solve a Problem

Entrepreneurs	Year	Problem	Solution	Company That Resulted
Arlene Harris	2006	Many cell phones are too complicated and the buttons are too small for seniors to use easily.	Design a cell phone for seniors that is easy to use, has large buttons, and has a single button that when pushed connects to an operator that can assist with a call.	GreatCall (http://www.jitterbug.com)
Scott Kliger	2006	411 (directory assistance) calls are expensive, costing from $1.25 to $3.75 per call, depending on your cellular provider.	Create a free, nationwide, advertiser supported directory assistance service.	Jingle Networks (http://www.free411.com)
David Bateman	2002	No way existed for apartment renters to pay their monthly rent online.	Create a software product that allows apartment complexes to enable their tenants to pay online.	Property Solutions (http://www.propertysolutions.com)
Lisa Druxman	2002	No fitness routine was available to help new mothers stay fit and be with their newborns at the same time.	Create a franchise organization that promotes a workout routine (which involves a 45-minute power walk with strollers) that mothers and their babies can do together.	Stroller Stride (http://www.strollerstride.com)
Richard Cole	1999	No service was available to help people with computer problems at home.	Create an organization that makes "house calls" and helps people solve computer problems in their homes.	Geeks On Call (http://www.geeksoncall.com)

location or aren't available at all. Part of the problem is created by large retailers, such as Wal-Mart and Costco, which compete primarily on price and offer the most popular items targeted toward mainstream consumers. Although this approach allows the large retailers to achieve economies of scale, it leaves gaps in the marketplace. This is the reason that clothing boutiques and specialty shops exist. These businesses are willing to carry merchandise that doesn't sell in large enough quantities for Wal-Mart or Costco to carry.

Product gaps in the marketplace represent potentially viable business opportunities. For example, in 2000, Tish Ciravolo realized that there were no guitars on the market made specifically for women. To fill this gap, she started Daisy Rock (http://www.daisyrock.com), a company that makes guitars just for women. Daisy Rock guitars are stylish, have feminine names (e.g., Atomic Pink, Power Pink, Rainbow Sparkle), and incorporate design features that accommodate a woman's smaller hands and build. A more common example of a company that filled a gap in the marketplace is provided by p.45 (http://www.p45.com), a women's clothing boutique in Chicago. The store carries innovative collections from young fashion designers, original pieces of jewelry made by Chicago area residents, unique shoes, and accessories that complement the clothing in the store. p.45 fills a gap in the marketplace by offering people with particular tastes a line of clothing and accessories that they couldn't find at a mainstream store. It is also located in an area of Chicago that has a sufficient critical mass of upscale shoppers to support the store.

Gaps in the marketplace are commonly recognized when people become frustrated because they can't find a product or service that they need, and they recognize that other people feel the same frustration. This scenario played out for Lorna Ketler and Barb Wilkins, who because frustrated when they couldn't find stylish "plus-sized" clothing that fit. In response to their frustration, they started Bodacious (http://www.bodacious.ca), a store that sells fun and stylish clothing for hard-to-fit women. Ketler and Wilkins' experience illustrates how compelling a business idea can be when it strikes just the right cord by filling a gap that deeply resonates with a specific clientele. Reflecting on the success of Bodacious, Wilkins said:

> It's so rewarding when you take a risk and it pays off for you and
> people are telling you every single day, "I'm so glad you're here." We've
> had people cry in our store. It happens a lot. They're crying because
> they'so so happy (that they're finding clothes that fit). One woman put
> on a pair of jeans that fit her, and she called me an hour later and said,
> "They still look good, even at home!" Sometimes people have a body
> change that happens, whether they have been ill or had a baby, and
> there's lots of emotion involved in it. If you can go out and buy clothes
> that fit, that helps people feel good about themselves.[8]

A related technique for generating new business ideas is to take an existing product or service and create a new category by targeting a completely different target market. This approach essentially involves creating a gap and filling it. An example is PopCap games (http://www.popcap.com), a company that was started to create a new category in the electronic games industry called "casual games." The games are casual and relaxing rather than flashy and action-packed and are made for people who want to wind down after a busy day. Currently, 90 percent of the company's customers are women 25 years old or older, which is a completely different demographic than the young males that the mainstream game manufacturers target.[9]

Another approach to filling gaps in the marketplace is to service an area that is lacking a particular product or service. For example, SPC Office Products (http://www.spcop.com) is a company that sells the same products as Staples and Office Depot but focuses on towns under 20,000 in population. As a rule of thumb, SPC doesn't like to open a store that's within 120 miles of a Staples or Office Depot.[10]

Other examples of companies that were launched to fill gaps in the marketplace are included in Table 2-3.

TABLE 2-3   Companies Started to Fill a Gap in the Marketplace

Gap in the Marketplace	Resulting New Business Opportunity	Companies That Resulted
No fitness centers designed specifically for women	Fitness centers that are just for women, featuring workouts and exercise machines designed specifically for women, and fitting the time and budgetary constraints of its female clientele	Curves, Contours Express, Lady of America
Lack of toys that focus on the intellectual development of a child	Toy stores, direct-sales organizations (such as Tupperware), and Web sites that sell educational toys	Discovery Toys, Kazoo & Company
No hair care, skin care, and body care stores that are fresher and more sophisticated than standard Bath and Body outlets but less upscale than high-end stores such as Nordstrom's and Sacks	Specialty boutiques that offer fresh, new natural and organic hair care, skin care, and body care products	Aveda, Origins, Sephora
Restaurants that are both fast and serve good food	Fast-casual restaurants that combine the advantages of fast-food (fast service) and casual dining (good food)	Panera Bread, Chipotle, Cosi, Bruegger's
Shortage of clothing stores that sell fashionable clothing for hard-to-fit people	Boutiques that sell fashionable clothing for hard-to-fit people, including plus-sized clothes, maternity clothes, or clothing for tall or short people	Casual Male, Ashley Stewart, Casual Plus, iGigi

TECHNIQUES FOR GENERATING IDEAS

The three sources of new business ideas are used by people in both subtle and overt ways. Some people recognize new business ideas through casual observation, intuition, or even serendipity or luck. Other people are more overt and use the three sources of business ideas to deliberately try to generate new business ideas, whether they have an idea of the type of business they want to start or whether they are starting from scratch. This section of the chapter focuses on three techniques that people use to explicitly try to generate new business ideas.

While considering these techniques, remember that business ideas take time to develop, so it's important to not become discouraged if an idea doesn't come to you quickly. It's also important to realize that the best ideas aren't necessarily the most original. It normally exceeds the budget of a new firm to educate the public about a revolutionary or original idea. The following Business Plan Insight box illustrates the most realistic categories of business ideas for new firms.

BRAINSTORMING

The most common way to generate business ideas is through brainstorming. The term **brainstorming** is a catch phrase that means different things to different people. Technically, a brainstorming "session" is targeted to a specific topic about

---

BUSINESS PLAN INSIGHT

Why the Most Original Ideas Aren't Always the Best Ideas

When considering business ideas, it's important to realize that the best ideas aren't always the most original ones. It normally exceeds the budget of a new firm to educate the public about a revolutionary new product or service idea.

The following table provides a quick visual depiction of the four categories of new business ideas and the most realistic categories for new firms. The simplest ideas (existing products in existing markets) are located in Box 1, and are generally undesirable because they are in crowded fields with stiff competition. The trickiest and the most expensive to implement ideas are in Box 4 (new products in new markets) and are usually avoided because they put a new firm too far out on a limb. The most practical ideas for most new businesses are located in either Box 2 or Box 3. The vast majority of new businesses referred to in this book are Box 2 or Box 3 startups.

	Existing Products	*New Products*
Existing Markets	1	2
New Markets	3	4

Adapted from PlanWare, "Getting New Business Ideas," accessed at http://www.planware.org, May 2, 2007.

which a group is instructed to come up with ideas. The leader of the group asks the participants to share their ideas. One person shares an idea, another person reacts to it, another person reacts to the reaction, and so on. A flip chart or white-board is typically used to record the ideas. A productive brainstorming session is freewheeling and lively. The session is not used for analysis or decision making—the ideas during a brainstorming session need to be filtered and analyzed, but this is done later.

Brainstorming sessions dedicated to generating new business ideas are often less formal. For example, Marcene Sonneborn, an adjunct professor in the Whitman School of Management at Syracuse University, uses a tool she developed called the "bug report" to help her students brainstorm business ideas. She instructs her students to list 75 things that "bug" them in their everyday lives. The number 75 was chosen because if forces students to go beyond thinking about obvious things that bug them (campus parking, roommates, scooping snow in the winter) and think more deeply. On occasion, students actually hold focus groups with their friends to brainstorm ideas and fill out their lists. Another particularly effective approach to brainstorming is to use the three sources for new business ideas as a way of organizing the discussion. Imagine you are part of a small group that is trying to brainstorm ideas for a new type of fitness center. You know the market is too crowded to support another generic center, so you're looking for novel ideas. You create three columns on a whiteboard labeled Changing Environmental Trends, Unsolved Problems, and Gaps in the Marketplace. You then start brainstorming specific ideas, looking at each category individually and then looking at how the categories interact with each other. After brainstorming dozens of ideas in each category, you start grouping the ideas into themes or patterns to create more solid ideas. One pattern jumps out at you: the population is aging, older people are increasingly interested in fitness, many of the exercise machines and classes taught in traditional fitness centers aren't suitable for older people, and there are no fitness centers designed specifically for the 50+ demographic. Based on this pattern, your first solid idea is to create a fitness center designed specifically for people 50 years old and older.

FOCUS GROUPS

A **focus group** is a gathering of 5 to 10 people who are selected because of their relationship to the issues being discussed. Although focus groups are used for a variety of purposes, they can be used to help generate new business ideas.

Focus groups typically involve a group of people familiar with a topic, who are brought together to respond to questions and shed light on an issue through the give-and-take nature of a group discussion. Focus groups usually work best as a follow-up to brainstorming, when the general idea for a business has been formulated, such as opening a fitness center for the 50+ demographic, but further refinement of the idea is needed. Usually, focus groups are conducted by trained moderators. The moderator's primary goals are to keep the group "focused" and to generate lively discussion. Much of the effectiveness of a focus group session depends on the moderator's ability to ask questions and keep the discussion on track. For example, to further explore the idea of opening a fitness center designed specifically for older people, a focus group might be assembled that consists of 10 people who are 50 years old or older and are members of generic fitness centers. The moderator might ask, "What is it that you don't like about your fitness center?" A 71-year-old man might say, "I don't like the classes that are offered. They include various types of aerobics and spinning, which I don't mind, but the music is too loud, the pace is too quick, and they are always taught by guys and gals in their twenties who have no idea of what I'm going through in life." The moderator may then ask the group, "How many of you would feel more comfortable if the classes in your fitness center were taught by people your own age?" If 7 out of the 10 hands shot up, you might have just discovered one refinement for your business idea.

On some occasions, hybrid focus group methodologies are used to achieve specific insights and goals. An example is **College Drop-Ins**. This approach involves paying a pair of college students to host a party at their campus and providing them a budget to buy food and snacks. During the party, the hosts interview and videotape other students about specific market issues or business ideas. Everything is up-front—the partygoers are told that the information is being collected for a market research firm (on behalf of a client). Most students are cooperative. One student, commenting on a College Drop-In party he attended, said "Everybody knows it costs a lot to throw a party and if all they have to do is give up 10 minutes of time to offer their opinions, it's a no-brainer!"[11]

LIBRARY AND INTERNET RESEARCH

A third approach to generate new business ideas is to conduct library and Internet research. A natural tendency is to think that an idea should be chosen, and the process of researching the idea should then begin. This approach is too linear. Often, the best ideas emerge when the general notion of an idea, like opening an innovative type of fitness center, is merged with extensive library and Internet research, which may provide insights into the best type of innovative fitness center to pursue.

Libraries are often underused as a source of information for generating business ideas. The best approach to using a library is to discuss your general area of interest with a reference librarian, who can point you to useful resources, such as industry-specific magazines, trade journals, and industry reports. Simply browsing through several issues of a trade journal on a topic can spark new ideas. Very powerful search engines and databases are also available through university libraries, which would cost hundreds or thousands of dollars to access on your own. An example is Mintel (http://www.mintel.com), a company that publishes market research on all major industries and subcategories within industries. Mintel is a fee-based site but is normally free if accessed through a university or large city library. Mintel has literally dozens of pages of information on the "Health and Fitness Club" industry alone. Spending time reading through the information could spark new ideas for fitness centers or help affirm an existing idea. Spending just a few minutes reading Mintel's report bodes well for the idea of opening a fitness center for the 50+ demographic. According to the report, while 45 percent of people say they exercise regularly, only 22 percent belong to fitness clubs, which suggests there are opportunities for membership growth. Households with higher income are more likely to belong to fitness clubs, which fits the 50+ demographic. Individuals who are 35 to 54 are the most likely candidates to join health clubs. Interestingly, 67 percent of the people who currently don't belong to a fitness club said they would join one if they knew the activities would keep them motivated. Mintel's summary of the fitness club industry concluded by stating "it is important for health clubs to tailor their offerings to their target market."[12] This is exactly what a fitness center for the 50+ demographic would do.

Internet research is also important. If you're starting from scratch, simply typing "new business ideas" into Google or Yahoo! will produce links to newspaper and magazine articles about the "hottest" and "latest" new business ideas. Although these types of article are general in nature, they represent a starting point if you're trying to generate new business ideas from scratch. If you have a specific idea in mind, like the fitness center concept we've been discussing, a useful technique is to set up a Google or Yahoo! "alert" using keywords that pertain to your topic of interest. Google and Yahoo! alerts are e-mail updates of the latest Google or Yahoo! results (i.e., Web site updates, press releases, news articles, blog postings) based on your topic. This technique, which is available free, will feed you a daily stream of news article and blog postings about a specific topic.

FIRST SCREEN

After a business idea, or several ideas, have been chosen, it is important to have a way to quickly assess the merits of the idea, before subjecting it to full feasibility and business planning. The **First Screen** provides a mechanism for quickly assessing the merits of a business idea.[*] As mentioned earlier, it is called the First Screen because it is an entrepreneur's (or group of entrepreneurs') first pass at assessing the feasibility of a business idea. If a business idea cuts muster at this stage, and the decision is made to pursue it, it will be subjected to a full feasibility analysis (Chapter 3) before a full business plan is written. Recall, these early steps are necessary to make sure that only ideas with sufficient potential enter the full business planning process. The First Screen template is provided in Appendix 2.1 at the end of this chapter.

Although completing the First Screen does take some research and analysis, it is not meant to be a lengthy process. It is also not meant to be a shot-in-the-dark. The best ideas are the ones that emerge from analysis that is based on facts and good information, rather than speculation and guesses. Appendix 2.2, at the

---

[*]Copies of the First Screen worksheet, in both MS Word and PDF format, can be obtained from the author's Web site at www.prenhall.com/entrepreneurship.

end of this chapter, contains the Internet Resource Table that may be particularly helpful in completing a First Screen analysis. Several of the most valuable resources, such as IBISWorld, Mintel, and ProQuest, are fee-based but are typically free if accessed through a university or major public library. It is well worth your time to learn how to use these resources—they are rich in terms of their content and analysis.

The First Screen contains 25 items and should be able to be completed in less than an hour. A mental transition needs to be made when completing the First Screen from thinking of a business idea as just an idea to thinking of it as a business. The First Screen is an assessment of a *business* idea rather than strictly a *product* or *service* idea. The mechanics of filling out the First Screen Worksheet are straightforward. The final section of the worksheet, "Overall Potential," includes a section that allows for suggested revisions to a business idea to improve its potential or feasibility. For example, a business might start out planning to manufacture its own product, but through the process of completing the worksheet, learn that the capital needed to set up a manufacturing facility is prohibitive in terms of the both the money that would need to be raised and the extended time to break even for the business. As a result, two of the five items in Part 5, "Initial Capital Investment" and "Time to Break Even," might be rated "low potential." This doesn't need to be the end of the story, however. In the column labeled "Suggestions for Improving the Potential," the founders of the business might write, "Consider contract manufacturing or outsourcing as an alternative to manufacturing the product ourselves." The value of the First Screen worksheet is that it draws attention to issues like this one and forces the founders to think about alternatives. If this particular suggestion is realistic and is determined to be a better way to proceed, a revised version of the First Screen might rate the two factors referred to previously, "Initial Capital Requirements" and "Time to Break Even," as "high potential" rather than "low potential" because of the change in the business concept that was made. Business ideas should always be see as fluid and subject to change. Little is lost if several versions of the First Screen are completed for the same business idea, however, there is much more to be lost if a startup gets half way through writing a business plan and concludes that the business isn't feasible, or actually launches a business without having all the kinks worked out.

A brief explanation of each section of the First Screen Worksheet follows.

PART 1: STRENGTH OF THE BUSINESS IDEA

High-potential ideas are typically drawn from one of the three sources of business ideas discussed in this chapter and are timely in terms of market introduction. In regard to timeliness, for an entrepreneur to capitalize on an idea, its window of opportunity must be open.[13] The term *window of opportunity* is a metaphor describing the time period in which a firm can realistically enter a new market. Once the market for a new product is established, its window of opportunity opens. As the market grows, firms enter and try to establish a profitable position. At some point, the market matures, and the window of opportunity closes. An important judgment call is whether the window of opportunity for a particular business idea is open or closed.

A new idea must "add value" for its buyer or end user in some appreciable way, like the ZUCA (backpack on rollers) adds value by allowing school kids to pull rather than carry their backpacks, and the IHearSafe earbuds add value by limiting the volume of music produced by an MP3 player. Value refers to worth, importance, or utility. A related topic is the extent to which consumers are already reasonably satisfied. If consumers, in general, are satisfied with the products or services that are similar to the ones you're thinking about producing, your job will be much harder than if people are ambivalent or dissatisfied. In addition, investors and others tend to be skeptical of ideas that require meaningful changes in behavior, and they shy away from them as a result. An example of what this means is provided by contrasting the adoption rate of TiVo (http://www.tivo.com) versus YouTube (http://www.youtube.com). TiVo users had to change their behavior quite a bit by purchasing a new product, learning how to use it, and paying a monthly subscription fee. As a result, even though many of TiVo's early adopters sang its praises, most people never signed up (and still haven't) because they either never quite understood what TiVo is or thought it would be too big of a hassle or too expensive to purchase and set up. In contrast, YouTube users didn't have to change their behavior much at all. Most of its users were already on the Internet, knew how to navigate Web sites, and quickly caught on to how to use YouTube and even post video clips.[14] The result is that YouTube took off much quicker than TiVo. Although this example is a simplification, it illustrates the basic point that requiring consumers to change their behaviors is a difficult task.

Several online resources, such as the Business & Company Resource Center, Mintel, and IBISWorld, provide information on industry trends. These discussions provide data on the most promising trends in an industry, which often helps affirm or refute the attractiveness of a potential business idea. Two particularly powerful search engines, ProQuest and MagPortal, are useful for gathering more general information about a product or service idea. Often, simply querying a product or service idea via one of these search engines produces magazine and newspaper articles that provide important insight.

PART 2: INDUSTRY-RELATED ISSUES

The industry that a company enters is extremely important. In various studies, researchers have found that 8 to 30 percent of the variation in firm profitability is directly attributable to industry factors. Among the most important factors for an industry are the number of competitors, the stage it's at in its life cycle, and its growth rate. Industries that are growing, are not crowded, and are in the emergence or growth stages of their life cycles are more receptive to new entrants than industries with the opposite characteristics. An important caveat to this set of heuristics is the target market that a new firm selects. There are markets within

TABLE 2-4 Average Net Income for Firms in Certain Industries

Industry	Average Net Income
Advertising	5.0%
Book publishers	7.5%
Electronics and appliance stores	2.5%
Food and beverage stores	2.2%
Pharmaceutical products	14.4%
Telecommunications	10.1%

older, crowded, slow-growth industries that defy the industry's norms and provide attractive opportunities for new firms.

The average operating margins for the firms in an industry are also important. Some industries simply provide more opportunities for profits than others. For example, BizStats records the average net income for firms in certain industries, according to the most recently reported information as shown in Table 2-4.[15] (If you're looking for net income estimates for an industry you're interested in, BizStats and IBISWorld are the best bets. BizStats is more limited than IBISWorld in terms of the number of industries that it follows.)

This chart provides a visual depiction of how much average profitability varies by industry.

Very detailed and comprehensive industry data, which is sufficient to make an informed judgment on each item in Part 2 of the First Screen, is available through Mintel, IBISWorld, and Standard & Poor's NetAdvantage. These resources are typically free if accessed through a university library Web site.

Part 3: Market- and Customer-Related Issues

The identification of the target market in which the firm will compete is extremely important. A target market is a place within a larger industry or market segment that represents a narrower group of customers with similar interests. Most new firms do not start by selling to broad markets. Instead, most start by identifying an emerging or underserved niche within a larger market. The ability to create "barriers to entry" is an important aspect of any firm's potential competitive advantage. A **barrier to entry** is a condition that creates a disincentive for another firm to enter a company's niche market. Barriers to entry can be created through a number of means, such as economies of scale, product differentiation, unique access to distribution channels, and intellectual property protection, such as patents.

Mintel publishes periodic reports that describe the purchasing power of various age and demographic groups, along with their spending patterns. In terms of the purchasing power of people in a specific geographic area, American Factfinder, drawing on census data, provides access to the medium household income for any city, county, or ZIP code in the United States. Similar, and often more current information, is provided by City-Data.com. The ease of making customers aware of a new product or service is another important consideration. A new firm typically does not have the resources to educate the public about a revolutionary new product or service, unless the firm is particularly savvy at using the blogosphere and other means to get the word out for free.

Another important issue is the growth potential of a firm's target market. Because a startup's target market is normally a small slice of a larger market, it's usually harder to get a feel for the growth potential of a target market than it is for a broader industry. For example, if you were interested in the growth rate of the pet food and supplies industry, that number would be fairly easy to get from IBISWorld, Mintel, or Standard and Poor's NetAdvantage. But if you planned to produce high-end organic pet food, the growth rate for that slice (or segment) of the industry isn't as easy to find. The best approach in this type of circumstance is to first read through the applicable industry reports through the sources mentioned previously to see if organic pet food is mentioned and discussed. The next step is to search articles on "organic pet food" through Lexis-Nexis Academic, ProQuest, MagPortal, Google, and other search services you are familiar with. Another excellent potential source of information is an industry trade association. This pursuit is somewhat of a scavenger hunt. For instance, in the organic pet food example just discussed, there are pet food trade associations, such as the American Pet Products Manufacturers Association (http://www.appma.org) and organic products trade associations, such as the Organic Trade Association (http://www.ota.com). Both associations may have useful information on the growth rate of organic pet food sales, either on their Web sites or by contacting them directly. Industry trade journals are another potential source of information.

If you're thinking about producing a product or service that doesn't exist, such as H20Audio did when it contemplated producing waterproof housings for the Apple iPod, your task is harder. Obviously, at that time, there wasn't a market for waterproof housing for the Apple iPod. In these instances, you have to be somewhat creative. Markets do exist for Apple iPod accessories and for water sport products. Using the approaches suggested earlier, you would try to learn as much as you could about the market for iPod accessories and the market for water sports, and then make an informed judgment.

PART 4: FOUNDER- (OR FOUNDERS-) RELATED ISSUES

This portion of the First Screen requires the potential founder or founders of the business to complete a self-assessment, so it is important to be honest and fair. Few firms, particularly if they are being started by younger people, will score high on each of the five dimensions. Still, the strength of the founding team is extremely important. An often-repeated phrase among investors is that they would rather invest in a strong founding team with a weak product idea, than a weak founding team with a strong product idea. The attributes that make for a strong founder (or founding team) is experience in the industry the new venture is entering, skills as they relate to the new venture's product or service, and broad social and professional networks in the industry the firm will be entering. It is also important that the new firm is consistent with the founder's (or founding team's) personal goals and aspirations.

A particularly important issue is the likelihood that a firm will be able to put together a team to launch and grow the new venture. As one expert has put it, "People are the one factor in product . . . that animates all the others."[16] A good start is for a firm to assemble an advisory board, which will assist in future recruitment and selection efforts.

PART 5: FINANCIAL ISSUES

The initial capital investment needed to start a firm is important. Although an exact estimate is not needed at this point, it is important to have a sense of the magnitude of the investment. According to the Wells Fargo/Gallup Small Business Index, the average small business is started for about $10,000, with the majority of the money coming from the owners' personal savings.[17] That figure cuts across all types of businesses, however, including home-based businesses. Many businesses cost much more to start. For a retail or service business, it is fairly easy to put together a good-faith estimate of the capital that will be needed. For a business that is developing a new product, it is much harder to estimate the development costs that will be incurred and the costs associated with securing distribution for the product. The best way to approach this task is to talk to industry experts, read industry-specific blogs and trade journals, and read through industry-specific reports available through the resources mentioned earlier. A directory of trade magazines, sorted by industry, is available by typing "trade show directory" into any major search engine.

If you're unsure of the capital requirements necessary to enter an industry, IBISWorld provides a discussion of the overall "cost structure" associated with owning firms in the industries that it follows. Other reporting services provide similar information. The information contained in these reports is often quite insightful. For example, IBISWorld reports that many firms in the fitness industry rent rather than own their facilities and often lease rather than purchase the exercise equipment they feature, such as treadmills and rowing machines. These factors lower the capital requirements necessary to enter the fitness club industry, which in part explains the large number of participants in the industry.

The number of revenue drivers that a business has is also important. For example, most electronics store have several revenue drivers, which include selling electronics products, selling extended warranties, servicing and repairing electronic products, and installing products, such as car stereos. Some of the revenue drivers may be loss leaders, such as a $299 27-inch color television, to get people in the store. Other items, like car stereos, may make very little money, but large margins might be available through an installation service. Startups don't want to lose focus by creating multiple revenue drivers, but typically the financial potential of a firm is greater if it has several ways of generating sales.

The time it takes a firm to break even or recoup its initial investment is also important. Businesses that have a fairly low initial investment break even fairly quickly, as the income generated by the business pays back the initial investment. The time to break even is lengthier and the risk is higher for businesses with high capital investments or lengthy product development cycles.

The next issue to consider for this part of the First Screen is to assess the financial performance of businesses similar to the one you are contemplating to get a feel for the type of sales and financial returns to anticipate. Both ReferenceUSA and the "Build a List" feature in Hoover's premium service provide estimates of the sales of privately owned firms, which are more likely to be similar to your start-up than publicly traded firms. Of course, you'll need to make adjustments based on the initial size of your firm compared to firms you're looking at and on other factors. Another approach is to search for newspaper and magazine articles on firms that are similar to the one you're thinking about starting. Often, the articles will comment on the sales and profitability of the firms they are focusing on.

The final item in Part 5 refers to your ability to fund the initial product (or service) development and initial startup expenses for your venture from personal funds or via bootstrapping. The salience of this item depends on how far along a firm is at the time it is preparing its business plan. If all a company has is an idea, it will be tough to get financing or funding. Normally, investors and lenders like to see a working prototype of an idea with customer feedback and preferably initial sales before they invest. As a result, a firm is much better off if it can self-fund and/or bootstrap its initial product development and startup costs before it tries to raise investment capital or borrow money.

Chapter Summary

1. The three most common sources of new business ideas include changing environmental trends, unsolved problems, and gaps in the marketplace.
2. The most important environmental trends to follow, in the context of discovering new business ideas, are economic trends, social trends, technological advances, and political action and regulatory changes.
3. Many companies have been started by people who have experienced a problem in their lives and then realized that the solution to the problem represented a business opportunity.
4. Gaps in the marketplace exist when there are products or services that consumers want but that aren't available through larger firms or aren't available at all.
5. Three techniques that entrepreneurs use to generate new business ideas include brainstorming, focus groups, and library and Internet research.
6. The most common way to identify business ideas quickly is through brainstorming. Technically, a brainstorming "session" is targeted to a specific topic about which a group is instructed to come up with ideas.
7. A focus group is a gathering of 5 to 10 people who are selected because of their relationship to the issues being discussed. Although focus groups are used for a variety of purposes, they can be used to help generate new business ideas.

8. Often, the best new business ideas emerge when the general notion of an idea is merged with extensive library and Internet research.

9. Once a business idea, or several ideas, have been chosen, it is important to have a way to quickly assess the merits of the idea before subjecting the idea to a full feasibility analysis. The First Screen provides a mechanism for quickly assessing the merits of a business idea.

10. Although completing the First Screen does take some research and analysis, it is not meant to be a lengthy process. It contains 25 items and should be able to be completed in less than an hour.

Review Questions

1. What are the three most common sources of new business ideas? Briefly describe how each of the sources spawns potential business ideas.

2. What four environmental trends provide the richest sources of new business ideas? List each environmental trend and provide an example of the type of business idea that it might create.

3. Explain how "unsolved problems" can create a business idea. Provide an example that was not mentioned in the chapter of a business that was created by solving an unsolved problem.

4. Explain how finding a gap in the marketplace can lead to new business ideas.

5. Describe the four categories of new business ideas and the most realistic categories for new firms.

6. Describe the brainstorming process. How can brainstorming be used to generate new business ideas?

7. Describe how a focus group is set up and how it can be used to generate new business ideas?

8. Explain how library and Internet research can be used to generate new business ideas?

9. Why is it necessary to quickly assess the merits of a business idea before conducting a feasibility analysis and writing a business plan?

10. Describe the makeup and the purpose of the First Screen.

Application Questions

1. Tim Jensen thinks he has identified a new e-commerce idea, but he wants to make sure that he isn't just following a hunch. What criteria can Tim use to make sure that his business idea has a fundamentally sound basis?

2. Megan Holms just finished reading this chapter and was struck by the idea of opening a fitness center for people 50 years old and older. She is interested in running with the idea, but first wants to make sure that it is consistent with changing economic trends, social trends, and technological advances. Make a table that lists these three environmental trends and the changes in these trends that work for and work against Megan's idea.

3. Think about the problems that you encounter in your everyday life. Select one problem, and describe how solving the problem might represent the basis for a new business idea.

4. A good friend of yours, who works for a large corporation, was just notified that his job will be phased out in three months. He is tired of working for large companies and wants to start his own business. He has several vague notions of businesses to start but nothing specific. Make some suggestions to your friend about how he might go about deciding on a business to start.

5. Complete the First Screen for the business idea you selected to answer Question #3. Which areas of the First Screen were the easiest to complete and which areas were the most difficult? Was the result the one you expected?

Endnotes

1. First Research homepage, http://www.firstresearch.com (February 3, 2007).

2. S. Cooper, and others "The Hot List," Entrepreneur.com, December, 2006.

3. D. Darlin, "The iPod Ecosystem," *The New York Times,* February 3, 2006.

4. D. Fuscaldo, "For Tech Firms, Sarbanes-Oxley Provides Revenue Opportunities," *The Wall Street Journal,* December 1, 2004, B2A.

5. P. Kotler, *Marketing Insights from A to Z* (New York: John Wiley & Sons, 2003), 128.

6. K. Spiller, "Low-Decible Earbuds Keep Noise at a Reasonable Level," *The Nashua Telegraph,* August 13, 2006.

7. S. Schubert, "Getting a Foothold in the Yoga Market," *Business 2.0,* July, 2006, 64.

8. Ladies Who Launch homepage, http://www.ladieswholaunch.com (May 4, 2007).

9. nPost homepage, http://www.npost.com, (May 4, 2007).

10. J. Bailey, "How One Small Store Thrives Among Giants," (StartupJournal). http://www.startupjournal.com (May 4, 2007).

11. S. Gold, "Have Insights, Will Party," *The Hub Magazine,* November 9, 2005, 18.

12. Mintel, 2007.

13. D. N. Snull, "The Three Windows of Opportunity," *Harvard Business Review Working Knowledge,* June 6, 2005.

14. D. Beisel, "Frameworking Changes in Consumer Behavior" (Genuine VC). http://www.genuinevc.com (August 1, 2006).

15. Biz Stats homepage, http://www.bizstats.com (May 6, 2007).

16 C. Read and others, *eCFO* (Chichester, UK: Joun Wiley & Sons), 117.

17. Wells Fargo/Gallup Small Business Index, "How Much Money Does It Take to Start a Small Business?" (Well Fargo Bank, August 15, 2006). http://www.wellsfargo.com (May 4, 2007).

First Screen

PART 1: STRENGTH OF THE BUSINESS IDEA

For each item, circle the most appropriate answer and make note of the $(-1), (0),$ or $(+1)$ score.

	Low Potential (-1)	Moderate Potential (0)	High Potential $(+1)$
1. Extent to which the idea: • Takes advantage of an environmental trend • Solves a problem • Addresses an unfilled gap in the marketplace	Weak	Moderate	Strong
2. Timeliness of entry to market	Not timely	Moderately timely	Very timely
3. Extent to which the idea "adds value" for its buyer or end user	Low	Medium	High
4. Extent to which the customer is satisfied by competing products that are already available	Very satisfied	Moderately satisfied	Not very satisfied or ambivalent
5. Degree to which the idea requires customers to change their basic practices or behaviors	Substantial changes required	Moderate changes required	Small to no changes required

Part 2: Industry-Related Issues

	Low Potential (−1)	Moderate Potential (0)	High Potential (+1)
1. Number of competitors	Many	Few	None
2. Stage of industry life cycle	Maturity phase or decline phase	Growth phase	Emergence phase
3. Growth rate of industry	Little or no growth	Moderate growth	Strong growth
4. Importance of industry's products and/or services to customers	"Ambivalent"	"Would like to have"	"Must have"
5. Industry operating margins	Low	Moderate	High

Part 3: Target Market and Customer-Related Issues

	Low Potential (−1)	Moderate Potential (0)	High Potential (+1)
1. Identification of target market for the proposed new venture	Difficult to identify	May be able to identify	Identified
2. Ability to create "barriers to entry" for potential competitors	Unable to create	May or may not be able to create	Can create
3. Purchasing power of customers	Low	Moderate	High
4. Ease of making customers aware of the new product or service	Low	Moderate	High
5. Growth potential of target market	Low	Moderate	High

PART 4: FOUNDER- (OR FOUNDERS-) RELATED ISSUES

	Low Potential (−1)	*Moderate Potential* (0)	*High Potential* (+1)
1. Founder or founders experience in the industry	No experience	Moderate experience	Experienced
2. Founder or founders skills as they relate to the proposed new venture's product or service	No skills	Moderate skills	Skilled
3. Extent of the founder or founders professional and social networks in the relevant industry	None	Moderate	Extensive
4. Extent to which the proposed new venture meets the founder or founders personal goals and aspirations	Weak	Moderate	Strong
5. Likelihood that a team can be put together to launch and grow the new venture	Unlikely	Moderately likely	Very likely

PART 5: FINANCIAL ISSUES

	Low Potential (−1)	*Moderate Potential* (0)	*High Potential* (+1)
1. Initial capital investment	High	Moderate	Low
2. Number of revenue drivers (ways in which the company makes money)	One	Two to three	More than three
3. Time to break even	More than two years	One to two years	Less than one year
4. Financial performance of similar businesses	Weak	Modest	Strong
5. Ability to fund initial product (or service) development and/or initial startup expenses from personal funds or via bootstrapping	Low	Moderate	High

Overall Potential

Each part has five items. Scores will range from −5 to +5 for each part. The score is a guide—there is no established rule-of-thumb for the numerical score that equates to high potential, moderate potential, or low potential for each part. The ranking is a judgment call.

	Score (−5 to +1)	Overall Potential of the Business Idea Based on Each Part	Suggestions for Improving the Potential
Part 1: Strength of Business Idea		High potential ☐ Moderate potential ☐ Low potential ☐	
Part 2: Industry-Related Issues		High potential ☐ Moderate potential ☐ Low potential ☐	
Part 3: Target Market and Customer-Related Issues		High potential ☐ Moderate potential ☐ Low potential ☐	
Part 4: Founder- (or Founders-) Related Issues		High potential ☐ Moderate potential ☐ Low potential ☐	
Part 5: Financial Issues		High potential ☐ Moderate potential ☐ Low potential ☐	
Overall Assessment		High potential ☐ Moderate potential ☐ Low potential ☐	

Summary—briefly summarize your justification for your overall assessment:

APPENDIX 2.2

Internet Resource Table

Resource to Help Complete the First Screen

Source	Description	Applicable Parts of First Screen	Cost/Availability
American Factfinder (http://www. factfinder. census.gov)	An easy-to-use portal for obtaining census data. One quick way to retrieve data is to get a "Fact Sheet" on a geographic area (by city, county, or ZIP code), which provides population, medium household income, demographic breakdown (age, gender, race), and other information.	Part 3	Free
BizStats (http:// www.bizstats.com)	Has a variety of detailed financial data on various retail categories. On the site, a user can type in the projected income of a firm, by industry, and receive a mock income statement in return.	Parts 2 and 5	Free
Business & Company Resource Center (http://www.gale. com/BusinessRC)	Access to information on the organization and structure of industries, current industry trends, and other information.	Parts 1 and 2	Fee based; typically free if accessed through a university library
City-Data.com (http://www. city-data.com)	Contains detailed information on cities, including median resident age, median household income, ethnic mix of residents, and aerial photos.	Part 3	Free
County Business Patterns (http:// www.census.gov/ epcd/cbp/view/ cbpview.html)	Good resources for looking at business activity, including the number of competitors, at a city, county, or state level. For example, you can find the number of drycleaners (or any other business) in a specific ZIP code or city.	Parts 2 and 3	Free

Source	Description	Applicable Parts of First Screen	Cost/Availability
Hoovers Online (http://www.hoovers.com)	Brief histories and financial information on companies, industries, people, and products. Premium service provides access to detailed financial information and 10-K reports for publicly traded firms.	Parts 2, 3, and 5	Free; premium version available on a fee basis or typically for free if accessed through a university library
IBISWorld (http://www.ibisworld.com)	Detailed reports available on hundreds of industries, including industry stats, trends, buyer behavior, and expected returns.	Parts 1, 2, 3, and 5	Fee based; typically free if accessed through a university library
Lexis-Nexis Academic (http://www.lexisnexis.com)	Provides access to sales data for public and private firms, which can be searched in a number of useful ways. Helps startups estimate the financial performance of similar businesses. Go to "Business" and then "Company Financial."	Part 5	Fee-based; typically free if accessed through a university library
MagPortal.com (http://www.magportal.com)	Search engine and directory for finding online magazine articles. Helps startups by providing access to magazine articles about their product/ service and industry of interest. This information may be helpful in all areas of feasibility analysis.	Parts 1, 2, 3, 4, and 5	Free
Mergent Online (http://www.mergentonline.com)	Provides near instant access to financial data, including income statements, balance sheets, and cash flows, on more than 10,000 U.S. public corporations.	Parts 2 and 5	Fee based; typically free if accessed through a university library
Mintel (http://www.mintel.com)	Detailed reports available on hundreds of industries, including industry stats, trends, buyer behavior, and expected returns.	Parts 1, 2, 3, and 5	Fee based; typically free if accessed through a university library

Source	Description	Applicable Parts of First Screen	Cost/Availability
ProQuest (no public Web site available)	Very robust search engine for searching publications such as the *Wall Street Journal* and the *New York Times*. Useful for all areas of feasibility analysis.	Parts 1, 2, 3, 4, and 5.	Fee based; typically free if accessed through a university library
Quickfacts (http://quickfacts.census.gov)	A very quick way to access census bureau data, including population, median household income, census breakdowns by age and other demographic characteristics, and so on.	Parts 2 and 3	Free
ReferenceUSA (http://www.referenceusa.com)	Provides contact information, estimated annual sales, credit rating score, year established, news, and other information on both public and private companies. Contains more information on private firms than many similar sites. Helps startups estimate the financial performance of similar businesses.	Part 5	Free
Standard & Poor's NetAdvantage (http://www.netadvantage.standardpoor. com)	Detailed reports available on hundreds of industries, including industry stats, trends, buyer behavior, and expected returns.	Parts 1, 2, 3, and 5	Fee based; typically free if accessed through a university library
Trade (and Professional) Association Directories (http://idii.com/resource/ associations.htm) (http://www.weddles.com/associations/index.cfm) (http://www.ipl.org/div/aon/)	Directories provide access to the Web site addresses of trade associations in all fields. The trade associations can be contacted to obtain information on all areas of feasibility.	Parts 1, 2, 3, 4, and 5	Free

Source	Description	Applicable Parts of First Screen	Cost/Availability
Yahoo! Industry Center (http://biz. yahoo.com/ic)	Provides a directory of industries, along with a list of the companies in each industry, the latest indus- try-related news, and per- formance data on the top companies in an industry.	Parts 2, 3, and 5	Free

CHAPTER

FEASIBILITY ANALYSIS

INTRODUCTION

This chapter focuses on assessing the feasibility of a business idea. **Feasibility analysis** is the process of determining if a business idea is viable. In Chapter 2, we introduced the First Screen, which is a tool for quickly assessing the merits of business ideas. A feasibility analysis is a more stringent test designed to take the best ideas that emerge from the First Screen and more fully assess their feasibility.

As mentioned in Chapter 1, the most effective business plans are part of a comprehensive process that includes (1) identifying a business idea, (2) screening the idea (or ideas) to determine their preliminary feasibility, (3) conducting a feasibility analysis to see if proceeding with a business plan is warranted, and (4) writing the plan. A visual reminder of the comprehensive nature of this process and where feasibility analysis fits in is provided in Figure 3-1. Recall, the sequential nature of the steps shown in Figure 3-1 cleanly separate the investigative portion of thinking through the merits of a business idea from the planning and selling stage of the process. Steps 2 to 3, which focus on feasibility analysis, are investigative in nature and are designed to critically assess the merits of a business idea. Step 4, the business plan, focuses on planning and selling. A properly conducted feasibility analysis lays the foundation for a well-reasoned and a well-researched business plan. The most compelling facts a company can include in a business plan are the results of its own feasibility analysis, particularly if the analysis includes feedback from industry experts and prospective customers.

This chapter presents a template for completing a feasibility analysis and describes each of the four steps in the feasibility analysis process.

FIGURE 3-1 **The Comprehensive Feasibility Analysis/Business Planning Process**

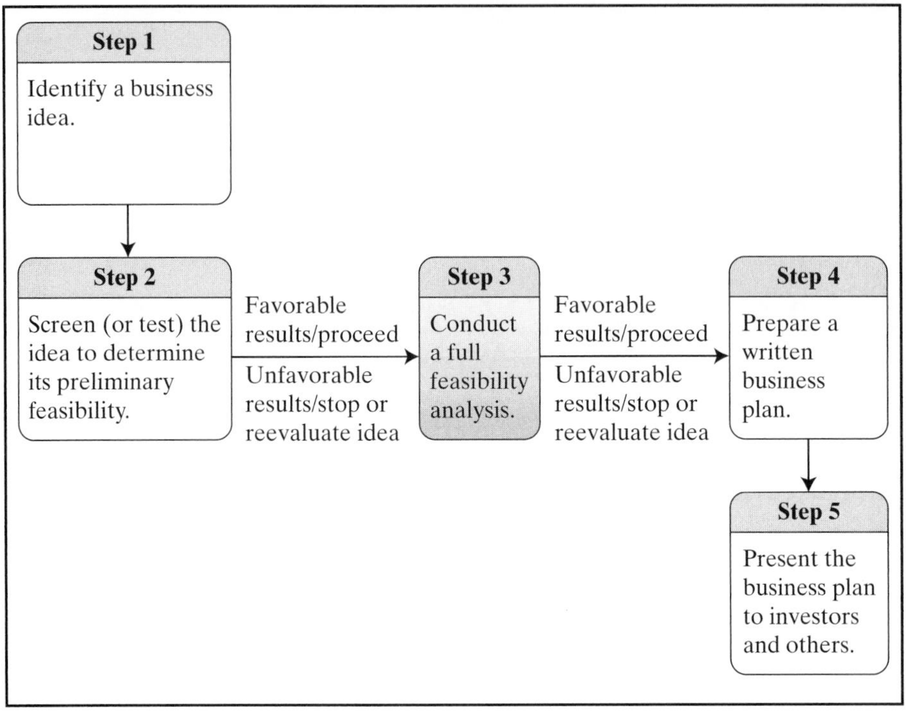

Note: Shaded step is covered in this chapter.

TEMPLATE FOR COMPLETING A FEASIBILITY ANALYSIS

The template for completing a feasibility analysis is shown in Table 3-1. It includes an introduction, the four parts of feasibility analysis (product/service feasibility, industry/market feasibility, organizational feasibility, and financial feasibility), and a summary and conclusion. A fuller version of the template, with instructions and assessment tools, is provided in Appendix 3.1 at the end of this chapter. It may be helpful to refer to Appendix 3.1 periodically when reading through the descriptions of each of the four forms of feasibility to visualize how the various parts of the feasibility analysis fit together and see what the assessment instruments look like.*

The template shown in Table 3-1 represents a full feasibility analysis. Whereas the First Screen should take only an hour or so to complete, completing a full feasibility analysis is a lengthier process. It requires both primary and secondary

---

*Copies of the feasibility analysis shown in the Appendix, along with each of the assessment tools mentioned in the chapter, can be obtained from the author's Web site at http://www.bus.ucf.edu/barringer.

| TABLE 3-1 Full Feasibility Analysis |

Introduction
A.   Name of the proposed business
B.   Name of the founder (or founders)
C.   One paragraph summary of the business

Part 1: Product/Service Feasibility
A.   Product/service desirability
B.   Product/service demand

Part 2: Industry/Target Market Feasibility
A.   Industry attractiveness
B.   Target market attractiveness
C.   Market timeliness

Part 3: Organizational Feasibility
A.   Management prowess
B.   Resource sufficiency

Part 4: Financial Feasibility
A.   Total startup cash needed
B.   Financial performance of similar businesses
C.   Overall financial attractiveness of the proposed venture

Summary and Conclusion

(Circle correct response.)

Product/Service Feasibility	Not feasible	Unsure	Feasible
Industry/Market Feasibility	Not feasible	Unsure	Feasible
Organizational Feasibility	Not feasible	Unsure	Feasible
Financial Feasibility	Not feasible	Unsure	Feasible
Overall Assessment	Not feasible	Unsure	Feasible
Suggestions for Improving Feasibility in One or More Areas			

research. **Primary research** is original research that is collected by the person or persons completing the analysis. It normally includes talking to industry experts, obtaining feedback from prospective customers, and administering surveys. **Secondary research** probes data that is already collected. The data generally includes industry studies, Census Bureau data, company reports, and other pertinent information gleaned through library and Internet research.

It should be emphasized that while a feasibility analysis tests the merits of a specific idea, it allows ample opportunity for the idea to be revised, altered, and changed as a result of the feedback that is obtained and the analysis that is conducted. The whole idea behind the feasibility analysis process is to take an abstract concept, like the idea of opening a fitness center for the 50+ demographic (introduced in Chapter 2), and put it to the test—by talking to industry experts, surveying prospective customers, studying industry trends, thinking through the financials, and scrutinizing it in other ways. These types of activities not only help determine whether an idea is feasible but also help shape and mold the idea. The importance of this notion is affirmed by R.G. Cooper, a widely published author in the area of new product development, who wrote:

> New product success is largely decided in the first few plays of a game— in those critical steps and tasks that precede the actual development of a product. The upfront homework defines the product and builds the business case for development.[1]

Although Cooper was referring specifically to developing new products, the same can be said for developing new companies. The most critical steps are the early ones, where the upfront homework (i.e., feasibility analysis and preparing a business plan) defines the business and provides sufficient evidence to build a compelling case for moving forward.

An integral part of the feasibility analysis described in this chapter is the set of assessment tools that helps organize the thinking of the people completing a feasibility analysis and helps them make final judgments regarding each area of feasibility. The assessment tools are referred to in the chapter and are shown in their entirety in Appendix 3.1 at the end of this chapter.

Now let's look at each of the four components of feasibility analysis and how each of the four components should be evaluated and assessed.

PRODUCT/SERVICE FEASIBILITY

Product/service feasibility is an assessment of the overall appeal of the product or service being proposed. Although there are many important things to consider when launching a new venture, nothing else matters if the product or service itself doesn't sell. There are two key issues to consider at this point: product desirability and product demand.

PRODUCT/SERVICE DESIRABILITY

The first component of product/service feasibility is to affirm that the proposed product or service is desirable and serves a need in the marketplace. The following questions speak to the basic appeal of the product:

- Does it make sense?
- Is it reasonable?
- Is it something that consumers will get excited about?
- Are there any fatal flaws in the product's basic design or concept?

The proper mindset at the feasibility analysis stage is to get a general sense of the answers to these and similar questions, rather than to try to reach final conclusions. One way to achieve this objective is to administer a concept test.

Concept Test. A concept test involves showing a preliminary description of a product or service idea, called a **concept statement,** to industry experts and prospective customers to solicit their feedback. It is normally a one-page document, which includes the following:

- A description of the product or service
- The intended target market
- The benefits of the product or service
- A description of how the product or service will be positioned relative to competitors
- A description of how the product or service will be sold
- A brief description of the company's management team (for purposes of completeness)

After the concept statement is developed, it should be shown to 5 to 10 people who are familiar with the industry that the firm hopes to enter and who can provide informed feedback. The temptation to show it to family members and friends should be avoided because these people are predisposed to give positive feedback. Instead, it should be distributed to people who will provide candid and informed feedback and advice. A short survey should be attached to the statement that asks the participants to (1) tell you three things that they like about the product or service idea, (2) provide you three suggestions for making it better, (3) tell you whether they think the product or service idea is feasible, and (4) share additional comments or suggestions. The information gleaned from the statements should be tabulated and carefully read. If time permits, the statement can be used in an iterative manner to strengthen the product or service idea. For example, you might show the statement to a group of industry experts, get feedback, tweak the idea, show it to second group for additional feedback, tweak the idea some more, and so on.

The concept statement for a fictitious company, named Prime Adult Fitness, is provided in Figure 3-2. The fitness center, as alluded to several times in the book, will target consumers who are 50 years old and older and will be the main focus of the business plan, discussed in Chapters 4 through 10. Prime Adult Fitness will feature exercise machines, classes, and workouts that are specifically designed for older people. It will also offer massage therapy and physical therapy services on site and will feature classes that focus on its members' mental fitness to complement the activities that focus on physical fitness. To help facilitate this goal, the company will maintain a well-stock game room and will facilitate small groups that meet to play Sudoku and similar games.

There are many variations on how entrepreneurs solicit feedback on their business ideas. Rather than developing a formal concept statement, some entrepreneurs conduct product/service feasibility analysis by simply talking through their ideas with people and gathering informal feedback. For example, during the development of Proactiv (http://www.proactiv.com), a popular acne medication, Dr. Katie Rodan, one of the company's cofounders, hosted dinner parties at her house to solicit feedback from guests about her product idea. The guests included business executives, market researchers, an FDA regulatory attorney, the chief

FIGURE 3-2 Concept Statement: Prime Adult Fitness

Product

Prime Adult Fitness will be a fitness center for people 50 years old and older. The center will be two-thirds the size of an average Bally Fitness Center or Gold's Gym and will feature exercise machines, classes, and workouts that are especially designed for its clientele. It will also feature access to massage and physical therapy services.

Prime Adult Fitness will provide an atmosphere that encourages older people to exercise and stay fit. Substantial evidence suggests that older people prefer to exercise with people their own age. In fact, according to one study, many older people would rather exercise alone than in a mixed group that includes younger people. As a result, there may be a large untapped market of older people who would like to join a fitness center but aren't interested in their current choices. Prime Adult Fitness will provide older people a fitness center designed specifically for them.

Target Market

Prime Adult Fitness will be located in Central Florida, one of the fastest growing areas for people 50 years old and older in the country. It will limit its membership to people 50 years old and older. Although the fitness industry itself is on a steady growth curve, we believe that existing fitness centers are not able to offer the environment, programs, or mix of classes that are optimal for older people. As shown by Curves International (just for women) and others, focusing on a single demographic is a viable and potentially profitable way of carving out a distinct target market in the fitness industry.

How Prime Adult Fitness Will Be Positioned Relative to Competitors

Prime Adult Fitness will be the only fitness center in Central Florida exclusively focused on people 50 years old and older. Its amenities will be equal to the major competitors in its target market, which include Life Time Fitness, LA Fitness, and the YMCA. The company's approach will free it to focus exclusively on the needs of its clientele.

Management Team

Prime Adult Fitness is led by its cofounders, Jeremy Ryan and Elizabeth Sims. Jeremy started a successful fitness center in South Florida and grew it to 38 units in 3 years before selling it to a major chain. Elizabeth Sims worked with Jeremy in his last venture and has 19 years experience as a certified public accountant.

financial officer of a major company, and others.[2] Similarly, Sharelle Klause, the founder of Dry Soda (http://www.drysoda.com), a company that makes an all natural soda that's paired with food the way wine is in upscale restaurants, tested her idea by first talking to her husband's colleagues, who were in the food industry, and then tapped into the professional network of a friend, who owned a bottled water company. Through this process, she met a chemist who was instrumental in helping her develop the initial recipes for her beverage. Klause also went directly to restaurant owners and chefs to ask them to sample early versions of her four flavors: Rhubarb, Kumquat, Lavender, and Lemongrass.[3]

Although not a complete approach, there is merit to the give-and-take that entrepreneurs like Rodan and Klause experienced by talking with prospective customers rather than just handing them a concept statement and asking them to complete a survey. As a result, the ideal combination is to have a written concept statement, like the one shown previously in Figure 3-2, with a survey to complete but also to engage in verbal give-and-take with as many industry experts and prospective customers as possible.

PRODUCT/SERVICE DEMAND

The second component of product/service feasibility analysis is to determine if there is demand for the product or service. A useful technique to gain a preliminary sense of the demand for a product or service is to administer a buying intentions survey.

Buying Intentions Survey.   A **buying intentions survey** is an instrument that is used to gauge customer interest in a product or service. It consists of a concept statement (or a similar description of a product or service) with a short survey attached. The statement and the survey should be distributed to 15 to 30 potential customers (do not include any of the people who completed the concept statement test). Each participant should be asked to read the statement and complete the survey. The survey typically features a question that looks something like this:

How likely would you be to buy a product (or service) like this, if we make it?

_____ Definitely would buy
_____ Probably would buy
_____ Might or might not buy
_____ Probably would not buy
_____ Definitely would not buy

The number of people who indicate that they *definitely* would buy is typically combined with the number who indicate that the *probably* would buy to gauge customer interest.

One caveat is that people who say that they intend to purchase a product or service don't always follow through, so the numbers resulting from this activity are almost always optimistic. The survey also doesn't normally tap a scientifically random sample. Still, the results give a potential entrepreneur a general sense of the degree of customer interest in the product or service idea.

Additional questions are often added to the buying intentions survey, depending on the nature of the product or service involved. Examples of the types of questions that are added include the following:

- How much would you be willing to pay for the product or service? This provides insight into pricing.
- Where would you expect to find this product or service for sale? This may provide insight into sales and distribution.

The survey should be kept short to maximize participation.

To find people to talk through a product or service idea or to react to a concept statement, entrepreneurs should contact industry trade associations and attend industry trade shows. Web sites that provide a directory of the trade associations in an industry and display a schedule of trade show dates and locations are included in the Internet Resources Table (Appendix 2.2) at the end of Chapter 2. Another online resource, Trade Show Central (http://www.tsnn.com), provides a searchable database of more than 50,000 trade shows, conferences, and seminars for various industries. Establishing a dialogue with a trade association and/or attending industry trade shows and conferences will put you directly in touch with people who are experts in the industry you are interested in.

INDUSTRY/TARGET MARKET FEASIBILITY ANALYSIS

Industry/target market feasibility is an assessment of the overall appeal of the industry and the target market for the product or service being proposed. There is a distinct difference between a firm's industry and its target market, which should be clearly understood. An **industry** is a group of firms producing a similar product or service, such as computers, cars, airplanes, or clothing. A firm's **target market** is the limited portion of the industry that it goes after or tries to appeal to. Most firms do not try to service their entire industry. Instead, they select or carve out a specific target market and try to service that market very well. Prime Adult Fitness's target market is people 50 years and older within the broader fitness industry.

It's important to assess both the broad industry you will be entering and your specific target market. If you want more detailed information on either of these topics, you can skip ahead to Chapters 5 and 6 of this book, which focus on the industry analysis and market analysis sections of the business plan.

INDUSTRY ATTRACTIVENESS

Industries vary in terms of their overall attractiveness. In general, the most attractive industries for startups are large and growing, are young rather than old, are early rather than late in their life cycle, and are fragmented rather than concentrated. You also want to pick an industry that's structurally attractive—meaning startups can enter the industry (in various target markets) and compete. Some industries are characterized by such high barriers to entry or the presence of one or two dominant players that potential new entrants are essentially shut out.

Other factors are also important. For example, the degree to which environmental and business trends are moving in favor rather than against the industry are important for the industry's long-term health and its capability to spawn new target or niche markets. For example, an increased awareness of the benefits of exercise is an extremely positive trend for the fitness industry. Another factor is how important the products or services an industry sells are to its customers. One of the reasons the pharmaceutical industry is so profitable is because there are no good substitutes for its products. Compare that to the movie industry, which is struggling. How many dozens of options do we have for spending our free time and money other than going to a movie?

The assessment tool provided in the feasibility analysis in Appendix 3.1 enables you to assess the industry you're thinking about entering. As you fill out this assessment tool, make sure to stick strictly to an assessment of your industry, not the specific portion of the industry you plan to target. Refer to the Internet

Resources Table in Appendix 2.2 at the end of Chapter 2 to identify sources that will help you make your assessments. IBISWorld, Standard & Poor's Net Advantage, and Mintel are particularly useful resources for this section of the feasibility analysis.

TARGET MARKET ATTRACTIVENESS

As mentioned, a target market is a place within a larger market segment that represents a narrower group of customers with similar needs. Most startups simply do not have the resources needed to participate in a broad market, at least initially. Instead, by focusing on a smaller target market, a firm can usually avoid head-to-head competition with industry leaders and can focus on serving a specialized market very well.

The challenge in identifying an attractive target market is to find a market that's large enough for the proposed business but is yet small enough to avoid attracting larger competitors. An example of a company that has targeted a market that meets these criteria is Dogster (http://www.dogster.com), a social networking site for dog owners. The site allows its users to create profiles for their dogs, participate in dog-related forums, post photos and video clips of their dogs, and perform a number of other activities. The site, which was started from scratch in 2004 with its sister site, Catster (http://www.catster.com), now has more than 275,000 human members, 340,000 photos of dogs and cats, and a collection of blue-chip advertisers, including Disney and Target. Although the firm operates in the $36 billion pet industry, it has carved out a specialized target or niche market for itself and is reported to be operating in the black and generating more than a million dollars a year in advertising revenue.[4] As the company gains momentum and financial resources, it may grow beyond this specialized market but has gotten off to a good start largely because it has remained laser-focused on a clearly defined target market (social networking for dog and cat owners) within a larger industry.

Although it's generally easy to find good information to assess the attractiveness of an industry, discerning the attractiveness of a small target market is tougher, particularly if the firm is pioneering the market. Often, under these circumstances, information from more than one industry and/or market must be collected and synthesized to make an informed judgment. For example, H2OAudio (http://www.H2OAudio.com), the company introduced in Chapter 2, makes waterproof housings for the iPod and the iPod nano. The waterproof housing permits iPod users to listen to their iPod while swimming, surfing, snorkeling, or engaging in any activity where the iPod might get wet. The question for a product like this is what market to assess? There are no SIC (Standard Industrial Classification) or NAICS (North American Industry Classification System) codes for the "waterproof iPod housing" industry or market. Obviously, a combination of markets must be studied, including the MP3 or iPod market, the iPod accessory market, and the market for water sports. It would be important to not only know how well iPod accessories are selling but also what the current trends in water sports are. If iPod accessories are selling like hotcakes, but water sports are on a sharp decline, the niche market that H2OAudio is pioneering would be much less attractive than if iPod accessories were selling well and interest in water sports was rapidly increasing.

A tool for assessing the validity and attractiveness of a target market is provided in the full feasibility analysis in Appendix 3.1. Again, make sure to focus this analysis strictly on the portion of your industry you plan to target.

MARKET TIMELINESS

The final step in industry/market feasibility analysis is to evaluate the timeliness of the introduction of the proposed product or service. There are two important considerations. The first consideration is to determine if the window of opportunity for the product or service is open or closed. As explained in Chapter 2, the term *window of opportunity* is a metaphor describing the time period in which a firm can realistically enter a new market. After the market for a new product is established, its window of opportunity opens. As the market grows, firms enter and try to establish a profitable position. At some point, the market matures, and the window of opportunity closes. An important judgment call is whether the window of opportunity for a particular business idea is open or closed.

The second consideration regarding market timeliness is to study the simple economics of the industry the firm plans to enter to determine whether the timing is right for a new entrant. For example, Cartridge World (http://www.cartridgeworld.com), a franchise organization, pioneered the idea to establish small storefronts to refill ink cartridges for printers. A consumer can walk into a Cartridge World store, wait while the cartridge is refilled, and leave with a full cartridge at about half the price of a new one. The company, which currently has more than 1,400 franchises, is successful and growing.[5] In the past two years, a number of new competitors have entered Cartridge World's industry, and recently Walgreens, Office Depot, and OfficeMax indicated that they plan to start offering cartridge refill services.[6] These trends suggest that now is not a good time to launch a new cartridge refill startup. A tool for assessing market timeliness is provided in the full feasibility analysis in Appendix 3.1.

Firms that do not conduct a thorough industry and target market analysis and enter a small part of an industry without knowing its size or potential, often find that the market is not large enough to maintain and grow the business. In these instances, firms must often scramble to find a complementary niche to expand the size of their business. Through this process, firms often learn their lesson and do better jobs assessing the attractiveness of the second target market than they did for the first one. This scenario played out for Gecko Head Gear (http://www.geckoheadgear.com), a British company, as described in the Business Plan Insight box. As illustrated in the Business Plain Insight box, a firm can recover from selecting too small of a target market initially if it can find a complementary target market fairly quickly that can be properly assessed and is more attractive.

A tool for assessing industry attractiveness is provided in the full feasibility analysis in Appendix 3.1.

Sometimes a Company Needs More Than One Target Market

In 1993, Jeff Sacree started Gecko, a small British company that made custom surf-boards for local surfers and retail shops. Having completed no industry or target market feasibility analysis, Sacree soon found that the surfboard market was too seasonal to sustain a business, and he started making lightweight, heat-retaining helmets for surfers. The helmets were specifically designed to prevent "ice cream headaches," a common complaint among people who surf in cold water. Although the helmets worked great, Sacree again found himself in a very small target market. There just weren't many surfers. He was confident that he had a well designed helmet but wasn't sure he could build a business in such a small niche market.

To grow his business, Sacree started researching other potential uses for his specially designed helmet. After a chance encounter with a lifeboat operator, he approached the Royal National Lifeboat Institution (RNLI), a volunteer organization in the United Kingdom and the Republic of Ireland that is dedicated to saving lives at sea. The organization mans over 230 lifeboat stations and provides personnel for 60 beaches in the UK and the Republic of Ireland to provide water safety instruction and rescue operations at sea.

The RNLI was instantly interested in Sacree's novel helmet. In fact, the RNLI was dissatisfied with the helmets that it was using, which were essentially motorcycle helmets. These helmets created a "bucket effect" when someone entered the water wearing one, which could cause drag on the neck and an injury. Although the RNLI was interested in Sacree's product, it was a tough customer. As a result, Sacree's approach to entering this market was different by necessity. To land the RNLI contract, he was required to put the helmet through a number of stringent usability and safety tests. In the process, Sacree learned how to build prototypes, learned how to partner with suppliers to improve his designs, and became much more sophisticated in his analysis of products and markets. The result—Gecko landed the RNLI contract, moved into a larger target market, and has iterated its helmet design several times since. Gecko Head Gear now has customers worldwide, primarily for its lifeboat helmets, and counts the British Ministry of Defense and the Australian Navy as customers.

Source: Gecko Headgear homepage (http://www.geckoheadgear.com). Accessed May 16, 2007.

ORGANIZATIONAL FEASIBILITY ANALYSIS

Organizational feasibility analysis is conducted to determine whether a proposed business has sufficient management expertise, organizational competence, and resources to successfully launch its business. There are two primary issues to consider in this area: management prowess and resource sufficiency.

MANAGEMENT PROWESS

A startup should assess the prowess, or ability, of its initial management team, whether it is a sole entrepreneur or a larger group. This task requires the individuals starting the firm to be honest and candid in their self-assessments. Two of the most important factors in this area are the passion that the sole entrepreneur or management team has for the business and the extent to which the people involved understand the markets in which the firm will compete. There are no practical substitutes for strengths in these areas.

A collection of additional factors help define management prowess, including prior entrepreneurial experience,[7] the depth of the professional and social networks of the people involved,[8] the degree of creativity among the members of the group, the extent of experience that the team has in cash flow management, and the extent to which the sole entrepreneur and members of the team have college degrees.[9] In most instances, not all of these qualities will be present. This is the reason that many startups fairly quickly add an industry veteran or an experienced entrepreneur to their team, or place one or more individuals with these credentials on their Board of Advisors. The prowess, or strength, of a startup's management team is normally given disproportionate weight when outsiders evaluate the desirability of a new venture, and most entrepreneurs know this.

A tool for assessing management prowess is provided in the full feasibility analysis in Appendix 3.1.

RESOURCE SUFFICIENCY

The second step in organizational feasibility analysis is to determine whether the proposed venture has or is capable of obtaining sufficient resources to move forward. The focus in organizational feasibility analysis is on nonfinancial resources because financial feasibility is considered separately. It is not necessary to develop an exhaustive list of nonfinancial resources. The objective is to identify the 8 to 12 most important and potentially problematic nonfinancial resources and assess whether they are available. An example is a startup that will require one or more wet labs to produce its products or perform its service. A **wet lab** is a space where chemicals, drugs, or other material or biological matter is tested or analyzed, and requires water, direct ventilation, and specialized piped utilities. Most wet labs are in buildings that are specifically designed to house them. If a firm plans to rent its wet labs, but no wet lab rental space is available in the community where the firm plans to locate, a serious resources sufficiency problem exists. Other nonfinancial resources, which often become issues due to concerns regarding their affordability or availability, include office space, light manufacturing space, key management employees, key support personnel, and support from state and local governments if applicable.

One important but easily overlooked resource sufficiency issue that new firms should consider is their proximity to similar firms. There are well-known **clusters** of high-tech firms, for example, in the Silicon Valley of California, on Route 128 around Boston, and in Austin, Texas. Clusters arise because they increase the productivity of the firms participating in them. Because these firms are located near each other, it is easy for their employees to network with each other, and it is easy for the firms to gain access to specialized suppliers, scientific knowledge, and technological expertise native to the area.[10] For example, there is a cluster of medical device companies in the Twin Cities area of Minnesota. As a result, a medical device firm that decided to locate in Des Moines, Iowa, for example, may have a decided disadvantage over a similar startup located in Minneapolis, which is just 240 miles to the north. Researchers have found that small manufacturing firms benefit more than larger firms by being physically close to a cluster of similar firms.[11]

An instrument to assess resource sufficiency is provided in the full feasibility analysis in Appendix 3.1.

FINANCIAL FEASIBILITY ANALYSIS

Financial feasibility analysis is the final stage of a comprehensive feasibility analysis. For feasibility analysis, a preliminary financial analysis is normally sufficient. More rigor at this point is typically not required because the specifics of the business will inevitably evolve, making it impractical to spend a lot of time early on preparing detailed financial statements. Still, it is important to have more than a cursory sense of the financial feasibility of a proposed business.

The most important issues to consider at this stage are total startup cash needed, financial performance of similar businesses, and the overall financial attractiveness of the proposed venture. If a proposed new venture moves beyond the feasibility analysis stage, more complete financial projections will be included in the business plan.

TOTAL STARTUP CASH NEEDED

The first issue refers to the total cash needed to prepare the business to make its first sale. An actual budget should be prepared that lists all the anticipated operating expenses and capital purchases that will be needed to get the business up-and-running. After a total figure is arrived at, an explanation of where the money will come from should be provided. Avoid cursory explanations such as "I'll borrow the money" or "I plan to bring equity investors on board." Although you may ultimately involve lenders or investors in your business, a more thoughtful account is required of how you'll provide for your initial cash needs.

If the money will come from friends and family or is raised through other means, such as credit cards or a home equity line of credit, a reasonable plan should be stipulated to repay the money. Showing how a new venture's startup costs will be covered and repaid is an important issue. Many new ventures look promising as ongoing concerns but have no way of raising the money to get started or are never able to recover from the initial costs involved. When projecting startup expenses, it is better to overestimate rather than underestimate the costs involved. Murphy's Law is prevalent in the startup world—things will go wrong. It is a rare startup that doesn't experience some unexpected expenses during the startup phase.

A form for estimating total startup expenses is included in the full feasibility analysis in Appendix 3.1.

FINANCIAL PERFORMANCE OF SIMILAR BUSINESSES

The second component of the financial feasibility analysis is estimating a proposed startup's potential financial performance by comparing it to similar, already established businesses. Obviously, this effort will result in approximate rather than exact numbers. There are several ways of doing this, all of which involve a little ethical detective work. First, substantial archival data is available online, which offers detailed financial reports on thousands of individual firms. The easiest data to obtain is on publicly traded firms through Hoovers or a similar source. These firms are typically too large, however, for meaningful comparisons to proposed new ventures. The trick is to find the financial performance of small, more comparable firms. A listing of Web sites that are helpful in this regard are provided in the Internet Resources Table in Appendix 2.2 at the end of Chapter 2. ReferenceUSA, for example, provides revenue estimates for many private firms. Both Mintel and IBISWorld provide data on the average sales and profitability for the firms in the industries they track. On the expense side, a very useful site is BizStats.com, where an entrepreneur can type in the projected revenue of his or her firm, by industry classification, and receive a mock income statement in return that shows the average profitability and expenses percentages of U.S. small businesses in the same category. IBISWorld also normally provides a chart of the average expenses (as a percentage of net sales) for major items like wages, rent, and utilities for firms in the industries they follow. Another source to help estimate a firm's sales and net profit is BizMiner (http://www.bizminer.com). BizMiner provides a printout of the average sales and profitability for firms in the industries they follow, which provides more detail than similar reports. BizMiner is a fee-based site, and the reports cost between $69 and $99.

There are additional ways to obtain financial performance data on smaller firms. Some industry trade associations publish data on the sales and profitability of the firms in their industries. If the data can't be easily found, you can call or e-mail a trade association to ask if the data is available. Similarly, if startup entrepreneurs identify a business that is similar to the one they want to start, and the business isn't likely to be a direct competitor, it's not inappropriate to ask the owner or manager of the business to share sales and income data. Even if the owner or manager is only willing to talk in general terms (i.e., "our annual sales are in the $2 million range, and we're netting between $150,000 and $200,000 per year"), that information is certainly better than nothing.

Simple Internet searches are also often helpful. If you're interested in the fitness industry, simply typing "fitness industry sales" and "fitness industry profitability" in the Google search bar will invariably result in links to stories about fitness companies that will discuss sales and profitability data.

A final way to obtain sales data for similar businesses is through simple observation and legwork. This approach works in some cases, and in some cases, it doesn't. For example, if you were proposing to open a smoothie shop, you could gauge the type of sales to expect by estimating the number of people, along with the average purchase per visit, who patronize similar smoothie shops in your area. A very basic way of doing this is to frequent these stores and count the number of customers who come in and out of the stores during various times of the day.

The assessment tool associated with this topic is included in the full feasibility analysis that appears in Appendix 3.1.

OVERALL FINANCIAL ATTRACTIVENESS OF THE PROPOSED VENTURE

A number of other factors are associated with evaluating the financial attractiveness of a proposed venture. Again, at the feasibility analysis stage, the extent to which a proposed business appears positive relative to each factor is based on an estimate or forecast rather than actual performance. Important factors in this category include the extent to which sales can be expected to grow during the first one to years of the venture, the percentage of recurring revenue to anticipate (it's cheaper to serve a small number of loyal customers than to continually have to find new customers), the likelihood that internally generated funds will be available within two years to finance growth, and the availability of exit opportunities for investors if applicable.

An instrument to assess the overall financial attractiveness of the proposed venture is provided in the full feasibility analysis in Appendix 3.1.

In summary, feasibility analysis is a vital step in the process of both validating and developing business ideas. Although the process described in this chapter will not give an entrepreneur a final answer regarding the potential feasibility of a business idea, it should provide substantial clarity and insight. The ultimate goal of the process is that only well-researched, well-thought out, and potentially feasible ideas enter the business planning process.

Chapter Summary

1. Feasibility analysis is the process of determining if a business idea is viable.
2. Primary research is original research that is collected by the person or persons completing the analysis. It normally includes taking to industry experts, obtaining feedback from prospective customers, and administering surveys.
3. Secondary research probes data that is already collected. The data generally includes industry studies, Census Bureau data, company reports, and other pertinent information gleaned through library and Internet research.
4. Product/service feasibility is an assessment of the overall appeal of the product or service being proposed. Its two components are product/service desirability and product/service demand.
5. A concept test involves showing a preliminary description of a product or service idea, called a concept statement, to industry experts and prospective customers to solicit their feedback.
6. A buying intentions survey is an instrument used to gauge customer interest in a product or service. It consists of a concept statement (or a similar description of a product or service) with a short survey attached.

7. Industry/target market feasibility is an assessment of the overall appeal of the industry and market for the product or service being proposed. Its three components are industry attractiveness, target market attractiveness, and market timeliness.

8. Organizational feasibility analysis is conducted to determine whether a proposed business has sufficient management expertise, organizational competence, and resources to successfully launch its business. Its two components are management prowess and (nonfinancial) resource sufficiency.

9. Clusters of firms arise because of the increase in the productivity of the firms participating in them. Because the firms are located near each other, it is easy for the employees to network with each other, and it is easy for the firms to gain access to specialized suppliers, scientific knowledge, and technological expertise native to the area.

10. Financial feasibility analysis is conducted to determine if a new venture is feasible from a financial perspective. Its three components are total startup cash needed, financial performance of similar businesses, and overall financial attractiveness of the proposed venture.

Review Questions

1. What is a feasibility analysis? How does a feasibility analysis differ from a business plan?
2. What are the four individual components of a full feasibility analysis?
3. What is the difference between primary research and secondary research? Are both types of research necessary to complete a full feasibility analysis?
4. Describe the purpose of product/service feasibility analysis. Briefly describe its two components.
5. Describe the purpose of a concept test and how it should be executed. Also, describe the purpose of a buying intentions survey and how it should be distributed and assessed.
6. Explain the purpose of industry/target market feasibility analysis. Briefly describe its three components.
7. What is a target market? Why do most startups start in target markets rather than broader markets that have more customers?
8. Describe the purpose of organizational feasibility analysis. Briefly describe its two components.
9. What is an industry "cluster?" Why might a semiconductor startup, for example, decide to launch in a geographic area where there are other semiconductor firms, rather than another area?
10. Describe the purpose of a financial feasibility analysis. Briefly describe its three components.

Application Questions

1. Ann Bennett, a friend of yours, recently inherited $150,000 from an elderly aunt and is about to sign a three-year lease on a small storefront in an upscale

mall. Ann has always wanted to open a cosmetics store for women and feels now is her chance—she has the money she needs and the space in the mall is available. You ask Ann if she has conducted a feasibility analysis and a business plan for her business, and she said that she bought a business plan software package online and plans to look at it soon but needs to get the lease signed first and isn't familiar with what a feasibility analysis is. When you give Ann a quizzical look, she pauses and says, "Am I doing something wrong?" What would you tell her?

2. Three recent startups, Greasecar Vegetable Fuel Systems, ZUCA, and Ingemi Corp. (the maker of the IHearSafe earbuds) were mentioned in Chapter 2. Pick one of these companies and write a concept statement for it.

3. Yogitoes, another company introduced in Chapter 2, makes nonslip rugs for yoga enthusiasts. Describe how you would have conducted an industry/target market feasibility analysis for this startup.

4. Kyle Smith has developed a new software product that helps the owners of independent bookstores better track their inventory and sales. Kyle is now wondering whether this is a good time to launch the product. What factors should Kyle consider in making this determination?

5. Using one or more of the resources included in the Internet Resources Table in Appendix 2.2 at the end of Chapter 2, investigate the health and growth potential of the spa industry in the United States.

Endnotes

1. R.G. Cooper, *Product Leadership: Creating and Launching Superior New Products* (Reading, MA: Perseus Books, 1998), 99.

2. B. R. Barringer and R. Duane Ireland, *Entrepreneurship: Successfully Launching New Ventures* (Upper Saddle River, NJ: Prentice-Hall, 2008).

3. G. Galant and S. Klause, "VV Show #35" (Venture Voice). http://www.venturevoice.com (March, 2006).

4. T. McNichol, "A Startup's Best Friend? Failure." CNNMoney.com, April 4, 2007.

5. Wikipedia homepage, http://www.wikipedia.org (May 15, 2007).

6. Pui-Wing Tam, "A Cheaper Way to Refill Your Printer," *The Wall Street Journal,* January 26, 2006, D1.

7. D. Politis, "The Process of Entrepreneurial Learning: A Conceptual Framework," *Entrepreneurship Theory and Practice,* 29 (2005): 399–424.

8. D. M. DeCarolis and P. Saparito, "Social Capital, Cognition, and Entrepreneurial Opportunities: A Theoretical Framework," *Entrepreneurship Theory and Practice* 30 (2006): 41–56.

9. A. C. Cooper, F. J. Gimeno-Gascon, and C. Y. Woo, "Initial Human and Financial Capital as Predictors of New Venture Performance," *Journal of Business Venturing* 9, no. 5 (1994): 371–395.

10. P. B. Doeringer and D.G. Terkla, "Business Strategy and Cross-Industry Clusters," *Economic Development Quarterly* 9 (1995): 225–237.

11. M. Rogers, "Networks, Firm Size and Innovation," *Small Business Economics* 22, no. 2 (2004): 141–153.

Full Feasibility Analysis

Note: All fields can be expanded to provide additional space to respond to the questions. A copy of this template, along with each of the assessment tools, is available in MS Word and PDF format at the authors' Web site at http://www.bus.ucf.edu/barringer.

INTRODUCTION

A. Name of the proposed business
B. Name of the founder (or founders)
C. One paragraph summary of the business

PART 1: PRODUCT/SERVICE FEASIBILITY

ISSUES ADDRESSED IN THIS PART

A. Product/service desirability
B. Product/service demand

ASSESSMENT TOOLS

Concept Statement Test

- Write a concept statement for your product/service idea. Show the concept statement to 5 to 10 people. Select people who will give you informed and candid feedback.

- Attach a blank sheet to the concept statement, and ask the people who read the statement to (1) tell you three things they like about your product/service idea, (2) provide three suggestions for making it better, (3) tell you whether they think the product or service idea is feasible (or will be successful), and (4) share any additional comments or suggestions.

- Summarize the information you obtain from the concept statement into the following three categories:
  - Strengths of the product or service idea—things people who evaluated your product or service concept said they "liked" about the idea
  - Suggestions for strengthening the idea—suggestions made by people for strengthening or improving the idea
  - Overall feasibility of the product or service concept—report the number of people who think the idea is feasible, the number of people who think it isn't feasible, and any additional comments that were made
  - Other comments and suggestions

■ **70** ■

Buying Intentions Survey

- Distribute the concept statement to 15 to 30 prospective customers (do not include any of the people who completed the concept statement test) with the following buying intentions survey attached. Ask each participant to read the concept statement and complete the buying intentions survey. Record the number of people who participated in the survey and the results of the survey here.

- Along with the raw data recorded here, report the percentage of the total number of people you surveyed that said they would probably buy or definitely would buy your product or service if offered. This percentage is the most important figure in gauging potential customer interest.

- One caveat is that people who say that they intend to purchase a product do not always follow through, so the numbers resulting from this activity are almost always optimistic. Still, the numbers provide you with a preliminary indication of how your most likely customers will respond to your potential product or service offering.

How likely would you be to buy the product or service described above?

_____ Definitely would buy
_____ Probably would buy
_____ Might or might not buy
_____ Probably would not buy
_____ Definitely would not buy

Additional questions may be added to the buying intentions survey.

Conclusion (expand fields and report findings, in discussion form, for each area)
A. Product/service desirability
B. Product/service demand
C. Product/service feasibility (circle the correct response)
   Not Feasible   *Unsure*   *Feasible*
D. Suggestions for improving product/service feasibility.

PART 2: INDUSTRY/MARKET FEASIBILITY

ISSUES ADDRESSED IN THIS PART

A. Industry attractiveness
B. Target market attractiveness
C. Timeliness of entry into the target market

ASSESSMENT TOOLS

Industry Attractiveness

- To the extent possible, assess the industry at the five-digit NAICS code level your potential business will be entering. Use a broader industry category (less NCICS digits) if appropriate (http://www.census.gov/epcd/www/naicstab.htm).

- Assess the attractiveness of the industry the potential business plans to enter on each of the following dimensions.

Industry Attractiveness Assessment Tool

(used to assess the broad industry, rather than the specific target market, you plan to enter)

	Low Potential	*Moderate Potential*	*High Potential*
1. Number of competitors	Many	Few	None
2. Age of industry	Old	Middle aged	Young
3. Growth rate of industry	Little or no growth	Moderate growth	Strong growth
4. Average net income for firms in the industry	Low	Medium	High
5. Degree of industry concentration	Concentrated	Neither concentrated nor fragmented	Fragmented
6. Stage of industry life cycle	Maturity phase or decline phase	Growth phase	Emergence phase
7. Importance of industry's products and/or services to customers	"Ambivalent"	"Would like to have"	"Must have"
8. Extent to which business and environmental trends are moving in favor of the industry	Low	Medium	High
9. Number of exciting new product and services emerging from the industry	Low	Medium	High
10. Long-term prospects	Weak	Neutral	Strong

Target Market Attractiveness

- Identify the portion or specific market within your broader industry that you plan to target.

- Assess the attractiveness of the target market on each of the following dimensions.

Target Market Attractiveness Assessment Tool

(used to assess the specific target market, rather than the broader industry, you plan to enter)

	Low Potential	*Moderate Potential*	*High Potential*
1. Number of competitors in target market	Many	Few	None
2. Growth rate of firms in the target market	Little to no growth	Slow growth	Rapid growth
3. Average net income for firms in the target market	Low	Medium	High

	Low Potential	Moderate Potential	High Potential
4. Methods for generating revenue in the industry	Unclear	Somewhat clear	Clear
5. Ability to create "barriers to entry" for potential competitors	Unable to create	May or may not be able to create	Can create
6. Degree to which customers feel satisfied by the current offerings in the target market	Satisfied	Neither satisfied or dissatisfied	Unsatisfied
7. Potential to employ low cost guerrilla and/or buzz marketing techniques to promote the firm's product or services	Low	Moderate	High
8. Excitement surrounding new product/service offerings in the target market	Low	Medium	High

Market Timeliness

- Determine the extent to which the "window of opportunity" for the proposed business is open or closed based on the following criteria.
- Determine the timeliness of entering a specific target market based on other criteria.

Market Timeliness Assessment Tool

	Low Potential	Moderate Potential	High Potential
1. Buying mood of customers	Customers are not in a buying mood	Customers are in a moderate buying mood	Customers are in an aggressive buying mood
2. Momentum of the market	Stable to losing momentum	Slowly gaining momentum	Rapidly gaining momentum
3. Need for a new firm in the market with your offerings or geographic location	Low	Moderate	High
4. Extent to which business and environmental trends are moving in favor of the target market	Low	Medium	High
5. Recent or planned entrance of large firms into the market	Large firms entering the market	Rumors that large firms may be entering the market	No larger firms entered the market or are rumored to be entering the market

Conclusion (expand fields and report findings, in discussion form, for each area)

A. Industry attractiveness
B. Target market attractiveness
C. Market timeliness
C. Industry/market feasibility (circle the correct response)
   Not Feasible   Unsure   Feasible
E. Suggestions for improving industry/market feasibility.

PART 3: ORGANIZATIONAL FEASIBILITY

ISSUES ADDRESSED IN THIS PART

A. Management prowess
B. Resource sufficiency

ASSESSMENT TOOLS

Management Prowess

- Use the following table to candidly and objectively rate the "prowess" of the founder or group of founders who will be starting the proposed venture.

Management Prowess Assessment Tool

	Low Potential	*Moderate Potential*	*High Potential*
1. Passion for the business idea	Low	Moderate	High
2. Relevant industry experience	None	Moderate	Extensive
3. Prior entrepreneurial experience	None	Moderate	Extensive
4. Depth of professional and social networks	Weak	Moderate	Strong
5. Creativity among management team members	Low	Moderate	High
6. Experience and expertise in cash flow management	None	Moderate	High
7. College graduate	No college education	Some college education but not currently in college	Graduated or are currently in college

Resource Sufficiency

- The focus in this section is on nonfinancial resources. Use the following table to rate your "resource sufficiency" in each category.

- The list of resources is not meant to be exhaustive. A list of the 6 to 12 most critical nonfinancial resources for your proposed business is sufficient.

An explanation of the rating system used in the first portion of the table is as follows:

① Available
② Likely to be available: will probably be available and will be within my budget
③ Unlikely to be available: will probably be hard to find or gain access to, and may exceed my budget
④ Unavailable
⑤ NA: not applicable for my business

Resource Sufficiency Assessment Tool

Ratings	Resource Sufficiency
① ② ③ ④ ⑤	Office space
① ② ③ ④ ⑤	Lab space, manufacturing space, or space to launch a service business
① ② ③ ④ ⑤	Contract manufacturers or outsource providers
① ② ③ ④ ⑤	Key management employees (now and in the future)
① ② ③ ④ ⑤	Key support personnel (now and in the future)
① ② ③ ④ ⑤	Key equipment needed to operate the business (computers, machinery, delivery vehicles)
① ② ③ ④ ⑤	Ability to obtain intellectual property protection on key aspects of the business
① ② ③ ④ ⑤	Support of local and state government if applicable for business launch
① ② ③ ④ ⑤	Ability to form favorable business partnerships

Ratings: Strong, Neutral, or Weak

_____	Proximity to similar firms (for the purpose of knowledge sharing)
_____	Proximity to suppliers
_____	Proximity to customers
_____	Proximity to a major research university (if applicable)

Conclusion (expand fields and report findings, in discussion form, for each area)

A. Management prowess
B. Resource sufficiency
C. Organizational feasibility (circle the correct response)
   Not Feasible   Unsure   Feasible
D. Suggestions for improving organizational feasibility

PART 4: FINANCIAL FEASIBILITY

ISSUES ADDRESSED IN THIS PART

A. Total startup cash needed
B. Financial performance of similar businesses
C. Overall financial attractiveness of the proposed venture

ASSESSMENT TOOLS

Total Start-up Cash Needed

- The startup costs (which include capital investments and operating expenses) should include all the costs necessary for the business to make its first sale. New firms typically need money for a host of purposes, including the hiring of personnel, office or manufacturing space, equipment, training, research and development, marketing, and the initial product rollout.

- At the feasibility analysis stage, it is not necessary for the number to be exact. However, the number should be fairly accurate to give an entrepreneur an idea of the dollar amount that will be needed to launch the firm. After the approximate dollar amount is known, the entrepreneur should determine specifically where the money will come from to cover the startup costs.

- The total startup cash needed can be estimate using the following table.

Total Startup Cash Needed (to Make First Sale)

Capital Investments	Amount
Property	_____
Furniture and fixtures	_____
Computer equipment	_____
Other equipment	_____
Vehicles	_____

Operating Expenses	Amount
Legal, accounting, and professional services	_____
Advertising and promotions	_____
Deposits for utilities	_____
Licenses and permits	_____
Prepaid insurance	_____
Lease payments	_____
Salary and wages	_____
Payroll taxes	_____
Travel	_____
Signs	
Tools and supplies	_____
Starting inventory	_____
Cash (working capital)	_____
Other expense 1	_____
Other expense 2	_____
Total Startup Cash Needed =	_____

Comparison of the Financial Performance of Proposed Venture to Similar Firms

- Use the following tables to compare the proposed new venture to similar firms in regard to annual sales (Year 1 and Year 2) and profitability (Year 1 and Year 2).

Comparison of the Financial Performance of Proposed Venture to Similar Firms Assessment Tool

Annual Sales

Estimate of Proposed Venture's Annual Sales—Year 1	Explanation of How the Estimate Was Computed
Estimate of Year 1 Sales _____	_____
Summary: How proposed annual sales, on average, compares to similar firms (circle one)	_____ _____
Below Average Average Above Average	_____
Estimate of Year 2 Sales _____	_____
Summary: How proposed annual sales, on average, compares to similar firms (circle one)	_____ _____
Below Average Average Above Average	_____

Net Income

Estimate of Proposed Venture's Net Income — Year 1	Explanation of How the Estimate Was Computed
Estimate of Year 1 Net Income _____	_____
Summary: How proposed net income, on average, compares to similar firms (circle one)	_____ _____
Below Average Average Above Average	_____
Estimate of Year 2 Net Income _____	_____
Summary: How proposed net income, on average, compares to similar firms (circle one)	_____ _____
Below Average Average Above Average	_____

Overall Financial Attractiveness of the Proposed Venture

- The following factors are important in regard to the overall financial attractiveness of the proposed business.
- Assess the strength of each factor in the following table.

Overall Financial Attractiveness of Proposed Venture Assessment Tool

	Low Potential	Moderate Potential	High Potential
1. Steady and rapid growth in sales during the first one to three years in a clearly defined target market	Unlikely	Moderately likely	Highly likely
2. High percentage of recurring income — meaning that once you win a client, the client will provide recurring sources of revenue	Low	Moderate	Strong
3. Ability to forecast income and expenses with a reasonable degree of certainty	Weak	Moderate	Strong
4. Likelihood that internally generated funds will be available within two years to finance growth	Unlikely	Moderately likely	Highly likely
5. Availability of exit opportunity for investor if applicable	Unlikely to be unavailable	May be available	Likely to be available

Conclusion (report finding for each area)

A. Total startup cash needed
B. Financial performance of similar businesses
C. Financial feasibility (circle the correct response)
   Not Feasible   Unsure   Feasible
D. Suggestions for improving financial feasibility

OVERALL FEASIBILITY: SUMMARY AND CONCLUSION

	Overall Feasibility of the Business Idea Based on Each Part	*Suggestions for Improving the Feasibility*
Product/Market Feasibility	Not feasible ☐ Unsure ☐ Feasible ☐	_____ _____ _____
Industry/Market Feasibility	Not feasible ☐ Unsure ☐ Feasible ☐	_____ _____ _____
Organizational Feasibility	Not feasible ☐ Unsure ☐ Feasible ☐	_____ _____ _____
Financial Feasibility	Not feasible ☐ Unsure ☐ Feasible ☐	_____ _____ _____
Overall Assessment	Not feasible ☐ Unsure ☐ Feasible ☐	_____ _____ _____

Conclusion—briefly summarize your justification for your overall assessment.

CHAPTER 4

INTRODUCTORY MATERIAL, EXECUTIVE SUMMARY, AND DESCRIPTION OF THE BUSINESS

INTRODUCTION

As discussed throughout the book, a **business plan** is a written document (usually 25 to 35 pages) that carefully explains every aspect of a new business venture. An entrepreneur provides the business plan to an investor or other interested party to describe why the business is starting and how it will make money. If properly prepared, the business plan also relays the passion and energy that the individuals who wrote the plan have for the proposed business venture.

This chapter begins our discussion of how to write a business plan. Although experts vary on the order of the topics in a business plan, most plans follow a fairly standard format. The first two steps in a business plan, the executive summary and the company description, will be discussed in this chapter, along with the title page, the table of contents, and how to select a name for a business. The executive summary and the company description are arguably the most important sections of a business plan because if the reader's interest isn't captured early on, the plan won't get read. The title page, the table of contents, and the name of a business are also important issues. A new venture's name is often the first thing that someone associates with the business, and the title page and table of contents are the first things people observe in a business plan. As a result, to get off to a good start, all of these items should be given careful consideration.

Two quick points before we get started. First, as mentioned in Chapter 1, a business plan should be written with extreme empathy for the reader. Most of the people who will read your plan are extremely busy, so it's important that the plan is clear, concise, and easy to follow. It should also be interesting—a topic that we'll stress throughout the book. If the plan is dull, contains too much jargon, or simply plods along, it's unlikely to get completely read. Second, remember that as your readers evaluate your plan, they're not only evaluating the plan, but they're forming judgments about you. If the plan looks sharp, reads well, is backed up by solid research, and has a professional and upbeat tone, it's easy for the reader to associate those same attributes with you. In contrast, if the plan has the opposite qualities, it may not matter how good the business idea is or how sharp you really are, the reader may simply tune out. Never underestimate the importance of this latter set of points. Even though a business plan explains how a new business will be set up, most readers realize that the plan will change and evolve and that the business may look very different a year from now than it does today. As a result, what's more important than the specific details of the plan, which will invariably change, is the sense of competence, passion, and attention-to-detail that it projects.

Now let's begin by looking at the cover page and table of contents.

COVER PAGE AND TABLE OF CONTENTS

As mentioned in Chapter 1, to make the best impression, a business plan should follow a conventional format. This advice starts with the cover page and the table of contents.

COVER PAGE

The **cover page** should include the name of the company, its street address, its e-mail address, its phone number (land based and cell), the date, the contact information for the lead entrepreneur, and the company's Web site address if it has one. This information should be centered at the top of the page. The bottom of the page should include information alerting the reader to the confidential nature of the plan. If the company already has a logo or trademark, it should be placed somewhere near the center of the page.

It may also be appropriate to place a sketch or photo of your product or service on the cover page if you have one and it looks sharp. In some instances, a generic stock photo will do. If you don't have one, many Web sites, such as INMAGINE, (http://www.inmagine.com), provide access to royalty-free photos. For example, if you plan to open a dance studio, many digital photos of ballerinas and other dancers are available at the INMAGINE site. Placing an image on your cover page that depicts the type of dancer that your studio will train may make a valuable contribution to the plan.

The single most important item on the cover page is the contact information for the authors of the plan. You want to make it extremely easy for anyone reading the plan to be able to contact you.

TABLE OF CONTENTS

A **table of contents** should follow the cover page. It should list the main sections, subsections, and appendices to the plan along with their corresponding page numbers. The goal is to make it easy to find anything in the plan. Some plans include tabs, which makes it easier to go directly to a section. A carefully developed table of contents can draw attention to areas of the plan you want to emphasize. For example, if your business plan is for a restaurant, and you have several attractive sketches of what the exterior and interior of the restaurant will look like, creating a subsection labeled "artist depiction of what the restaurant will look like" under the appropriate section of the plan may cause someone who is glancing at the table of contents to turn directly to that part of the plan. These types of items are often overlooked in a quick perusal of a plan.

The table of contents for the Prime Adult Fitness business plan, which represents the format of the business plan described in this book, is provided in Figure 4-1. It's always a good idea to double-check the page numbers included in the table of contents to make sure they correspond with the page numbers in the plan before you send it out. It's easy to forget last-minute additions to the plan that can throw off the page numbers in the table of contents.

EXECUTIVE SUMMARY

The **executive summary** is the first item that appears in a business plan. This short overview of the entire plan provides a busy reader with everything that needs to be known about the new venture's distinctive nature. In many instances, an investor will first ask for a copy of the executive summary and will request a copy of the full business plan only if the executive summary is sufficiently convincing. The executive summary, then, is arguably the most important section of the business plan.[1] If it doesn't interest and excite the reader, it's unlikely that the reader will look any further.

The most important thing to remember when writing an executive summary is that it's not an introduction or a preface to the business plan. Instead, it is meant to be a summary of the plan itself. After reading the executive summary, the investor or other interested party should have a good sense of the entirety of the plan. The executive summary for Prime Adult Fitness is shown in Figure 4-2.

FORMAT

An executive summary shouldn't exceed two single-spaced pages. The cleanest format for an executive summary is to provide an overview of the business plan on a section-by-section basis, as shown previously in Figure 4-2. The topics should

FIGURE 4-1 Table of Contents (Prime Adult Fitness Business Plan)

Table of Contents

be presented in the same order as they are presented in the plan. Two identical versions of the executive summary should be prepared—one that's part of the business plan and one that's a stand-alone document. The stand-alone document is used to accommodate people who ask to see the executive summary before they decide whether they want to see the full plan. Make sure to place your contact information on any stand-alone executive summaries that you send out.

FIGURE 4-2   Executive Summary (Prime Adult Fitness Business Plan)

Introduction
The fitness industry grew to over $21 billion in 2006, up substantially from 2001. The indus-
try's growth has been driven largely by middle-aged and older people, who are increasingly
concerned about their health and fitness. A gap in the industry is the lack of fitness centers
that focus exclusively on people 50 years old and older, who prefer a different type of
fitness experience than younger people. Prime Adult Fitness will fill that gap in Center
Florida by opening a fitness center that focuses exclusively on that clientele.

Company Description
Prime Adult Fitness is proposing to operate a 21,600 square foot facility in Oviedo, FL, a
suburb of Orlando. Oviedo is an ideal community for the center—it has a higher percentage of older people with a higher income than national averages. The center will feature
a carefully selected assortment of fitness machines, classes, and programs, all tailored
specifically for people 50 years old and older. There will also be seminars and workshops
on nutrition, sleep, neurobics (brain exercises), and similar topics.

Designing and operating a fitness center for older people is a unique challenge. It
requires an extreme sensitivity to their needs, both physical and emotional. As a result, the
operations of the center will be geared to (1) providing an uplifting environment for the
members, (2) providing high-quality classes and equipment, and (3) encouraging people
to socialize and make Prime Adult Fitness one of the centerpieces of their lives.

Industry Analysis
Prime Adult Fitness will compete in the "Fitness and Recreational Sports Centers" industry
(NAICS 71394). The $21 billion industry is in the growth stage of its life cycle. Growth is
being driven primarily by an increased awareness of the importance of fitness and exercise.
The industry's biggest challenge is competing for the leisure time of its customers.

The industry is competitive. Fitness centers, on average, earn around a 9 percent net
profit (IBISWorld, May, 2007). The key success factors are location, having the right mix of
classes and activities, motivating members to stay engaged, and having an informed and
proactive staff.

Market Analysis
Prime Adult Fitness's trade area will be Seminole County, FL, which is the county in which
Oviedo is located. Its market analysis indicates that approximately 65,400 people 50 years
old and older live in its trade area, and 9,800 of these people currently belong to a fitness
center.

Prime Adult Fitness's membership and income goals are as follows:

Year	Membership Goal	Total Projected Income
2009	2,100 units	$1,690,398
2010	2,226 units	$2,416,514
2011	2,360 units	$2,561,955
2012	2,502 units	$2,716,124

The company, through focus groups and a study conducted by its Customer Advisory
Board, believes that 50 percent of its membership will come from people who already
belong to a fitness center, and 50 percent will be new members, drawn in by its unique
concept. If 50 percent of revenues come from the existing market, that means Prime Adult
Fitness will need to capture an 11.44 percent share of the 50+ market for people in
Seminole Country, FL, who currently belong to a fitness center. The company is confident
that its membership goals are achievable.

FIGURE 4-2   (continued)

Marketing Plan

The overall objective of Prime Adult Fitness's marketing strategy will be to make people 50 years old and older aware of the benefits of exercise, and to sell them on the idea of Prime Adult Fitness as the best place for them to either start or to continue exercising.

The company's points of differentiation are as follows:

- Only fitness center in its target market exclusively for people 50 years old and older
- Strong emphasis placed on the social aspect of belonging to a fitness center
- Well trained staff that cares about the needs and lives of older people

The company's promotional activities will include a mixture of traditional and grassroots marketing techniques. The company has established cobranding relationships with Central Florida Health Food and Oviedo Doctor's and Surgeon's Medical practice. Talks are currently underway to solidify the specifics of these relationships.

Management Team and Company Structure

A five-member management team is in place, led by cofounders Jeremy Ryan, age 46, and Elizabeth Sims, age 49. Ryan started a fitness franchise in South Florida and grew it to 38 units before selling to a larger company. He has 14 years of additional experience in the industry. Elizabeth Sims, who worked with Ryan in his former venture, is a CPA with more than 19 years of experience.

Prime Adult Fitness has a five-member Board of Directors, a four-member Board of Advisors, and a 10-member Customer Advisory Board.

Operations and Development Plan

Prime Adult Fitness has signed a seven-year lease, subject to funding, for the 21,600 square foot facility it plans to occupy. The lease includes an option to buy the facility at the end of the term.

The 21,600 square foot building will require $1 million in retrofitting. Preliminary plans for the retrofitting have been developed by an architect experienced in designing buildings suitable for an older clientele. The retrofitting of the building will be done with extreme sensitivity to the company's target market.

Financial Projections

The business plan includes a full set of pro forma income statements, balances sheets, and cash flows (five years income statements and balance sheets, and four years cash flows). The company projects an operating loss for 2009 (its initial year of operations) and steady gains from that point forward. Projected ROS is 13.1 percent in 2010, 10.5 percent in 2011, and 11.3 percent in 2012. Net income is projected to be $317,740 in 2010 and $269,670 in 2011. The company will remain cash flow positive throughout its startup period.

Funding Sought

The company is seeking $515,000 in investment capital.

One thing to be prepared for is that an increasingly common practice among investors and others is to ask for a short PowerPoint overview of a business plan rather than an executive summary. Investors do this because clicking through a dozen or so slides is an even quicker way to size up a business idea than reading an executive summary. In these instances, the executive summary should be boiled down to the 10 to 15 slides that are usually requested. Tips for how to prepare PowerPoint slides to send or present to an investor are provided in Chapter 11.

BUSINESS PLAN INSIGHT

Write the Pitch and Then Write the Plan

Guy Kawasaki, a well-know investor and entrepreneur, has an interesting theory about business plans and PowerPoint presentations (or pitches). Kawasaki says that the pitch should come before the plan. Here's what he means.

Many people, according to Kawasaki, write their business plan and then together a PowerPoint presentation that's an abbreviated version of the plan. He sees that sequence as backwards. Kawasaki thinks that it's best to put the PowerPoint presentation together first and then use it as a guide in writing the plan. Here's the rationale. Kawasaki is a big believer in trying things out. He tells entrepreneurs to develop a pitch, whether it's a PowerPoint presentation or another format, of their business idea and try it out in front of as many groups as possible before they write their business plan. Why? Because it's easier to revise a 15-slide PowerPoint presentation than it is a 25- to 35-page business plan. And you get immediate feedback on a pitch, whereas you're unlikely to get feedback on a business plan until it's finished.

Kawasaki makes a good point. Although you shouldn't let the pitch dictate your plan, any feedback you can get before the plan is written is a good idea. By putting together the first cut of your PowerPoint presentation before you write the plan, you have an ideal tool to solicit feedback and try out your plan before it's written. You'll also have a head start on preparing a polished PowerPoint overview of your plan when it's finished.

Guy Kawasaki writes a blog titled "How to Change the World" that is very colorful and focused on entrepreneurship and related issues. The blog is available at http://blog.guykawasaki.com.

Source: Guy Kawasaki Blog, "The Zen of Business Plans," posted January 21, 2006. The blog is available at http://blog.guykawasaki.com.

More information about the value of developing a PowerPoint overview of your business plan is provided in the following Business Plan Insight box.

Even though the executive summary appears at the beginning of the business plan, it should be written last. The plan itself will evolve as it's written, so not everything is known at the outset. In addition, if you write the executive summary first, you run the risk of trying to write a plan that fits the executive summary rather than thinking through each piece of the plan independently.[2]

CONTENT

Each section of the executive summary should contain a short synopsis of the material that's provided in the same section of the broader plan. To fit all of the material into two pages, each section must be crisp and concise. The section headings should be labeled in boldfaced type to allow them to stand out from the text.

The primary goal of an executive summary is to capture the reader's attention. To do this, the tone should be businesslike yet convey a sense of excitement and anticipation. Each section should be factual and well written and should show that you have conducted research to ensure that your assumptions are correct. You should avoid using a lot of technical or industry-specific jargon, unless you're writing for a very specific audience, such as a group of angel investors specializing in your industry. You should also try to connect with your readers on both an objective and an emotional level, if possible. For example, in the executive summary shown in Figure 4-2, we quote a 71-year-old man who participated in the buying intentions survey that we administered as part of our feasibility analysis. The heartfelt statement made by the man illustrates the value that he sees Prime Adult Fitness playing in his life. Statements like this can cause a reader to pause and think, "I bet there are a lot of people out there that think like that. Prime Adult Fitness just might be a hit."

It's also important that the first section of the executive summary, which covers the company description, begins by describing the opportunity and then shows how the proposed business meets the opportunity. For example, it's not very effective to start by saying something like "Prime Adult Fitness, incorporated in the state of Florida, will open a fitness center for people 50 years old and older. The center will feature exercise machines, classes, and other activities that are specifically designed for its clientele." This type of statement invites a "so what?" sort of response. It doesn't say anything about the fitness industry or the opportunities that exist. It only says what you want to do. A better way to start is to say something like, "The fitness center industry grew to over $20 billion in 2006, up substantially from 2001. The industry's growth has been driven largely by middle-aged and older people, who are increasingly concerned about their health. A gap in the industry is a lack of fitness centers that focus exclusively on people 50 years an older, who prefer a different type of fitness center experience than younger people. Prime Adult Fitness will fill that gap in Central Florida by opening a fitness center that focuses exclusively on people 50 years old and older." This opening creates a better tone. It first describes the opportunity and then shows how Prime Adult Fitness will meet the opportunity.

Most experts recommend that if a new venture is seeking financing or funding, the executive summary should state the amount of funds being requested. Some plans will state how much equity a business is willing to surrender for a certain amount of investment capital. In these instances, the executive summary will conclude with a section labeled "Status and Offering" as shown earlier in the executive summary in Figure 4-2. The Prime Adult Fitness executive summary indicates that the firm is prepared to offer a 20 percent ownership position in exchange for a $515,000 investment. Some entrepreneurs are more leery about how much equity they are willing to surrender and leave their plans intentionally vague on this point.

COMPANY DESCRIPTION

The main body of the business plan begins with a general description of the company. Although at first glance this section may seem less critical than others, it is extremely important. It demonstrates to your reader that you know how to translate an idea into a business. There are also issues within this section that take a lot of thought and planning, such as your company's mission and its legal form of business ownership.

A company description for Prime Adult Fitness is provided in Figure 4-3. The description shows the major headings that are included in the section. The headings are labeled in boldfaced type to make them to stand out from the text.

FIGURE 4-3   Company Description (Prime Adult Fitness Business Plan)

Introduction
Prime Adult Fitness is proposing to operate a 21,600 square foot fitness center, specifically for people 50 years old and older, in Oviedo, FL, a suburb of Orlando. The center will pioneer a new concept in fitness—it will be for exclusively for people 50 years old and older.

Prime Adult Fitness's cofounders are Jeremy Ryan, age 46, and Elizabeth Sims, age 49. The company is located at 1990 Palm Drive, Oviedo, FL. Jeremy Ryan can be reached by phone at 407-760-6325 or via e-mail at Jeremy@primeadultfitness.com

Company History
In the summer of 2007, Jeremy Ryan, a cofounder of Prime Adult Fitness, was making a presentation at a fitness industry conference in Atlanta. During the Q&A period following his presentation, a member of the audience asked, "Why isn't there a fitness center concept designed specifically for older people? Curves hit a home run by pioneering a fitness center just for women. Why not a fitness center just for older people?"

That question changed Jeremy Ryan's life. A longtime fitness industry veteran and advocate of fitness for older people, he had never thought of opening a fitness center exclusively for older people. In November and December of 2007, a feasibility analysis was completed, which validated the idea for the center. On January 8, 2008, Prime Adult Fitness was incorporated.

Mission Statement
The mission of Prime Adult Fitness is to make exercise and fitness a vibrant and satisfying part of the lives of people who are 50 years old and older.

Tagline
The company's tagline, which will be an important part of its branding strategy, is "Meet Your Dreams." The tagline, which emerged from a focus group session, captures the essence of what fitness ultimately accomplishes for people of all ages. It helps people feel better, live longer, and lead more satisfying lives.

Product and Services
The design of the Prime Adult Fitness offering has been guided by the results of its feasibility analysis. To properly determine the interests and preferences of its potential clientele, in November 2007, the company distributed its concept statement and a questionnaire to a random sample of 196 people 50 years and older in its trade area. It has also conducted three focus groups.

Based on the results of these efforts and its ongoing research, Prime Adult Fitness will offer its members the following mix of programs and amenities:

- *Exercise Machines.* A full complement of exercise machines selected specifically for our clientele.

FIGURE 4-3 (continued)

- *Fitness Classes and Programs.* Fitness classes and programs will be offered at various times during the day. The classes will include water aerobics, low impact land aerobics, yoga, Pilates, body sculpting, and several others. Nontraditional classes will also be offered, such as outdoor "walking" classes where members will walk in classes throughout Central Florida neighborhoods.
- *Seminars and Workshops.* Seminars and workshops will be offered on nutrition, sleep, neurobics (brain exercises), avoiding back and neck pain, aging with dignity, and other topics.
- *Massage and Physical Therapy.* Massage and physical therapy services, by fully certified personnel, will be offered at the center.
- *Safety.* Attention to detail in regard to safety and support for the needs of older people will be evident throughout the center.
- *Emotional Support.* Prime Adult Fitness will feature a caring staff that is dedicated to meeting the needs of its older clientele in an uplifting, motivating, and fun atmosphere.

Current Status

Prime Adult Fitness is poised to commence operations on January 1, 2009. Since it was incorporated on January 8, 2008, the following milestones have been completed, and the following milestones remain to be completed for the company to start operations.

Milestones Completed

- Feasibility analysis, prospect survey, and three focus groups completed
- Business plan completed
- Five-member management team in place
- Board of directors, general advisory board, and customer advisory board in place
- Seven-year lease, subject to funding, signed on 21,600 square foot building
- $325,000 invested by management team
- $175,000 invested by angel investor
- $60,000 grant obtained from Healthy After 50, an organization supportive of the mission and goals of Prime Adult Fitness

Milestones Remaining to Be Completed

- Obtain additional funding (see specifics below)
- Retrofit building
- Select exercise equipment, plan programs and classes, hire personnel
- Prepare for grand opening

Funding Sought

As described in detail in the business plan, Prime Adult Fitness is seeking $515,000 in investment capital.

Legal Status and Ownership

Prime Adult Fitness is a Limited Liability Corporation incorporated in the state of Florida. It is currently owned by its management team and angel investor. A detailed schedule of ownership is provided in the "Management Team and Company Structure" section of the plan.

The company description should start with a brief introduction, which provides an overview of the company and reminds the reader of the reason it is starting. Demographic information should be also provided, including the names of the founders, the address of the company's headquarters, and contact information for the lead entrepreneur.

There are two important points to be mindful of as you start writing this section and prepare to tackle the rest of the plan. First, a business plan is at its core a story about an opportunity and how a person (or group of people) plans to start a business to take advantage of the opportunity. It's also about how the business plans to deliver value to its customers, compete in the marketplace, and make money. This basic storyline should be evident throughout the plan. If the story isn't consistent, or the plan is a hodgepodge of loosely related material, it will be ineffective. Second, you build credibility with your readers by backing up assumptions with facts and research. The Internet resources suggested in Chapter 2, along with the results of your feasibility analysis, should provide you ample information to validate your claims. For instance, there is no reason to make a statement like "the fitness industry is large and growing." This statement may be true, but it is insufficient. Exactly how big is the fitness industry? How much is it growing? What are industry experts saying about its future? Including this type of information strengthens your statements and builds credibility in your plan.

The following is a discussion of each of the five individual elements of the company description.

COMPANY HISTORY

The Company History section should be brief, but should explain where the idea for the company came from and the driving force behind its inception. If it is a startup, simply mention that the company is in its startup stage. If the story of where the idea for the company came from is interesting or heartfelt, tell it. For example, in Chapter 2, we introduced Christine Ingemi, the mother who created the IHearSafe earbuds. You'll recall that Ingemi became concerned about how loud her children were playing their MP3 players when she could hear music coming from their earphones while she was driving her van with the music on. After she and her husband, Rick, did some research and interviewed several audiologists, she invented the IHearSafe earbuds, which limits the volume of sound that can enter an individual's ears from an iPod or similar device. Ingemi's story is interesting and is one that anyone can relate to. It might even cause the person reading the plan to pause and think, "My daughter blasts away on her iPod constantly. I wish she had a product like that." By telling a story, you place a human face on the business plan and potentially connect with readers on an emotional level.

If you don't have an interesting story to tell, you can talk briefly about how your idea will meet a compelling need. If the company has been in business for a while, you should provide a brief timeline in narrative form and talk about its major achievements. You should also talk about its history of revenues, net income, and sales growth.

MISSION STATEMENT

A **mission statement** defines why a company exists and what it aspires to become.[3] If carefully written and used properly, a mission statement can define the path a company takes and act as its financial and moral compass. For a business plan, a well-written mission statement demonstrates that your business is focused and you can articulate its purpose clear and distinctly.

The trick to writing an effective mission statement is to articulate the mission or purpose of the company in as few words as possible. A short mission statement is easier to remember than a longer one and is usually more effective. The mission statement should also be more than empty words. It should be the driving force behind the company and the major decisions that it makes. Many resources are available on the Internet and elsewhere that provide advice for how to write an effective mission statement. Several rules-of-thumb for writing an effective mission statement are as follows. Your mission statement should

- Not be a mini-overview of the business
- Describe what makes your company different
- Be honest—don't claim to be something you aren't
- Convey passion and stick in the mind of the reader
- Define your "reason for being"
- Be risky and challenging but achievable
- Use a tone that best reflects your company's culture
- Be something that everyone involved with the firm can relate to
- Involve everyone in your team in its creation

Examples of several mission statements are shown in Table 4-1.

TABLE 4-1 Examples of Mission Statements

Google
Organize the world's information and make it universally accessible and useful.

Southwest Airlines
The mission of Southwest Airlines is dedication to the highest quality of Customer Service delivered with a sense of warmth, friendliness, individual pride, and Company Spirit.

eBay
eBay's mission is to provide a global trading platform where practically anyone can trade practically anything.

Intel
Delight our customers, employees, and shareholders by relentlessly delivering the platform and technology advancements that become essential to the way we work and live.

Dell
Dell's mission is to be the most successful computer company in the world at delivering the best customer experience in markets we serve.

Along with a mission statement, some companies have mottos or taglines that are effective in conveying their purpose and building the brand. Examples of famous mottos or taglines include Google — "Don't be evil"; Nike — "Just do It!"; MySpace — "A space for friends"; and Nokia — "Connecting people." Some companies, such as Nike and Nokia, have built their entire branding campaigns around their taglines. If your company has a motto or tagline, it should be mentioned in this section of the plan.

There is no set procedure for how to come up with a mission statement or tagline. Often, the founders and early employees of a company get together and simply brainstorm ideas. The following anecdote about how Google came up with the motto "Don't be evil" may be helpful to you in thinking about how to come up with a mission statement or motto for your company. In July 2001, as Google was becoming larger, and the founders were worried that it might lose its corporate identity, Stacy Sullivan, the head of Google's HR department, rounded up a cross section of employees with the mission of clarifying Google's core values. According to a well-regarded book on the early history of Google, the meeting sputtered some, as the people in the room suggested generic clichés like "treat everyone with respect" and "be on time for meetings." The following picks up the description of the meeting directly from the book:

> The engineers in the room were rolling their eyes. Patel (a Google employee) recalls: "Some of us were very anticorporate, and we didn't like the idea of all of these specific rules. And engineers in general like efficiency — there had to be a way to say all these things in one statement, as opposed to being so specific." That's when Paul Buchheit, another engineer in the group, blurted out what would become the most important three words in Google's corporate history. Paul said, 'All of these things can be covered by just saying, Don't be evil,' Patel recalls. "And it just kind of stuck."[4]

The story goes on to explain that to reinforce the phrase, Patel scribbled "Don't be evil" in the corner of nearly every whiteboard in the company. The phrase caught on and became the rallying cry for Google's employees. Commenting on the importance of "Don't be evil," which is still prominent at Google today, Larry Page, one of the company's cofounders, said, "When you are making a decision, it causes you to think. I think that's good."[5]

PRODUCTS AND SERVICES

The Products and Services section should include an explanation of your product or service, beyond what you said in the executive summary. Include a description of how your product or service is unique and how you plan to position it in the marketplace. A product or service's **position** is how it is situated relative to its rivals. If you plan to open a new type of coffee shop, for example, you should explain how your coffee shop differs from others and how it will be positioned in its market in terms of the products it offers, its location, and its price range. You should also identify who your clientele will be and why they would patronize your coffee shop instead of Starbucks or another existing chain.

The product/service description is the ideal place for you to start reporting the results of your feasibility analysis. If the concept test and buying intentions survey produced meaningful results, they should be reported here. It's appropriate to allow your reader insight into how you shaped the ideas for your product or service and how you determined its positioning strategy. For example, in the coffee shop example, you might report, "A concept statement that outlined the company's initial business concept was distributed to 15 industry experts who suggested that we broaden our product line in select areas. As a result, we plan to complement our menu of coffee, tea, specialty coffees, lattes, and desserts with bottled drinks such as Honest Tea and Jones Soda and a limited line of smoothies. To affirm our revised business concept, we queried a new set of 10 industry exerts who responded very favorably to our expanded product mix for our upscale target market."

You should explain any proprietary aspects to your product or service and the extent to which you have protected your intellectual property. If your product or business method is patentable, at the minimum, you should file a provisional patent application, which grants "provisional rights" for up to one year. Instructions for filing are available at the U.S. Patent and Trademark Office's (USPTO) Web site (http://www.uspto.gov). If there is nothing proprietary about your product or service, you should briefly mention how you will create barriers to entry to prevent it from being quickly copied. Without adequate barriers to entry, it will be easy for a larger competitor to copy what you are doing.

This later point raises an important issue. The realization that your product or service idea can be copied by a larger competitor, absent any intellectual property protection, will be recognized by a savvy reader of the plan. At exactly this type of juncture, your business plan either gains or loses credibility. If you duck the issue and say nothing, you'll lose credibility. The reader of the plan will know that a lack of barriers to entry could be a huge problem for your firm and will notice that you didn't address it. In contrast, if you confront the issue head-on and offer a plausible explanation or say that an inability to create barriers to entry is a major risk, you'll gain credibility. You should also think creatively about risk. In some cases, introducing a product or service that is likely to attract the interest of larger firms is just what you want. It may make your company an attractive acquisition target and provide a liquidity event for your investors. The overarching point is that you must confront difficult issues head-on and offer plausible explanations or disclose major risks. If you don't, your business plan will lose credibility quickly.

CURRENT STATUS

The Current Status section should reveal how far along your company is in its development. A good way to frame this discussion is to think in terms of milestones. If you have selected and registered your company's name, completed a feasibility analysis, written a business plan, and established a legal entity, you have already cleared several important milestones. Any similar activities that you have accomplished or about to accomplish should be mentioned.

Three issues are particularly important for this section: the current composition of you management team, early customer reaction to your product or service, and your company's financial status. In regard to your management team, if you're an early-stage venture, and the company consists of just you or a small group of people, that's okay, but you should mention your future staffing plans. If you've put together or are putting together a board of advisors, you should mention that. In regard to your product or service, if you have conducted a feasibility analysis and have feedback from potential customers, you should summarize any results that indicate how enthused people are about your product idea and how close it is to being marketable. Similarly, if you have attended trade shows or have solicited feedback on your product or service idea in a similar way, you should report the results.

Finally, in regard to the financial status of your company, your readers will want to know how the company has been funded up to this point, and if you have any debt or have surrendered any equity in the firm. If you are seeking funding, briefly indicate how much funding you are seeking and for what purpose. You'll be able to expand on all of these points in the financial section of the plan.

LEGAL STATUS AND OWNERSHIP

The Legal Status and Ownership section should indicate who owns the business, how the ownership is spit up if more than one individual is involved, and whether a founder's agreement has been set up. A **founder's agreement** (or shareholders' agreement) is a written document that deals with issues such as the relative split of the equity among the founders of the firm, how individual founders will be compensated for the "sweat equity" they put into the firm, and how long the founders will have to remain with the firm for their shares to be vested. If you don't have a founder's agreement (and more than one founder is involved), you should indicate that this step is pending to alert the reader that you are thinking about it and recognize its importance.

You should also indicate what your current form of business ownership is. If you've done nothing in this regard, you're a sole proprietorship or a general partnership by default, which is an untenable position for any length of time. A much better choice is to form a subchapter S corporation, a C corporation, or a Limited Liability Company (LLC). You should retain an attorney to help you resolve this manner. Again, if you haven't selected a form of business ownership, you should at the minimum state that this matter is pending to alert your reader that you understand the importance of this task.

The next section of the chapter deals with selecting the name for a business. This discussion is included here because selecting a name for a business is an activity that often goes hand-and-hand with feasibility analysis and the early stages of preparing a business plan. It is also an issue that makes a lot of difference for a firm, so should be considered carefully.

SELECTING THE NAME FOR A BUSINESS

Although selecting a name for a business isn't part of the formal business planning process, it's an important activity. A company's name is normally the first thing that people associated with a business, and it is a word or phrase that will be said thousands or hundreds of thousands of times during the life of a business. It is also an integral part of a company's branding strategy. A company's **brand** is the unique set of attributes that allow consumers to separate it from its competitors. As a result, it is important for a business to choose its name carefully so that it will facilitate rather than hinder how the business plans to differentiate itself in the marketplace. You don't want someone mentally questioning the wisdom of your company's name before they even start reading the business plan.

PRIMARY CONSIDERATION IN NAMING A BUSINESS

The primary consideration in naming a business is that the name should complement the type of business the company plans to be. It is helpful to divide companies into four categories to discuss this issue.

CUSTOMER-DRIVEN COMPANIES

If a company plans to focus on a particular type of consumer, its name should reflect the attributes of its clientele. For example, an online store that sells clothing for big and tall men and boys is named Big and Tall Guys (http://www.bigandtallguys.com). Similarly, a company that installs cameras in day care centers and allows parents to log on to a password-protected Web site to see their children during the day is called ParentWatch (http://www.parentwatch.com). These companies have names that were chosen to appeal specifically to their target market or clientele.

PRODUCT- OR SERVICE-DRIVEN COMPANIES

If a company plans to focus on a particular product or service, its name should reflect the advantages that its product or service provide. Examples include 1-800-FLOWERS, XM Satellite Radio, Whole Foods Markets, and Jiffy Print. These companies have names that were chosen to reflect the distinctive attributes of the product or service the company offers, regardless of the clientele.

INDUSTRY-DRIVEN COMPANIES

If a company plans to focus on a broad range of products or services in a particular industry, its name should reflect the category it is participating in. Examples include General Motors, Linens N Things, Kraft Foods, and Home Depot. These companies have names that are intentionally broad and are not limiting in regard to a target market or a product selection.

PERSONALITY- OR IMAGE-DRIVEN COMPANIES

Some companies are founded by individuals who put such an indelible stamp on the company that it may be smart to name the company after its founder. Examples include Ben & Jerry's Homemade, Charles Schwab, Dell Inc., Liz

Claiborne, and Magic Johnson Enterprises. These companies have names that benefit from a positive association with a popular or distinctive founder. Of course, this strategy can backfire if the founder falls out of favor in the public eye.

LEGAL ISSUES

Many legal issues are involved in naming a business, and these should be addressed before the business plan is finalized. The general rule for business names is that they must be unique. In other words, in most instances, there may not be more than one business per name per state. In addition, a new business may not adopt a name that is confusingly similar to an existing business. This regulation prevents a new overnight deliver company from naming itself FedExtra, for example, which FedEx would undoubtedly claim is confusingly similar to its name.

To determine whether a name is available in a particular state, the entrepreneur must usually contact the secretary of state's office to make the inquiry. If the name is available, the next step is to reserve it in that state. After an available name has been reserved, it should be trademarked along with the company's logo, if a logo has been created. Instructions for how to go about obtaining a trademark on name and a logo are available at the USPTO Web site (http://www.uspto.gov). A quick way to see if a name has been trademarked is to visit the USPTO Web site, and follow the instructions for performing a search. For example, the name of the company that we made up for this book, Prime Adult Fitness, is not trademarked. A shorter version of the name, Prime Fitness (http://www.primefitness.com), is trademarked and is an actual business located in Bonney Lake, Washington. As a result, we couldn't use that name if we were starting a real business.

The process of finding a name for a business can be frustrating because the most obvious names are often already taken. For example, if you wanted to start a quick printing company, almost every possible combination of the names "quick" and "print" are taken. These combinations include quick-print, jiffy-print, instant-print, swift-printing, fast-print, and so on. In fact, according to the USPTO database, the word *print* appears in 3,739 registered trademarks. A complicating factor is getting an Internet domain name that is the same as a company's name. Because no two domain names can be exactly the same, frustrations often arise when a company tries to register its domain name, and the name has already been taken. Still, a little imagination goes a long way in selecting a company name and an Internet domain name. For instance, the Internet domain name for Prime Adult Fitness (http://www.primeadultfitness.com) was available so we registered it on Godaddy.com for $8.95 per year.

You must also be careful to pick a name that won't be a problem in a foreign culture if your business expands. The classic example of this is the Chevy NOVA. After much advertising and fanfare, the car received a very cool reception in Mexico. It turned out that the phrase *No Va* in Spanish means "Doesn't go." Not surprisingly, the NOVA didn't sell well in Mexico.

A brief mention should be made in the business plan that a company's name has been registered and trademarked, and that the Internet domain name has been secured. If these activities have not been completed, you should mention that they are pending so the reader of the plan knows you are aware of their importance.

Chapter Summary

1. The executive summary and the company description are arguably the most important sections of a business plan because if the reader's interest isn't captured early on, the plan is unlikely to get read.
2. The cover page should include the name of the company, its street address, its e-mail address, its phone number (land based and cell), the date, the contact information for the lead entrepreneur, and the company's Web site address if it has one.
3. The table of contents should follow the cover page and should list the main sections, subsections, and appendices to the plan along with their corresponding page numbers.
4. The executive summary is the first item that appears in a business plan. It is a short overview of the entire plan that provides a busy reader with everything about the new venture's distinctive nature.
5. The most important thing to remember when writing an executive summary is that it's not an introduction or a preface to the business plan. Instead, it is meant to be a summary of the plan itself.
6. Even though the executive summary appears at the beginning of the business plan, it should be written last. The plan itself will evolve as it's written, so not everything is known at the outset.
7. The main body of the business plan begins with a general description of the company. Although at first glance this section may seem less critical than others, it is extremely important. It demonstrates to your reader that you know how to translate an idea into a business.
8. The subsections under the Company Description category are Company History, Mission Statement, Products and Services, Current Status, and Legal Status and Ownership. It is best to follow this order.
9. A mission statement defines why a company exists and what it aspires to become.
10. The primary consideration in naming a business is that the name should complement the type of business the company plans to be.

Review Questions

1. Why is it important for a business plan to have a cover page? What information should the cover page contain?
2. What is it important for a business plan to have a table of contents? What are the attributes of an effective table of contents?
3. What is an executive summary? Why is it often called the most important part of a business plan?

4. At what point in the process of putting together a business plan should the executive summary be written?
5. Why would in investor ask for a PowerPoint overview of a business plan rather than an executive summary or the full plan?
6. Explain the statement "the primary goal of an executive summary is to capture the reader's attention."
7. What are the subsections that are included under the company description section of a business plan?
8. What is the purpose of a mission statement? Why is it important to include a mission statement in a business plan?
9. To what extent should the results of a company's feasibility analysis be reported in its business plan?
10. Why is selecting a company's name a critical issue?

Application Questions

1. Jeremy and Susan Kramer are friends of yours. You were at their house recently and noticed a copy of a business plan on their kitchen table. You knew that Jeremy and Susan talked to their banker a month or so ago about the business, and he asked them to complete a business plan as part of the process of applying for a loan. Jeremy noticed that the business plan caught your eye and said, "Take a look at our plan, we'd like your feedback." In paging through the plan, you noticed that it appeared to be well written and had lots of facts but didn't have a cover page and table of contents, and wasn't divided into sections. It was basically a 35-page continuous narrative. After a few minutes, Jeremy sat down at the table across from you and said, "So, what do you think?" What would you tell him?

2. John Ryan is part of a five-person group that wants to start a biodiesel firm. He and his partners have been meeting daily for the past three weeks to hammer out a business plan, which they plan to send to an angel investor who specializes in alternative fuels. John volunteered to keep careful notes on everything that was decided in the meetings and actually write the plan. When the discussions were over, John put the plan together and distributed copies to everyone in the group. Amy, a member of the group, called Paul, another member, a couple of hours after she received the plan with a somewhat desperate tone in her voice. She said, "John got the essence of our plan right, and the writing is okay, but it looks sloppy. There are typos throughout the plan, several misspelled words, and the major headings are in 12-point font in some places and 14-point font in others. I confronted John about it, and he got real defensive. He said 'If the facts are all there and the plan is well written, what difference does it make if the font sizes vary or there are a couple of misspelled words?' What do think we should do, Paul? I'm really worried about it." Is Amy justified in her concern? If you were Paul, what would you say to her? What would be an appropriate course of action for Amy and Paul to take?

3. Mary Campbell is planning to open a retail store that sells upscale cookware. She spent the past three months writing a business plan and is very proud of it. It is well written, includes detailed industry analysis, and contains three years of pro forma financial statements that a CPA helped her develop. Mary is targeting an angel investor in her city, who has funded retail startups before. She met the investor at a Chamber of Commerce function a month ago, and he seemed interested in her plans. Mary just exchanged e-mail messages with the investor and is disappointed. She offered to FedEx him a copy of her plan, but he asked for a 10-slide PowerPoint overview instead. She doesn't even have a PowerPoint overview of the plan and will now have to scramble to prepare one. Is Mary's disappointment justified? Should she be worried that the request for a PowerPoint overview instead of the plan is an indication of lukewarm interest on the part of the investor?

4. Scott and Rebecca Wheeler's youngest daughter, Emily, has struggled with asthma since she was born. In caring for Emily over the years, Rebecca designed and made a variety of cards, posters, notes, and even decorated lunch bags that encouraged Emily, educated her about her condition, and reminded her to take her medicine on time. Scott and Rebecca are in a support group for parents with asthmatic children, and many of the parents have encouraged Rebecca to start a company to make the items she made for Emily available to other parents. Rebecca has decided to go for it and is writing a business plan for the company. One thing she's unsure about is how much of her personal story to include in the plan. Should she talk about how she developed the items for her own daughter, Emily, or should she stick to the facts? If Rebecca asked you for your advice, what would you tell her?

5. Suggest an alternative name for the fictitious fitness club, Prime Adult Fitness, discussed in the chapter. The Internet domain name must be available for the alternative name that you suggest. Explain the rationale for the name you choose.

Endnotes

1. J. Tommons, A. Zacharakis, and S. Spinelli, *Business Plans That Work,* (New York: McGraw-Hill, 2004).
2. E. Siegel, B. Ford, and J. Bornstein, *The Ernst & Young Business Plan Guide* (New York: John Wiley & Sons, 1993).
3. J. Barney and W. Hesterly, *Strategic Management and Competitive Advantage* (Upper Saddle River, NJ: Prentice Hall, 2006).
4. J. Battelle, *The Search,* (New York: Portfolio, 2005), p. 138.
5. J. Battelle, *The Search,* (New York: Portfolio, 2005), p. 138.

CHAPTER 5

INDUSTRY ANALYSIS

INTRODUCTION

An **industry** is a group of firms producing a similar product or service, such as airplanes, music, electronic games, or fitness club memberships. Industries vary along many dimensions, including size, growth rate, structure, financial characteristics, and overall attractiveness. The trends affecting an industry also matter. For example, as the U.S. population ages, the growth of the fitness center industry is likely to depend increasingly on its ability to attract and retain people 50 years old and older. Fitness centers that are on top of this trend and adjust accordingly are likely to outperform those that aren't.

This chapter introduces and describes the industry analysis portion of the business plan. It's important that this section focus *strictly* on a firm's industry rather than its industry and its target market simultaneously. A firm's **target market** is the limited portion of an industry that it goes after or tries to appeal to at a certain point in time. Most firms do not try to service their entire industry. Instead, they focus on serving a specialized portion of the market well. Prime Adult Fitness's target market within the fitness industry is people 50 years old and older.

Separating the analysis of a firm's industry and its target market is important because it's premature for a new firm to select, or even talk about, a specific target market until an understanding of the broader industry is obtained. For example, if you were interested in starting a company to produce a new type of pesticide for orange trees, your target market would be orange growers. But before you make the decision to pursue that market, you should understand the pesticide industry in general. Is the industry large or small? Is it growing or shrinking? Is it dominated by large firms or small firms? Are firms in the industry making or losing money? What impact is organic farming having on pesticide sales? The answers to these and similar questions will determine whether the pesticide industry in general is an attractive industry to enter, and which segments within the industry offer the most promise. Your analysis will also give you a read on whether starting a firm to target orange growers is a good idea or whether other segments within the pesticide industry have greater potential.

The industry analysis should appear early in a business plan because it logically precedes the analysis of a firm's target market and marketing strategy. It also helps set up and support the remainder of the plan. The analysis normally includes, for example, an indication of the average growth in sales for the firms in an industry. This information helps a firm construct its own financial forecasts and justify its numbers. Similarly, the other major portions of a firm's plan, such as product selection, target market, and operations plan, are guided by the industry's characteristics and trends. For example, the increase in the number of upscale women's clothing boutiques, first mentioned in Chapter 2, is tied directly to factors and trends in the broader women's clothing industry. These factors and trends include the following:[1]

- The industry is growing.
- As more women have entered the workforce, the demand for business attire has increased.
- Opportunities are increasing for women's clothing retailers to compete in niche markets such as petites, plus-sized clothing, evening wear, casual wear, sportswear, and upscale clothing.
- The industry is made up of a large number of small companies.
- The capital costs associated with opening a single store are relatively low.
- The only barriers to entry associated with opening a single store are brand awareness and the level of competition in a local area.
- Mass merchandisers tend to focus their offerings on younger women, whereas boutiques tend to focus on middle-aged and older women who tend to have more discretionary income. In addition, older women have the most trouble finding the right clothes, making the personalized service offered by boutiques attractive.

Together, these factors and trends point directly toward opportunities to open specialty clothing stores or boutiques and suggest the types of stores that are the most prevalent. This type of information provides a solid foundation for the business plan for a company such as Olivine (http://www.olivine.net), the single-store women's clothing boutique in Seattle introduced in Chapter 2. It takes an understanding of an industry's characteristics and trends, however, to properly identify and justify these types of opportunities.

Now let's look at the first major section in an industry analysis and why it's important.

INDUSTRY DEFINITION

The first section of the industry analysis should briefly (no more than several sentences long) describe the firm's industry. The industry's SIC code and NAICS code should be provided. The older SIC system was replaced by the NAICS in 1997, although SIC codes are still used. The NAICS systems expanded the number of industry sections from 10 to 20 to reflect the broader number of industries that have come into existence. A nice side-by-side display of both systems is available at the U.S. Census Bureau's Web site at http://www.census.gov/epcd/www/naicstab.htm. You can identify your industry's SIC code and its NAICS code at this site.

Although it may seem like identifying a company's industry is a simple task, it's actually a tough call in many instances. A firm's industry can be defined narrowly or broadly. For instance, is Prime Adult Fitness in the fitness center industry or the recreation industry? Is JetBlue in the airline industry or the transportation industry? Is Olivine in the retail trade industry or the women's clothing industry? The distinction is important because it defines the scope of a company's industry analysis and helps identify its overall sphere of concern. The most practical approach for a business plan is to define a company's industry narrowly and include an analysis of the trends that influence broader industry categories if necessary. In the illustrations in this chapter, Prime Adult Fitness defines itself narrowly as part of the Fitness and Recreational Sports Center Industry (NAICS 71394). In a subsequent part of its industry analysis, it could have provided an analysis of trends of the broader industry—Arts, Entertainment and Recreation (NAICS 71), but it wasn't necessary in this instance.

If your firm operates in two or more industries, you should identify all the industries that it participates in, and recognize that you will need to conduct an industry analysis for each of the industries. For example, if a company makes computer software for doctor's offices, it should state that it operates in the computer software industry and the health care industry and provide an industry analysis for both industries. Some discretion is allowed regarding the weight placed on the individual analyses. In some instances, when a firm operates in more than one industry, it may be appropriate to conduct a full analysis on the primary industry the firm operates in and an abbreviated analysis on the other.

Sometimes it's difficult to identify an industry that matches an innovative new product or service. An example is H20Audio (http://www.h20audio.com), the firm that makes waterproof housings for the Apple iPod. If you had been asked to write the company's original business plan, it wouldn't have been clear how to define the industry or industries it participates in. Currently no NAICS codes exist for the Apple iPod, MP3 players, or iPod accessories. In cases like this, you have to either define a new industry or improvise by selecting the industries that represent the closest fit and then include additional pertinent information. (There are more than 1,800 NAICS coded industries to choose from.) In the case of H20Audio, the industries that represent the closest fit are Sporting and Athletic

FIGURE 5-1 Industry Definition (Prime Adult Fitness Business Plan)

Prime Adult Fitness will compete in the "Fitness and Recreational Sports Centers in the US" industry (NAICS 71394 and SIC 7991). The industry is comprised of establishments engaged in fitness instruction and facilities management. Well-know companies in the industry include Curves International, Life Time Fitness, and Gold's Gym. The industry includes fitness centers and specialized facilities such as tennis clubs, weight-training centers, ice skating rinks, and dance studios. The largest segment of the industry, fitness centers, represents 41.1 percent of industry revenues.

Goods Manufacturing (NAICS 33992), Sporting Goods Stores (NAICS 45111), and Electronic Shopping and Mail-Order Houses (NAICS 45111). Each of these industries relates to a piece of what H20Audio does, and collectively they define the bulk of H20Audio's competitive landscape. If you go this route, you should list each of the industries and indicate that you plan to expand your analysis to include additional information, such as current trends in iPod and iPod accessory sales. The advantage of this approach is that it anchors your analysis in established NAICS categories, where plentiful information is available online and elsewhere to assist you in your analysis. If you define a new industry, such as the iPod accessory industry, your industry definition may be more precise, but it will be more difficult to accumulate good quality information for your industry analysis. You also run the risk that your reader will not see the industry you define as a legitimate industry.

The best Internet resources to assist in helping identify industries, and in completing all sections of the industry analysis, are IBISWorld, Mintel, and Standard & Poor's NetAdvantage. All three of these resources are available free through most university library Web sites. They are also highlighted in the Internet Resources Table in Appendix 2.2 at the end of Chapter 2. IBISWorld, in particular, provides a 20- to 40-page analysis for nearly every industry at the five-digit NAICS code level. Each analysis starts with a very distinct description of the respective industry, which may be helpful to you in completing this section of your business plan.

The Prime Adult Fitness industry definition is shown in Figure 5-1.

INDUSTRY SIZE, GROWTH RATE, AND SALES PROJECTIONS

This section of the industry analysis briefly discusses the size (in dollars), the growth rate (in percent), and future sales projections for the industry or industries your firms will be entering. It's important that this section consist of more than just numbers. Unless you are defining a new industry, such as the iPod accessories industry, the numbers are fairly easy to find. The key is to make sense of the numbers and present them in a way that builds the credibility of your business plan.

There are four general rules of thumb for completing this section. First, you should always display financial information, such as industry sales and growth rate, in a multiyear format, making it easy to spot trends. Reporting a single number, such as "the women's clothing industry generated $37.5 billion in sales in 2005," is insufficient. In addition to that figure, your reader wants to know whether industry-wide sales are growing or declining, and the rate of growth or decline. The best approach is to report three to five years of industry-wide sales and industry-wide growth rates. Always provide a citation for where your information came from.

The second rule of thumb is to display your information graphically if possible. Guy Kawasaki, the entrepreneur and investor introduced earlier in the book, has said that one of the most effective ways to make a business plan stand out is to include diagrams and graphics.[2] There is a risk in overdoing this, but supplementing the raw data for industry-wide sales and sales growth with attractive graphs that visually depict the same data is an ideal opportunity.

The third rule of thumb is to provide information about your industry on a regional or local basis if appropriate. You don't need to go into detail—an analysis of your target market and competitors is provided in the next section of the plan, covered in Chapter 6. Still, in many industries, industry-wide sales are not evenly distributed across the United States. In these instances, it might be of interest to your readers to know where the majority of the sales take place and where the largest increase or decrease in sales is expected.

The final rule of thumb is to avoid the temptation to report only positive or flattering information about your industry. This approach not only undermines the credibility of your plan, but it also is not intellectually honest. The numbers that are reported should also be viewed in their proper context. Just because an industry's numbers aren't glowing doesn't mean that good opportunities aren't available. Many average industries have product or service gaps that provide exciting opportunities for new businesses. If you believe that your company has the potential to outperform the average companies in its industry, state your industry's numbers fairly and honestly, regardless of how poor they look, and in the "trends" portion of the industry analysis, start laying the groundwork for why a company like yours might outperform the industry. You will have the opportunity in the next section of your business plan to describe your specific target market and the promise it offers.

The industry size, growth rate, and sales projection portion of the Prime Adult Fitness industry analysis is shown in Figure 5-2.

INDUSTRY SIZE

An industry's size is normally displayed in dollars over a three to five year period, as shown in the Prime Adult Fitness industry analysis in Figure 5-2. Some business plans also report the number of firms in their industry. The ideal size of an industry for a startup is large enough to allow different competitors to serve different segments profitably but small enough that it isn't attracting the immediate attention of larger potential competitors. There are no good rules of thumb or heuristics for what this size is—it's strictly a judgment call.

FIGURE 5-2   Industry Size, Growth Rate, and Sales Projections (Prime Adult Fitness Business Plan)

Industry Size

	2002	2003	2004	2005	2006
Industry Sales	$16.1 billion	$17.3 billion	$18.4 billion	$19.7 billion	$21.0 billion
Number of Establishments	48,284	49,544	50,523	51,245	51,831
Employment	464,418	486,739	506,879	516,843	531,964

Industry Growth Rates

	2002	2003	2004	2005	2006
Industry Sales	8.2%	5.4%	3.5%	3.9%	3.6%
Number of Establishments	−0.7%	2.6%	2.0%	1.4%	1.1%
Employment	5.2%	4.8%	4.1%	2.0%	2.9%

Industry Sales Projections

	2007	2008
Industry Sales	$21.8 billion	$22.5 billion
Growth Rate	3.7%	3.3%

Graphs

Source for all information: IBISWorld, May 25, 2007.

Summary
The industry is in the growth phase of its life cycle. Growth is being driven primarily by an increased awareness of the importance of fitness and exercise. The industry's biggest challenge is competing for the leisure time of its customers. Time strapped customers are less likely to frequent a fitness club or other recreational sports center.

The largest segment of the industry, fitness centers, is growing at a more rapid rate than the industry as a whole. According to the International Health, Racquet & Sportsclub Association (IHRSA), the number of fitness clubs (in the United States) grew by 14.0 percent from 2003 to 2004 and 8.3 percent from 2004 to 2005.

The Fitness and Recreational Sports Centers industry is growing at a faster rate than three industries that compete for its customer's dollars—Sporting and Athletic Goods Manufacturing (which makes home fitness equipment), Golf Course and Country Clubs, and Marinas.

TABLE 5-1 Women's Clothing Industry Breakdown	
Segment	*Percent of Sales*
Tops (including t-shirts, shirts, blouses, and sweaters)	32.0%
Pants, jeans, shorts, and skirts	24.0%
Dresses	18.0%
Coats, jackets, and suits	17.0%
Sports apparel (including swimwear, sweat tops, etc.)	6.0%
Other apparel	3.0%

If your industry is broken down into easily identifiable segments, it may be appropriate to report the share (in percentage) of each segment. For example, the $37.5 million women's clothing industry is broken down as shown in Table 5-1.[3]

IBISWorld provides this information on industries that are identified by NAICS codes. It's a judgment call as to whether this level of detail is appropriate for your plan.

Some plans also report the contribution that a specific industry makes to its larger industry sector. For example, for Prime Adult Fitness, the industry it will participate in, Fitness and Recreational Sports Centers (NAICS 71394), generated 10.2 percent of the sales of its larger industry sector, Arts, Entertainment, and Recreational Services (NAICS 71).

INDUSTRY GROWTH RATE

An industry's growth rate should be reported on a percentage basis, as shown in the Prime Adult Fitness industry analysis in Figure 5-2. You should provide an interpretation of what the numbers mean. There are many ways to do this. Some plans comment on how the industry growth rate compares to similar industries. Note that in its industry analysis, Prime Adult Fitness compares the growth rate of its industry, fitness centers, to three industries that compete for its industry's dollars—Sporting and Athletic Goods Manufacturing (which makes home fitness equipment), Golf Courses and Country Clubs, and Marinas. The fact that Prime Adult Fitness's industry is growing faster than these competing industries is a positive sign. Although you don't want to cherry-pick information that places your industry in a positive light relative to others, you do want your reader to share your enthusiasm for the industry you are about to enter. Prime Adult Fitness's favorable comparison of its industry to others is an appropriate way of doing that.

If you are defining an industry, such as iPod accessories, that isn't being actively tracked by a reliable source (for example, IBISWorld or Standard & Poor's NetAdvantage), finding good sales data requires creativity and persistence. It normally involves searching for newspaper or magazine articles that report the industry's sales and sales growth or finding an industry trade association that tracks and reports the numbers. Mintel, one of the databases mentioned earlier, in an appendix to each of its industry analyses, provides the names, phone numbers, and Web site addresses of the major trade associations related to a particular industry. If you define a new industry, such as iPod accessories, you could search the industry analyses of related industries that Mintel follows to try to find a trade association that might track iPod accessory sales as part of its larger mission. You could then call or e-mail the trade association to ask if it tracks iPod accessory sales or to ask where to find the information.

A fuller list of suggestions for how to track down sales and sales-growth data for a newly defined industry, such as the iPod accessories industry, is provided in the Business Plan Insights box.

BUSINESS PLAN INSIGHTS

Finding Industry Sales Data by Knocking On Doors

If you're defining a new industry, such as iPod accessories, one challenge you'll encounter is finding good sales data and sales-growth information. In these cases, finding the information becomes somewhat of a scavenger hunt. And like in a scavenger hunt, a willingness to knock on doors and dogged determination make a big difference.

Here are some suggestions of the doors you might metaphorically knock on to get sales data and sales-growth information for the iPod accessories industry. Your industry might be much different from the iPod accessories industry, but the types of resources included in this list represents a good place to start:

- Type "iPod accessories industry" into the Google or Yahoo! search bar to see if the information has already been compiled by a reliable source.

- Try to determine if there is a trade association or an annual trade show for iPod accessory manufacturers, and contact the relevant organization to ask if industry-wide sales data is available.

- Search for newspaper and magazine articles on iPod accessories using public search engines such as Find Articles (http://www.findarticles.com) and MagPortal (http://www.magportal.com), and more powerful search engines such as ProQuest and LexisNexis, which are normally available through a university library Web site.

- Search industry-specific trade magazines. For example, an obvious place to look for articles about iPod accessories is in *MacWorld*, a magazine dedicated to covering the entire Apple Inc. ecosystem. If you can't find an article, contact *MacWorld,* and ask if they have run an article on iPod accessories industry sales.

- Contact a company in the industry to ask for leads on finding industry-wide sales data information. Don't be bashful. H20Audio, for example, lists its phone number and e-mail address on its Web site.

One thing you'll need to be careful about is discerning the credibility of your sources of information. Don't be afraid, however, to cite personal conversations if the information is credible. For instance, it's perfectly appropriate to cite a personal conversation with the director of a trade association if you feel reasonably confident the information you're being provided is credible.

INDUSTRY SALES PROJECTIONS

This section should report future sales projections for your industry. If you are reporting on an established industry, IBISWorld, Standard & Poor's NetAdvantage, Mintel, and similar sources report their predictions. You can quote from these reports, but you should do so sparingly. Most of the readers of your plan are more interested in what you think than in what Standard & Poor's or Mintel thinks. As indicated earlier in the book, a business plan not only lays out facts, but it also demonstrates to your reader how you think and interpret data.

You should include concrete numbers for what you think your industry's sales and sales growth rate will be for the next one to three years. If you project the numbers yourself, explain how you arrived at your estimates. A sensible approach, which works in most instances, is to simply extrapolate from the historic trend data you have available. In all cases, you should comment on what the predictions mean. If you are predicting a sharper increase in sales than would be expected by looking at historic trends, you should provide a rationale for your prediction. In most instances, you will point to improving industry trends as part of your justification for higher numbers. Briefly mention the key improving trends here, but do not elaborate. The third section of your industry analysis deals exclusively with industry trends.

INDUSTRY CHARACTERISTICS

This section talks about the structure of your industry and lays out its competitive landscape. The four key issues to deal with are industry structure, the nature of the participants in an industry, key ratios, and the industry's key success factors. Although you could comment on much more, it's simply impossible to include all the potential topics within the context of a 25- to 35-page business plan. Part of the art of writing a business plan is determining what to include and what to leave out. You will experience the frustration of having to leave out potentially important information as you write this section of your industry analysis.

The industry characteristics portion of the Prime Adult Fitness industry analysis is shown in Figure 5-3.

INDUSTRY STRUCTURE

This topic is particularly important. An industry's size and its growth rate, regardless of how positive they are, are basically moot points if an industry isn't structurally attractive for a startup. **Industry structure,** in the context of a business plan, refers to how concentrated or fragmented the industry is and whether the industry's competitive landscape is in general attractive or unattractive.

In regard to industry concentration, you should report how **concentrated** or **fragmented** your industry is. Concentrated industries are dominated by a few large firms, whereas fragmented industries include a large number of smaller companies. Normally, an industry is concentrated if large capital requirements

FIGURE 5-3 Industry Characteristics (Prime Adult Fitness Business Plan)

Industry Structure

The industry is fragmented, with the top four firms accounting for only 13 percent of industry sales. There are many small fitness centers, dance studios, gymnasiums, ice skating rinks, and similar facilities, which decreases industry concentration. Barriers to entry are high at the high-end of the market (full-service fitness centers) due to the high cost of real estate and equipment, and low at the lower-end of the market (smaller fitness clubs and dance studios), due to the plentiful nature of rental space available in strip malls.

Other structural characteristics of the industry include the following:

- *The Aging of the Population.* Approximately 25 percent of fitness club members are 55 years old or older, as are 23 percent of all Americans. As time goes on, older Americans will make up even a larger percentage of the population, while those aged 25–44 will decline in numbers. As a result of these trends, the industry is shifting its emphasis away from a focus on the younger demographic to an equal focus on the needs of younger and older patrons. Because older patrons have more discretionary income and free time, the industry is gearing up to serve an older clientele.

- *Competition.* Competition throughout the industry is strong. For-profit fitness and recreational centers must compete against centers that are nonprofit, such as the YMCA, and fitness facilities subsidized by local governments, hospitals, and businesses for their employees.

- *The Impact of Curves International.* Curves, which was founded in 1992, introduced the notion of tightly focused (Curves is just for women), low-overhead, well-run "neighborhood" fitness centers to the industry. As a result of Curves and similar companies, the industry has become more bifurcated, with the most desirable positions at the high-end of the market, represented by full-service fitness centers, and the low-end, where tightly focused centers serve a specific clientele. "Low-end" does not imply a diminished experience. Low-end centers such as Curves deliberately feature smaller facilities and fewer amenities in exchange for a lower monthly membership fee and the ability to locate their facilities closer to their members. Curves, and similar low-end centers, offer a simple combination of a 20–40 minute preplanned workout and a judgment-free atmosphere, which has struck a positive cord with their clientele.

- *Costs and Site Selection.* The best sites for full-service, high-end fitness centers are in densely population suburban areas with an affluent population. This fact presents a challenge because these areas also have the highest real estate prices. Site selection is easier at the lower end of the market, where fitness centers such as Curves and Cuts (Cuts is just for men) locate primarily in rented facilities in strip malls.

- *Basis for Competition.* At the high end of the market, firms compete on the basis of state-of-the art equipment and multiple classes. This method of competition implies a high cost of doing business. At the low end of the market, firms compete by serving their target market well and providing personalized service.

Nature of Participants

Firms in the Industry. The industry is comprised of a wide variety of participants, ranging from large, full-service fitness centers run by large chains, to small, single-employee dance studios and ice skating rinks. No single firm captures more than 5 percent of industry sales. The largest firm in the industry is Bally Total Fitness (5%), followed by 24 Hour Fitness Worldwide (4%), Life Time Fitness (2%), and Curves International (2%).

Segmentation. The most common way to segment the industry is by product/service as shown below.

FIGURE 5-3   (continued)

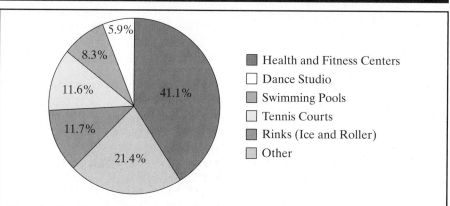

- ■ Health and Fitness Centers
- ☐ Dance Studio
- ■ Swimming Pools
- ☐ Tennis Courts
- ■ Rinks (Ice and Roller)
- ☐ Other

Clientele. The clientele of the industry is segmented as follows.

Age		Annual Household Income	
Age	**Share of Market**	**Income**	**Share of Market**
6–11 years old	4%	<$24,999	8%
12–17 years old	8%	$25,000 to $49,999	19%
18–34 years old	35%	$50,000 to $74,999	23%
35–54 years old	33%	$75,000 and over	50%
55 and older	20%		

Key Ratios
To gain as vivid a picture of the industry as possible, the following ratios were obtained from the sources cited.

Operating and Financial Ratios

	2003	**2004**
Total Revenue/Center	2.07 million	2.17 million
EBITDA % of Total Revenues	8.00%	16.6%
EBIT % of Total Revenues	0.00%	5.7%
Average Members/Center	3,091	3,174
Total Payroll as a % of Sales	43.8%	43.0%
Rate of Member Retention	67.7%	69.2%
Revenue/Member	$683.00	$719.00
Indoor Square Foot/Member	14.3	13.3
Revenue/Indoor Square Foot	$46.98	$48.81
Non-Dues Revenue as a % of Revenue	27.2%	28.1%

EBITDA—earnings before interest, taxes, depreciation, and amortization
EBIT—earnings before income taxes

Average Club Prices (enrollment fees are one-time fees)

	Enrollment Fee	**Monthly Dues**
Regular Individual (single adult)	$150.00	$55.00
Corporate Individual	$97.50	$48.00

FIGURE 5-3   (continued)

	Enrollment Fee	Monthly Dues
Couple	$199.00	$89.00
Family	$199.00	$89.00
Junior	$99.00	$39.00
Senior Citizen	$100.00	$44.62

Source: Survey of 196 fitness clubs collected by the International Health, Racquet & Sportsclub Association (IHRSA). The IHRSA is a nonprofit trade association that represents 6,500 fitness clubs and recreational facilities worldwide. Numbers are reported on a yearly basis.

Cost Structure Ratios

Item	Percent of Cost
Wages	29.3%
Purchases	18.2%
Depreciation	15.5%
Rent	12.5%
Advertising	5.0%
Utilities	3.4%
Other	7.1%
Profit	9.0%

Source: IBISWorld, May 25, 2007.

Key Success Factors
The key success factors for the industry are as follows:

- *Location and Income.* It is important to locate in an area that has a high percentage of people who earn $75,000 or more. These people are most likely to support fitness and recreational sports centers. An exception may be a tightly focused, lower-overhead center such as Curves, which charges a lower monthly fee and draws from a broader income range.
- *Right Mix of Classes and Activities.* Because fitness and recreational centers must compete for their customer's leisure time, and because an increasing number of centers are targeting a specific clientele, it is important to carefully match the classes and activities to the clientele.
- *Member Motivation.* According to a survey commissioned by Mintel, motivation remains the key to winning new members and keeping new members engaged. A total of 67 percent of people who currently do not belong to a fitness center said they would join if they knew the activities would keep them motivated.
- *Informed and Proactive Staff.* It is important that members feel like they can get help when they are having trouble with a fitness machine or have a question about a class. Many fitness centers tout the customer service skills and qualifications of their staff as a basis of differentiation.
- *Tightly Focused Target Market.* Since people vary in terms of the exercise machines and classes they find the most useful, a number of centers are opting to focus on a single clientele. Women and older people are more likely to report feeling out of place or intimidated in a traditional fitness center. As a result, single-gender and centers restricted to certain age groups are likely to grow in numbers.
- *Prices Charged for Use of Facilities.* Prices vary widely between centers, depending on the age and type of equipment provided, the number of classes offered, the location of the center, and the amentias provided. It is easy for consumers to comparison shop. It is important that a center's prices be similar to its competitors.

are necessary to participate, or it has matured and a substantial amount of consolidation has taken place. An industry is typically fragmented if it's in the emergence stage of its life cycle, and/or the cost of entry is relatively low. If you're launching into a fragmented industry, nothing more typically needs to be said—most startups launch into fragmented markets. If you're launching into a concentrated market, you'll need to provide a clear rationale in the next section of the plan (which focuses on your target market) of how you plan to compete. Some startups are able to launch into concentrated industries by finding target or niche markets that are less expensive to compete in or by lowering the overall capital requirements necessary to enter the industry through some innovative means. For example, many microbreweries have successfully entered the highly concentrated brewery industry by brewing their beer locally and relying on a local niche market clientele. Although this approach limits the nationwide potential of the microbrewery, at least initially, it lowers the costs of branding and distribution. Similarly, some companies are able to lower the capital requirements of entering an industry on a broader scale through innovative approaches. An example is DayJet (http://www.dayjet.com), an airline startup that will soon start offering "air taxi" services in the southeast part of the United States and will compete directly against regional airlines. The key to the company's business plan is that it will fly a new generation of planes called "very light jets," which are much cheaper to buy and operate than commuter planes, and will make use of community airports, which are less expensive.

The second topic regarding industry structure is the general attractiveness (or lack of attractiveness) of an industry's competitive landscape. A structurally attractive industry, according to Harvard professor Michael Porter's "five forces" model, should have relatively high barriers of entry to keep competitors out, not enough rivalry to create cutthroat competition, no good substitutes for the basic product or service the industry sells, limited power of suppliers to negotiate input prices up, and limited power of buyers to force selling prices down.[4] You normally won't comment on each of these points in a brief industry analysis, but you should allude to the most salient ones.[*] For example, if you're entering an industry with high barriers to entry, that's good; high barriers to entry deter competitors, so you should highlight that aspect of your industry in this section of your industry analysis. Of course, if the entry barriers are high, you'll have to explain, not here but in the next section of the plan that deals with your target market, how you're able to enter.

NATURE OF PARTICIPANTS

The next section of this portion of your business plan deals with the nature of the participants in an industry. Your reader will already know whether the industry is consolidated or fragmented. In this brief description, you want to provide your

---

[*] If you're unfamiliar with Michael Porter's five-forces model, you should familiarize yourself with the model and what it means while writing this portion of your industry analysis. A description of the model is provided in any strategic management textbook.

reader with a "feel" for the nature and mixture of firms in your industry. Who are the major players in the industry? What percentage of market share do they control? Are the major competitors online firms or traditional firms? You also want your reader to visualize how your firm will fit in or see the gap that your firm will fill. Although the industry analysis does not talk about your firm per se, the reader knows what your company is by reading the previous sections of the plan. Draw a mental map for your reader that shows exactly where your firm will fit into the industry.

You should also discuss how the industry is segmented. This discussion can get fairly complex because industries can be segmented in different ways. For example, the computer industry can be segmented by product type (i.e., handheld computers, laptops, PCs, minicomputers, and mainframes) or by customer segments served (i.e., individuals, businesses, schools, and government). Similarly, you can segment the fitness and recreational sports center industry by type of club (i.e., health and fitness club, ice and roller rink, tennis courts, swimming pools, squash and racquetball clubs) or by type of ownership (i.e., commercial, nonprofit, corporate, hotel/resort, spa). The best approach is to segment your industry by your point of entry. So if you're starting a company to sell specially designed computers for elementary schools, it would make the most sense to segment the computer industry by customers served, as shown previously. As you discuss the different segments of your industry, if you know which segment is growing the fastest and/or is the most profitable, that's good information to convey. There are also industries that have clearly bifurcated, with the most successful companies serving either the top end of the market (in terms of quality of goods and price range) or the bottom end. This trend is seen in industries such as grocery stores, where most of the money is being made by high-end stores such as Whole-Food Markets and Trader Joe's and low-end providers such as Wal-Mart and Costco.[5] The worst place to be, in bifurcated industries, is right in the middle. Again, if you're able to identify the most promising areas of an industry, or the areas to avoid, that information should be reported.

RATIOS

It's important to report an industry's key financial ratios and other ratios of interest. This information not only provides further insight into the structure and attractiveness of an industry, but it also provides a point of reference to compare a company's financial and nonfinancial projections against. For example, if a company reports in its industry analysis that the average firm in its industry earns a 6 percent net profit, and in later parts of the plan indicates it will earn 12 percent for its first three years, the firm will need to explain how it plans to generate over twice the net income of the average firm. Similar comparisons can be made with the other numbers.

KEY SUCCESS FACTORS

Key success factors in every industry define what an organization in the industry has to be good at to be successful. Most industries have 6 to 10 key factors. Most of the successful firms in an industry are competent in all of their industry's key success factors, and they try to differentiate themselves by excelling in two or three areas.

You should identify the key success factors for your industry and report them in the industry analysis. If they aren't readily apparent, reading through IBISWorld and Mintel industry profiles and looking at industry trade journals and magazines should reveal them. A technique that some people find helpful in identifying an industry's key success factors is to pose the rhetorical question, "For a company to be successful in this industry, it must be good at . . . (list 6 to 10 items)". The answer to this question is a good starting point in ascertaining the key success factors for an industry.

The key success factors vary widely by industry—they are not generic concepts. For example, the key success factors for the electronic games industry are as follows:

- Product features and playability
- Brand name recognition
- Compatibility of products with popular platforms
- Access to distribution channels
- Quality of products
- Ease of use
- Price
- Marketing support
- Quality of customer service

As you can see, this list is very specific to the electronic games industry. A different industry would have a much different list.

Knowing the key success factors for an industry is important because any firm in an industry can be judged by the degree to which it covers its bases on each factor and excels (or has plans in place to excel) at one or more factors.

INDUSTRY TRENDS

The final portion of an industry analysis deals with industry trends. This is arguably the most important section of an industry analysis because it often lays the foundation for a new business idea in an industry (i.e., older people are becoming increasingly interested in fitness—thus, maybe a fitness club just for adults makes sense), and it typically provides the justification for claims made earlier in the industry analysis, such as why industry-wide sales should be expected to continue to increase or decrease.

The two types of trends that are the most important to focus on are environmental trends and business trends. The best place to look for trend information is industry trade journals, industry-specific magazines, industry reports from

FIGURE 5-4 Industry Trends (Prime Adult Fitness Business Plan)

There are a number of environmental and business trends affecting the growth and attractiveness of the fitness and recreational sports center industry. They are as follows.

Trends That Favor the Industry

- Americans are increasingly aware of the need for exercise, weight control, good nutrition, and a healthy lifestyle among both adults and children.
- Nationwide economic conditions are strong, which boosts consumer confidence and makes it easier for industry participants to borrow money.
- An increased emphasis on wellness is evident across many sectors of society. In particular, positive press about the benefits of yoga, Pilates, and similar activities cause people to seek out businesses that offer those services.
- The increasing costs of other sports and recreational activities, such as golf and boating, can result in people opting out of those activities in favor of joining a fitness club or other recreational sports center.
- Increasing health care costs are motivating corporations to invest in corporate wellness programs. Many corporations now support their own fitness centers or offer fitness centers memberships as a benefit.

Trends Working Against the Industry

- Leisure time is becoming less available. Time-strapped consumers find it harder to make time to frequent a fitness center.
- Increasing prices for gasoline and health care are lowering consumers' disposable income.
- Americans are becoming more and more obese, with 34.1 percent of all adults aged 20 to 74 considered overweight. Many of these individuals may not see themselves as fit enough to work out.

resources such as IBISWorld and Standard & Poor's NetAdvantage, and through talking to industry participants. The Internet Resource Table in Appendix 2.2 at the end of Chapter 2 provides Web site addresses that are helpful in identifying the sources of this information. Many industries also have interest groups that sponsor Web sites to promote their industry and talk about current trends. For example, the Web site Style.com (http://www.style.com) is a fashion industry site that has a special section dedicated to "news and trends" in fashion.

The industry trends portion of the Prime Adult Fitness industry analysis is provided in Figure 5-4.

ENVIRONMENTAL TRENDS

As discussed in Chapter 2, environmental trends are very important. The strength of an industry often surges or wanes not so much because of the management skills of the firms in an industry, but because environmental trends shift in favor of or against the products or services sold by the firms in the industry.

The most important environmental trends are economic trends, social trends, technological advances, and political and regulatory changes. You should think through each area to determine if there are trends that are positively or negatively affecting your industry that should be commented on. For example, any industry that relies on the consumption of fossil fuels, such as the trucking industry and the airline industry, is being adversely affected by high fuel prices. In contrast, any industry that provides products or services to older people, such as health care and travel, stands to benefit by the aging of the population. Sometimes there are multiple environmental changes at work that set the stage for an industry's future. This point is illustrated in the following statement from Standard & Poor's NetAdvantage assessment of the future of the leisure products industry. This is the industry, in Standard & Poor's vernacular, that sells products such as golf clubs, boats, home fitness equipment, tennis racquets, and so forth.

> While we see the longer-term outlook for leisure products stocks as generally favorable, we expect to see a wide variances among companies. During the next decade, as the population bubble of baby boomers continues to advance, we believe the outlook for areas such as boating and golf, which tend to be favored by middle-aged and older Americans should improve, while pursuits that involve more vigorous physical activity, such as skiing and tennis, may see a corresponding decline. We believe that the factors driving long-term leisure spending include demographics, income levels and growth, consumer confidence, and the amount of free time available.[6]

This short statement illustrates the degree to which environmental change can affect one industry and the ebb and flow of the popularity of the segments within it. Similar forces are at work in all industries, which should be discerned and reported in your industry analysis.

Some industries experience slow or no growth for years and then experience sudden upswings in growth and popularity as the result of savvy industry incumbents and/or entrepreneurs who realized that environmental change has turned in favor of the industry. A recent example is the mattress industry. In *Business Week's* 2007 list of "The Best (100) Small Companies to Watch," two of the companies, Tempur-Pedic International (http://www.tempurpedic.com) and Select Comfort (http://www.selectcomfort.com) were mattress companies. Seriously, with all the high-tech and other interesting companies in the United States, would you have guessed that two mattress companies would make the list? Probably not. But if you study the mattress industry, your attitudes will change. A number of significant environmental trends are working in favor of the industry:[7]

- Rising incomes and a positive economic environment have led to increased mattress sales at the high end of the market.
- High shipping costs have limited imports (imports represent only 2.9 percent of U.S. mattress industry sales).
- The recent upswing in new housing construction and renovations to existing homes has led to increased bedroom numbers and sizes.

- A recent upswing in hotel and motel construction has resulted in a spike in mattress demand from that sector.

- There are approximately 2.7 million hospital and nursing home beds in the United States. These facilities typically purchase high-end mattresses with enhancements that allow them to be electronically adjusted. As the population ages, the healthcare market for mattresses will continue to expand.

- An increased emphasis on wellness has created new markets for mattresses that improve sleep quality and provide better neck and back support.

If you spend a few minutes browsing Select Comfort and Tempur-Pedic's Web sites, you'll see that they're tapping into these exact trends. The broader U.S. mattress industry grew by 8.8 percent in 2004 and 6.9 percent in 2005. That's better than either the women's clothing stores industry or the fitness and recreational sports center industry. The types of trends depicted in the preceding bullet points are the types of trends that you'll want to discern for your industry. An awareness of these trends can help startups develop more impressive industry analyses and potentially more successful business plans.

BUSINESS TRENDS

Other trends impact industries that aren't environmental trends per se but are important to mention. For example, are profit margins in the industry increasing or falling? Is innovation accelerating or waning? Are input costs going up or down? Are new markets for the industry's staple products opening up, or are existing markets being shut down by competing industries? You can't cover every possible fact affecting an industry, but you should mention the major trends.

LONG-TERM PROSPECTS

The industry analysis should conclude with a brief statement of your beliefs regarding the long-term prospects for the industry. No new information should be provided at this point. Instead, draw from the preceding sections of the industry analysis to support your conclusions. Your conclusions should be precise and to the point. No more than several sentences are required.

When you read through reports on your industry, from IBISWorld, Mintel, and Standard & Poor's NetAdvantage, the reports will include their assessments of the future prospects of the industry. Resist simply repeating what others are saying. Your assessment of the long-term prospects for your industry should reflect your thoughts and beliefs, and should be fully consistent with the information contained in the preceding sections of your industry analysis.

The Long-Term Prospects section for the Prime Adult Fitness industry analysis is shown in Figure 5-5.

FIGURE 5-5   Long-Term Prospects (Prime Adult Fitness Business Plan)

The industry is likely to maintain its current trajectory. An increasing interest in fitness and the emergence of new concepts such as Curves (just for women) and Cuts (just for men) will continue to spur growth, but the industry's growth rate isn't expected to exceed its recent 3.5 percent to 3.9 percent annual levels. The growth in the fitness center segment of the industry may be higher. The aging of the population is a long-term positive trend for the industry. Older people are becoming increasingly interested in fitness and have more money and spare time to devote to a fitness center. The nature of the industry is likely to change as a result of this development. Recreational centers that feature vigorous exercise, such as racquetball and tennis clubs, are likely to suffer, whereas fitness centers that offer specialized classes and equipment for older people are likely to benefit.

HOW THE INDUSTRY ANALYSIS AFFECTS AND IS AFFECTED BY OTHER SECTIONS OF THE PLAN

Industry analysis is a foundational aspect of evaluating the merits of a prospective business venture. The industry that a company participates in, as a result of its structural characteristics, historical conditions, and current trends, basically defines the playing field that a firm will participate in. A careful analysis of a firm's industry also lays out what is realistically possible and what isn't realistically possible for a startup to achieve. There are some firms, like Dell in the computer industry and Starbucks in the specialty restaurant industry, which basically turned their industries upside down by introducing new business models and outperforming their industries on most if not all metrics. However, these firms are the rare exception rather than the rule. Most startups are constrained enough by their industries that their performance falls in line with what you would expect after reading their industry analysis.

The industry analysis affects the other sections of the business plan in that it provides a point of reference to work from. Savvy business plan writers find themselves referring back to their industry analysis frequently when writing other parts of their plan. The analysis is an anchor that describes how the average firms in an industry are doing and what the overall trends are, and most business plan writers benefit by constantly comparing their plan against this anchor. It also helps temper the enthusiasm of business plan writers and provides a useful reference for a plan's readers. For example, if a startup projected a growth in sales of 17 percent per year for its first five years, and its industry is only growing at 5 percent per year, an obvious incongruity exists. A savvy reader will think, "Isn't the industry only growing at 5 percent per year? How is 17 percent possible?" There may be an explanation, but the incongruity between the industry's sales and the startup's projected sales must be explained in the plan.

Chapter Summary

1. An industry is a group of firms producing a similar product or service, such as airplanes, music, electronic games, or fitness club memberships.
2. Separating the analysis of a firm's industry and its target market is important because it's premature for a new firm to select, or even talk about, a specific target market until an understanding of the broader industry is obtained.
3. It's important that the industry analysis appear early in a business plan because it logically precedes the analysis of a firm's target market and its marketing strategy. It also helps set up and support the remainder of the plan.
4. The major sections of an industry analysis include industry definition; industry size, growth, and sales projections; industry characteristics; industry trends; and long-term prospects.
5. If your firm operates in two or more industries, you should identify all the industries that it participates in and recognize that it will be necessary to conduct an industry analysis for each of the industries. Some discretion is allowed regarding the weight placed on the individual analyses. In some instances, when a firm operates in more than one industry, it may be appropriate to conduct a full analysis on the primary industry that firm operates in and an abbreviated analysis on the other.
6. The key to the industry size, growth, and sales projections portion of the analysis is to not just report the numbers. Make sense of the numbers and present them in a way that builds the credibility of your business plan.
7. The four key issues to deal with in the industry characteristics section of the analysis are industry structure, the nature of the participants in an industry, key ratios, and the industry's key success factors.
8. The topic of industry structure is particularly important. An industry's size and its growth rate, regardless of how positive they are, are basically moot points if an industry isn't structurally attractive for a startup.
9. The industry trends portion of an industry analysis is arguably the most important section because it often lays the foundation for a new business idea in an industry, and it typically provides the justification for claims made earlier in the industry analysis.
10. The industry analysis should conclude with a brief statement of your beliefs regarding the long-term prospects for the industry.

Review Questions

1. What is an industry? Why is it important to include an "industry analysis" in a business plan?
2. Why is it important that the industry analysis focus strictly on a firm's industry rather than its industry and its target market simultaneously?
3. Why is it important for an industry analysis to appear early in a business plan?
4. Why is identifying a company's industry a tough call in many instances?

5. What should you do if your firm operates in more than one industry?
6. What are the four general rules of thumb for completing the industry size, growth, and sales projections portion of the industry analysis?
7. What topic should be discussed in the "industry structure" portion of an industry analysis? Why are these topics important?
8. Why is it important to know how an industry is segmented?
9. Why is knowledge of the key success factors in an industry important? How can an industry's key success factors be identified?
10. Why is the industry trends portion of the industry analysis arguably the most important section of the analysis?

Application Questions

1. You just reviewed a business plan for a company that will make athletic shoes with rollers on the bottom, which will allow its users to literally skate from place to place as if they were wearing roller skates. One thing you noticed is that the plan didn't include an industry analysis. When you asked Kevin, the author of the plan, why the industry analysis was left out he said, "Are you kidding? My industry is one of the hottest ones in America. Heelys, a company just like ours, has over two million users already. An industry analysis isn't necessary." Do you agree with Kevin? If he said to you, "Okay, persuade me that an industry analysis is necessary," what would you tell him?

2. Cybex International (http://www.cybex.com) is a company that makes premium exercise equipment for home and commercial use. What industry is Cybex in? (Provide both an SIC and NAICS code.) Report the industry's past three years of sales and sales growth, and make a prediction for its sales and sales growth for the next year. Is Cybex in the same industry as Prime Adult Fitness? Explain your answer.

3. Kelly Ryan, a high-school classmate of yours, is thinking about starting a company to compete with Cartridge World, the company that sell franchises to people who open small storefronts to refill printer ink cartridges for their customers. Kelly is writing a business plan and is working on the industry analysis. Kelly's having trouble nailing down the exact industry he will be competing in and is having trouble finding sources of information to help him discern the environmental trends that are impacting his industry. If Kelly asked you for your help, how would you help him determine the industry his cartridge refill company will participate in, and what suggestions would you give him for finding information on the environmental trends that are impacting his industry?

4. Cereality (http://www.cereality.com) is a company's that's launched an exciting new concept in the restaurant industry. Spend a few minutes looking at Cereality's Web site and studying its business concept. If the founders of Cereality had carefully studied the restaurant industry before coming up with their business idea, what factors about the industry might have led them to the idea for Cereality?

5. One industry mentioned in the chapter that is fairly "hot" is the mattress industry. Spend enough time studying the mattress industry to determine whether it is structurally attractive for new entrants. Report your conclusions.

Endnotes

1. "Women's Clothing Stores in the US: 44812" (IBISWorld Industry Report). http://www.ibisworld.com.au (February 13, 2007).
2. G. Kawasaki, *The Art of the Start* (New York: Portfolio, 2004).
3. "Women's Clothing Stores in the US: 44812" (IBISWorld Industry Report). http://www.ibisworld.com.au (February 13, 2007).
4. M. Porter, *Competitive Strategy: Techniques for Analyzing Industries and Competitors* (New York: Free Press, 1980).
5. M. J. Silverstein, *Treasure Hunt* (New York: Portfolio, 2006).
6. "Leisure Products" (Standard & Poor's). http://www.netadvantage.standardpoor.com (June 3, 2007).
7. "Mattress Manufacturing in the US: 33791" (IBISWorld Industry Report). http://www.ibisworld.com.au (February 15, 2007).

CHAPTER 6

MARKET ANALYSIS

INTRODUCTION

The industry analysis section of a business plan is normally followed by the market analysis. Whereas the industry analysis focuses on the broad business domain that a firm will participate in (i.e., airline industry, fitness and recreational sports industry, women's clothing industry), the **market analysis** breaks the industry into segments and zeroes in on the specific segment (or target market) that the firm will tackle. As mentioned in Chapter 5, most firms do not try to service their entire industry. Instead, they focus on servicing a specific market within the industry very well.

An important point to recognize at the outset of this chapter is that the market analysis section of a business plan is distinctly different from the marketing section. The market analysis section focuses on describing a firm's target market, customers, and competitors; how it will compete in the marketplace; and potential sales and market share. In contrast, the marketing section, which is covered in Chapter 7, focuses on the classic marketing functions that support a firm's product, including price, promotion, and distribution (product was covered earlier in the plan). Although some business plans commingle these two sections, it's much more effective to keep them separate.

The market analysis is an extremely important section of a business plan for two reasons. First, like the industry analysis, the market analysis helps define the nature of the business and the remainder of the plan. For example, the market analysis normally includes a forecast of a firm's sales, which directly impacts the size of its manufacturing operation, its marketing plan, the number of people it will need to hire, and the amount of money it will need. Similarly, the more a start-up understands the needs of its target market, the more it can match its product attributes to those needs. For instance, in conducting market analysis, GreatCall (http://www.jitterbug.com), the company that offers a cell phone service designed specifically for older people, found through a survey of cell phone users that the most important feature for users age 55 and older is just the ability to make or receive voice calls. As a result, GreatCall's phones are simple and easy to use and focus primarily on the ease of making and receiving calls. In contrast, another cell phone service startup, Helio (http://www.helio.com), is targeting the youth market. Consistent with the needs of its market, Helio is producing more stylish phones that offer advanced feature such as music downloads and text messaging.[1]

The second reason a market analysis is important, if done properly, is that it affirms that a company has a well thought out target market, understands its customers, and can generate sales in the face of competition. It also communicates the amount of potential that exists in a firm's target market. This latter point is particularly important because the potential of a firm's target market should be consistent with its overall goals and aspirations. If a firm wants to raise investment capital, for example, it must demonstrate that its target market has sufficient potential to enable it to rapidly increase sales and return to its investors an amount that is 5 to 20 times the original investment, which is what equity investors normally expect.[2] In contrast, if the business plan is for more of a lifestyle firm, such as a high-end woman's clothing boutique, and the goal is to qualify for an SBA guaranteed loan, then the target market will still need to demonstrate potential but at a level more commensurate with the type of financing desired.

Because of the stakes involved, a well-developed market analysis usually takes considerable time and effort to complete and is scrutinized carefully by discerning readers. The authors of a business plan must have a complete understanding of their target market, customers, and competitors; how they will compete in the marketplace; and their potential sales and market share. Gaining this degree of insight and knowledge generally requires entrepreneurs to conduct both primary and secondary research as they work through the individual sections of the market analysis.

Now let's look at the first major section in a market analysis and why it's important.

MARKET SEGMENTATION AND TARGET MARKET SELECTION

To succeed, a firm must answer the basic question: "Who are our customers, and how will we appeal to them?" To determine the customers, you first segment the industry that the firm will participate in and then identify the specific target market it will tackle.

In some cases, a firm will have two markets, and you should describe the characteristics of both markets. For example, if you plan to sell your products through a retail store, you have two markets—the retail stores and the end user of your product. You can use your judgment regarding how much weight to apply to each market analysis.

The market segmentation and target market selection portion of the Prime Adult Fitness market analysis is shown in Figure 6-1.

Market Segmentation

For the purpose of the Prime Adult Fitness business plan, the Fitness and Recreational Sports Centers in the U.S. industry is segmented by product type and age of buyer.

Product/Service	Share of Industry Sales	Age of Buyer	Share of Industry Sales
Health and Fitness Clubs	41.1%	6–11 years old	4%
Other	21.4%	12–17 years old	8%
Rinks (ice and roller)	11.7%	18–34 years old	35%
Tennis Courts	11.6%	35–54 years old	33%
Swimming Pools	8.3%	55 and older	20%
Dance Studios	5.9%		

Additional ways to segment the industry include by annual household income, by gender, and by sector (i.e., for-profit, not-for-profit, corporate).

Target Market Selection

Prime Adult Fitness will target the health and fitness club segment of the industry and people 50 years old and older. (Only people 50 years old or older will be granted membership.) The following factors led to the decision to select this market:

- *Industry analysis.* The industry analysis provides compelling evidence that older Americans are increasingly interested in fitness, have sufficient leisure time to engage in fitness activities, and have more disposable income than other age groups.
- *Additional evidence.* According to a 2002 report by the International Health, Racquet and Sports Club Association (IHRSA), fitness club membership for the 55+ age group jumped 114 percent from 1998 to 2001, whereas the number of 18- to 35-year-old members decreased. Although similar statistics are not available for the current period, all evidence points toward these trends continuing.
- *Older people prefer to exercise with people their own age.* Substantial anecdotal evidence suggests that older people, in particular, prefer to exercise with people their own age. In fact, according to a study published in the April 2007 issue of the *Annals of Behavioral Medicine,* many older people would rather exercise alone than in a mixed group that includes younger people. This statistic causes us to believe there is tremendous upside potential in terms of the number of older people who would join a fitness center if there was a center just for them.
- *Current fitness centers are not meetings the needs of older people.* As illustrated in the "Buyer Behavior" section shown below, all-purpose fitness centers are not able to offer the environment, programs, or mix of classes that are optimal for older people. As shown by Curves International and others, a potentially profitable business model in the fitness industry is to target a single demographic very well by offering a tailored environment and mixtures of classes and facilities.
- *Insurance subsidies.* An increasing number of health insurers are providing subsidies to Medicare-eligible individuals to join fitness centers.

Target Market Size

Prime Adult plans to open a single location in Oviedo, Florida. Oviedo is a suburb of Orlando. The following steps were taken to estimate the size of Prime Adult Fitness's target market.

FIGURE 6-1 (continued)

Step 1: Determine Prime Adult Fitness's trade area:

We feel that Seminole County, Florida, the county that Oviedo is located in, represents a reasonable approximation of Prime Adult Fitness's trade area. Most retail outlets obtain the majority of their business from a 5- to 10-mile radius of their location because people are not willing to drive further if a similar service is available. Because Prime Adult Fitness will offer a unique service, it may draw from a larger area. The company's initial location will not be more than 16 miles from any address in Seminole County.

Step 2: Determine the number of people 50 years old and older in Prime Adult Fitness's trade area.

According to the Metro Orlando Economic Development Commission, which has more current data available than the U.S. Census Bureau, there are 52,637 people 55 years old and older living in Seminole County. No breakdown is provided for the number of people 50 years old or older. We do know that there are 31,958 people who are 45 to 54 years of age. If 40 percent of those people are between 50 and 54, that amounts to an additional 12,783 people. Combining the two numbers, we estimate there are 65,420 people 50 years old and older living in Seminole County.

Step 3: Determine the percentage of the people 50 years old and older in Seminole County who already belong to a fitness club.

According to Simmons Research, as reported by *Fitness Management* magazine (http://www.fitnessmanagement.com), roughly 15.2 percent of Americans belong to a fitness club. This number is in sync with Mintel's Health & Fitness Club industry report, which reported that in 2005, 43.2 million people in the United States, or roughly 14.9 percent of the population, belonged to a fitness center. According to IBISWorld, Baby Boomers (age 43–61) and older Americans are well represented in regard to fitness club membership. As a result, we can reasonable assume that 15 percent of Seminole County's 65,420 people 50 years or older, or 9,813 people, belong to a fitness center. To substantiate this number in its local market, Prime Adult Fitness distributed its concept statement and buying intentions survey to a random sample of 196 residents of Seminole County 50 years old or older. A total of 17.8 percent of the respondents indicated that they belong to a fitness center.

Step 4: Determine the total size (in dollars) of Prime Adult Fitness's target market for 2008.

Fitness clubs have three revenue drivers.

Revenue Driver #1: Monthly membership dues.

The average cost of belonging to a fitness center, of all varieties, in Seminole County is $65 per month. $65 per month × 9,813 people (the estimated number of people in Seminole County that are 50 years old or older that belong to a fitness center) × 12 months per year = $7,654,140].

Revenue Driver #2: One-time enrollment fees.

The average one-time enrollment fee for joining a fitness center in Seminole County is $100 (all types of centers). Fitness centers, on average, turn over approximately 33 percent of their membership per year. As a result, if 33 percent of the total members are new, that would result in additional income of 3,238 new members per year (9,813 members × .33) paying the $100 fee, for a total additional income of $323,800.

Revenue Driver #3: Additional sources of income.

Fitness clubs have additional sources of income, which vary by center. Examples include massage services (which usually cost extra), tanning salons, coffee and smoothie bars, and childcare. According to the "key ratios" analysis in our industry report, the average fitness center's nondues revenue equals 27.2 percent of its sales. Based on conversations with owners and managers of Seminole County fitness centers, we've backed this number down

FIGURE 6-1   (continued)

to 20 percent. Thus, 20 percent on top of the income from revenue drivers #1 and #2, which totals $7,977,940, is $1,595,588.

Summary:

$ 7,654,140	Membership dues
$ 323,800	One-time membership fees
$ 1,595,588	Other income
$ 9,573,528	Total size of fitness club market for Prime Adult Fitness's trade area

Step 5: Determine the total size (in dollars) of Prime Adult Fitness's target market for 2009, 2010, and 2011.

Mintel estimates that fitness club sales across the United States will grow by approximately 4.25 percent over the next several years. This is a stronger growth rate than the broader Fitness and Sports Centers in the U.S. industry, as reported in the industry analysis section of this business plan. A 5 percent figure is used below, accounting for the higher percentage of people 50 years old and older that live in Seminole County compared to the national average.

2008: $ 9,573,528
2009: $10,052,205*
2010: $10,554,814
2011: $11,082,554

* Prime Adult Fitness plans to open on January 1, 2009.

MARKET SEGMENTATION

In many instances, a firm will already have shown how its industry is segmented in the industry analysis portion of the business plan. If this circumstance applies to your plan, simply recapping that analysis in this section may be appropriate. If you're starting from scratch, you should explain that market segmentation is the process of dividing a market into distinct subsets (or segments) that behave in the same way or have similar needs.[3] An important decision you'll need to make is to how to segment your market. Markets can be segmented in many ways, such as by geography (city, state, country), demographic variables (age, gender, family size, income), psychographic variables (personality, lifestyle, values), behavioral variables (benefits sought, product usage rate, brand loyalty), and product type (varies by product). Sometimes a firm segments its market on more than one dimension to drill down to a specific market segment that the firm thinks it is uniquely capable of serving. For example, in its market analysis, GreatCall, the cell phone service provider for older people, probably segmented the cell phone market by age and by benefits sought. Helio used this same segmentation strategy by targeting younger users and featuring a more sophisticated set of options.

To test whether you have segmented your market successfully, the requirements for successful market segmentation are as follows:

- Homogeneity of needs and wants appears within the segment.
- Heterogeneity of needs and wants exists between the segments.
- Differences within the segment should be small compared to differences across segments.
- The segment should be distinct enough so that its members can be easily identified.
- It should be possible to determine the size of the segment.
- The segment should be large enough to be profitable.

If you are satisfied that you have segmented your market in a way that meets the criteria shown in the preceding list and makes sense given your business concept, you can stop here. As shown in Figure 6-1, Prime Adult Fitness segmented its market by product type and by age of buyer.

If you're unfamiliar with how to segment your market, both IBISWorld and Mintel provide suggestions for segmenting the industries that they follow. Another good choice is to consult industry trade journals and trade associations. You may also want to talk to some of the major participants in your industry, such as suppliers, distributors, and customers. One of the richest sources used to understand the segmentation of the fitness club industry, for the purpose of completing the Prime Adult Fitness business plan, was information obtained from the International Health, Racquet & Sportsclub Association (http://www.ihrsa.org), a nonprofit trade association that represents more than 6,500 fitness clubs and recreational facilities worldwide. Information from these types of sources should be sought out and used.

An exciting aspect of the entrepreneurial process is that it often results in the identification of new segments of an industry that weren't previously considered. For example, Curves International (http://www.curves.com), the fitness center for women, created a new segment in the fitness industry by segmenting the market by gender. Following the lead of Curves, now firms are segmenting the fitness industry in other innovative ways. An example is Velocity Sports Performance (http://www.velocitysp.com), a chain of fitness centers that has segmented its market by benefits sought, which focuses strictly on helping athletes in every sport, at all ages and skill levels, realize their athletic potential through advanced sports training programs.

SELECTING A TARGET MARKET

As alluded to previously, after a firm segments its market, it selects a segment within the market to target. If a firm does not have a preconceived notion about the market it plans to target, it will usually select the segment that represents the best prospects for entry. Even in these instances, the segment that represents the best prospects for entry (in terms of sales growth and profitability) might not be chosen because it isn't consistent with founders' passions and/or core competencies. In these cases, the founders normally select the target market that represents the best fit for them both professionally and personally.

The biggest mistake that people make when selecting a target market is to define their target market too broadly or to try to target more than one segment simultaneously. Startups are usually best served by segmenting their industry carefully and zeroing in on a specific market segment. An exception may be a firm that targets two or more extremely small but related segments. It's simply too difficult and expensive, in the vast majority of cases, to adopt a more aggressive strategy, at least initially. This sentiment is affirmed by Joel Kurtzman, the founder and chairman of Kurtzman Group, a small business-consulting firm, and author of the book *Startups That Work*. Commenting on this issue, Mr. Kurtzman wrote:

> A lucid and articulate business plan will identify specific market segments and individual customers, and offer a blueprint for attacking the marketplace. Our research shows that startups often go after too many market segments simultaneously, trying to be all things to all people and fail to satisfy anyone.[4]

For a new firm, focusing intently on a single market rather than several markets (or a larger market) makes sense because it allows a firm to become an expert in a specialized area, rather than trying to spread itself too thin, as alluded to by Mr. Kurtzman. An example of a firm that has benefited by maintaining a narrow focus is Prometheus Laboratories, a small firm that sells diagnostic services to the 15,000 doctors in the United States specializing in gastroenterology and rheumatology. Explaining the firm's strategy of developing worldwide expertise in a specialized area, Prometheus CEO Michael Walsh said, "We want to be an inch wide and a mile deep."[5]

Before settling on a specific target market, a firm should assess the size of the market and study the trends that are affecting that market to make sure it is large enough and healthy enough to meet the firm's objectives. This subject is covered in the next section of the chapter.

TARGET MARKET SIZE AND TRENDS

Estimating the size of a target market can be a tricky proposition. In many cases, you need to literally invent a methodology for making your estimate. The first rule of thumb is to not make frivolous predictions. Although there may be occasions when you have to make an educated guess or estimate, the key is to explain the path that led you to your conclusions. If the reader of your plan discerns that you are simply guessing, with no clear rationale for your guess, the credibility of your plan will be compromised.

If you are producing a product that is an enhanced version of something that is already available, such as a new type of toy or electronic game, the numbers will be fairly easy to get. IBISWorld, Mintel, Standard & Poor's NetAdvantage, and similar resources track the sizes of industries and segments within industry on a broad basis. You can also consult industry trade journals and trade associations as mentioned previously. Sometimes the size of a market segment isn't stated exactly in an industry report, but the number is easy to compute if you read through the report. For example, if you developed a new type of soccer ball and wanted to know the size of the market for soccer balls in the United States, that number is relatively easy to determine. IBISWorld reports that the Sporting and Athletic Goods Manufacturing in the U.S. industry (NAICS 33992), which soccer balls are part of, reported sales of $12.8 billion dollars in 2006. The sales of soccer balls and related equipment accounted for 1.4 percent of industry sales.[6] Thus, the market for soccer balls is roughly $18 million per year in the United States.

Estimating the size of a target market for a market that doesn't exist, or a market that is specific to a particular location or geographic area, is harder. You will probably need to do some marketing research. For example, to determine the size of its target market, Prime Adult Fitness, which will open a single location in Oviedo, Florida (a suburb of Orlando), used the approach carefully articulated in its business plan. Readers will normally judge a projection like this based on (1) the reasonableness of the assumptions made, (2) the degree to which the numbers are anchored in facts and sound analysis rather than guesses or speculation, and (3) the extent to which it appears that a good faith effort was made to make as accurate of a projection as possible, given normal time and budget constraints. All readers know that a projection is just that, a projection, and some latitude is normally provided. But there is no fooling a savvy reader if a projection is just a set of guesses that looks hastily prepared. Following that approach seriously undermines the credibility of a business plan.

A projection, like the one shown in Figure 6-1, must also be melded with common sense to arrive at a final judgment. For example, the numbers in Prime Adult Fitness's projection of its target market size are likely to be conservative because they estimate the dollar value of the *existing* fitness center market for people 50 years and older in its trade area. Prime Adult Fitness may be able to bring new people into the industry as the result of the unique nature of its offering (i.e., exclusively for 50+ aged adults), similar to how Curves brought new people into the fitness center industry by opening the first fitness centers exclusively for women. In the final section of the market analysis, which describes how a startup forecasts its initial sales, we'll show how much of its available target market, along with new people brought into the market, Prime Adult Fitness believes it can garner during the startup years.

A similar process is used to estimate the size of a new target market for a company that plans to produce a product and sell it nationwide. Again, the key is to follow a sensible process based on the best available data and conduct primary research if necessary. If you get stuck and can't find the information you need, the best recourse is to talk to a reference librarian to see if there are information sources that you are overlooking, and then talk to people in the industry you are interested in. The best place to start in regard to industry participants is to talk to the editors of industry-specific trade journals and the directors of industry trade associations. Industry participants, such as suppliers and distributors, are other good sources of information. Most people are flattered to be asked for their insights and opinions.

Along with reporting the approximate size of a firm's target market, this section of the market analysis should also comment on industry trends that have the potential to affect the target market positively or negatively, if the information has not already been sufficiently reported. The authors of Prime Adult Fitness's business plan, for example, did not include a section in its market analysis on target market trends because the information was already adequately covered. The same process for discerning trends discussed in Chapter 5, which covered industry analysis, can be applied here. An example of the type of trend that should be reported is a trend that is currently taking place in the electronic games industry. The industry is increasingly spreading beyond its young male clientele, and new market segments are being pioneered. An example is PopCap Games (http://www.popcap.com), the electronic games startup mentioned in Chapter 2, which targets women 25 years old and older. Another example is HopeLab (http://www.re-mission.net), a nonprofit organization that makes an electronic game called Re-Mission, which is designed to encourage cancer patients. Both companies are reflective of the broader trend of extending the electronics games industry into new markets and are helping pave the way for new companies to take advantage of this trend.

The next section of the market analysis deals with buyer behavior within a company's target market. This section of the Prime Adult Fitness market analysis is shown in Figure 6-2.

FIGURE 6-2   Buyer Behavior (Prime Adult Fitness Business Plan)

The following are factors that affect the fitness club purchase decision for people in Prime Adult Fitness's target market:

- *Motivation.* Motivation remains the key to recruiting new members and keeping them engaged. According to a survey commissioned by Mintel, 67 percent of nonfitness club members said they would join a fitness club if they knew the activities would keep them motivated.
- *Income level.* People with incomes of $75,000 or more are most likely to join a fitness center, a statistic that works in favor of Prime Adult Fitness. A total of 39.5 percent of households in Seminole County, FL, have incomes levels of $75,000 or more, which is well above the national average.
- *Environment.* Older people prefer to exercise in an environment that is tailored for their specific needs and stage in life, as noted in the target market section. To illustrate how deep these emotions run, the following is a sample of quotations taken from our survey of 196 people in Seminole County, FL (all 50 years old and older), who were asked to comment on how they feel about fitness centers in general.
    "I enjoy my fitness center, but it caters primarily to people who are young and thin. To be honest with you, I've reached a point in my life where I want to be working out with people my own age." (Retired Homemaker, age 69)
    "I've tried several aerobics and exercise classes over the years, but the pace was always too quick. I enjoy water aerobics, but the classes don't meet at a convenient time for me. I think that because the people who run the place (the fitness center) are all in their 20s and 30s, they don't think too much about us older folks." (Insurance Agent, age 61)

FIGURE 6-2 (continued)

> *"My husband died when he was only 68. He was overweight and never exercised. That scares me. I'm 71 now, and I want to live long enough to see my grandchildren grow up. I should join a fitness center and start exercising, but the choices confuse me. I wish someone would take me by the hand and show me what to do."* (Retired School Administrator, age 71)

- *Programs and facilities.* Older people prefer a different mixture of programs and different types of fitness machines than the population in general. As a result, older people who belong to all-purpose fitness centers are frustrated with exercise machines and programs that often don't suit their specific needs. To illustrate this point, the following is a comparison of the 10 most popular program offered by all-purpose fitness centers opposed to the 10 programs preferred by the 196 Seminole County residents 50 years old and older in our survey. The survey illustrates the potential benefit of tailoring a fitness center specifically to 50+ individuals.

Top 10 Programs Offered by All-Purpose Fitness Clubs (in order of popularity)	Top 10 Programs Preferred by a Sample of 196 People 50 Years Old and Older in Prime Adult Fitness's Trade Area
1. Personal Training	1. Low Impact Aerobics
2. Step/Bench Aerobics	2. Personal Training
3. Fitness Evaluation	3. Yoga
4. Cardio Kickboxing or Similar Activity	4. Fitness Evaluation
5. Yoga	5. Strength Training
6. Strength Training	6. Nutrition and Lifestyle Classes*
7. Low Impact Aerobics	7. Indoor Walking Track*
8. High Impact Aerobics	8. Body Sculpting*
9. Group Cycling Classes	9. Massage*
10. Child Care	10. Pilates*

*Not in list of top 10 programs offered by all-purpose fitness centers.

Source for Top 10 Programs Offered at Fitness Clubs: International Health, Racquet & Sportsclub Association (IHRSA).

- *Location of exercise.* People who are 55 years old and older are more inclined to exercise indoors than any other age group. This statistic is particularly important when considering a Florida audience, which may be more inclined to exercise indoors as a result of the heat and humidity.
- *Health concerns.* A total of 70 percent of people 50 years old and older have at least one chronic health condition. The most commonly reported conditions are back problems, spine problems, and arthritis (particularly in females). As a result, access to physical therapy and exercise regimes that address these problems is important to this age group.
- *Social interaction.* Older people often crave positive social interaction with their peer group. As a result, fitness centers that provide opportunities for social interaction and provide open spaces with tables and refreshments where people can gather and socialize have an advantage.

BUYER BEHAVIOR

It's important to include a section in the market analysis that deals directly with the behavior of the consumers in a firm's target market. As mentioned earlier, the more a startup knows about the consumers in its target market, the more it can gear products or services to accommodate their needs.

The brief discussion of buyer behavior in the Prime Adult Fitness market analysis, articulated as bullet points, is reflective of this. The company understands that the key to attracting people to its center is to provide an "environment" that motivates them to participate. As a result, in the marketing (Chapter 7) and operations (Chapter 9) sections of the plan, you'll see the specific steps that Prime Adult Fitness plans to take to tailor its center specifically for the needs of its clientele and make the center an uplifting and socially satisfying place to exercise. The Prime Adult Fitness plan highlights national statistics that show that people with annual incomes of $75,000 or more are the most likely to join a fitness center, a statistic that works in favor of Prime Adult Fitness. A total of 39.5 percent of households in Seminole County, Florida, the location of the first center, have income levels of $75,000 or more, which is well above the national average.[7]

There is additional information that Prime Adult Fitness knows about the consumers it will be servicing, which is reflective of the type of information you should include in this section of your market analysis. Prime Adult Fitness knows the types of classes and programs its potential members want because it conducted a survey of a random sample of people 50 years and older in its trade area. As shown in Figure 6-2, the mixture of classes and programs desired by the target market differs from what is offered by generic fitness centers. The company also knows that people who are 55 years old and older are more inclined to exercise indoors than any other age group.[8] A particularly important insight is the statistic that 70 percent of people 50 years old and older have at least one chronic health concern. This statistic prompted the founders of Prime Adult Fitness to include a physical therapy center within the fitness center. The company also knows that older people often crave positive social interaction. Again, in the marketing plan section and operations section of the business plan, you'll see how Prime Adult Fitness translates this insight into activities and business practices within the facility.

In this section of Prime Adult Fitness's business plan, the focus on the core needs of Prime Adult Fitness's target market, rather than the fitness industry in general, is particularly well done. A lot of information is available that explains why people, in general, join fitness centers and the types of activities they prefer. Some of this information applies equally to all age groups and should be included in Prime Adult Fitness's business plan. Prime Adult Fitness, however, is targeting the 50+ age group, not the population in general. So what's needed, mainly, is an understanding of what people 50 years and older want in a fitness center. Although this information is tougher to find, it's inclusion is essential, even if you have to collect it yourself.

Many other issues pertaining to buyer behavior may be important to cover in this section, depending on the nature of your business. For example, in many business-to-business startups, it's important to discern specifically who the "decision makers" are in the businesses you'll be trying to sell to. Similarly, the length of the customer's buying process is often an important concern. Many startups find it hard to sell products to public schools, for example, because purchase decisions are often made by committees (which draws out the decision-making process), and the funding often has to go through several levels of administrators to get approved. It's also important to know whether your product is a high-, medium-, or low-involvement purchase A **high-involvement purchase** is one for which the buyer is prepared to spend a considerable amount of time and effort searching. In contrast, a **low-involvement purchase** is one that a buyer makes with minimum thought because it does not have much impact on his or her life. Prime Adult Fitness's product is clearly a high-involvement purchase—people normally want to know a lot about a fitness center before they commit to a $50 to $100 per month membership. As a result, it would be prudent for Prime Adult Fitness to have staff members available to provide facility tours, to answer questions, to introduce prospects to current members, to host open houses, and so forth. This is also the reason that many fitness centers offer free trial memberships because it's hard to get some prospects to commit unless they are able to actually spend time becoming familiar with the facility.

COMPETITOR ANALYSIS

A competitor analysis is a detailed analysis of a firm's competition. It helps a firm understand the positions of its major competitors and the opportunities that are available to gain a competitive advantage in one or more areas. The competitor analysis also communicates to the readers of your business plan that you have a complete understanding of your firm's competitive environment. One thing you should never say is that you don't have any competitors. Even though a company like Prime Adult Fitness may be the only fitness center in its area that caters strictly to older people, its potential clientele can still spend their money in a million other ways.

The first item included in a competitor analysis is an identification of a firm's direct, indirect, and future competitors. This item is followed by the presentation of the firm's competitive analysis grid, which is a tool for organizing the information a firm collects about its major competitors.

Prime Adult Fitness's Competitor Analysis is shown in Figure 6-3.

IDENTIFICATION OF DIRECT, INDIRECT, AND FUTURE COMPETITORS

The first step in a competitor analysis is determining who the competition is. Depending on the nature of the business, this may be a more difficult task than you might think. For example, take a company such as Blue Nile (http://www.bluenile.com), the online jewelry store. Primarily, the company sells jewelry, but Blue Nile is not only in the jewelry business. Because jewelry is often given for

FIGURE 6-3 Competitor Analysis (Prime Adult Fitness Business Plan)

Direct Competitors

There are 32 fitness centers in Seminole county, FL. They are broken down as follows:

- 10 all-purpose large centers, including three YMCAs, one Bally Total Fitness Center, two Gold's Gyms, and two LA Fitness Centers
- 18 smaller, more tightly focused centers, including 9 Curves fitness centers
- 4 smaller centers

There are no fitness centers in Seminole county that focus strictly on the 50+ demographic. The benefits of this demographic, however, are apparent to all centers, which are starting to offer more programs with older people in mind. In addition, many centers are attempting to become more "senior" friendly in a variety of ways. For example, Gold's Gyms, the Southern California-based chain that touts its young celebrity clients, is now showing older people in its ads. Many Gold's Gyms also participate in Silver Sneakers, the fitness program offered through health insurers to Medicare recipients. Still, for the most part, the larger fitness chains cater primarily to a young demographic. Many of the tightly focused centers, such as Curves, are not equipped to offer specialized services to an older clientele. Prime Adult Fitness is poised to establish a competitive advantage in Seminole county by focusing strictly on the 50+ demographic.

Indirect Competitors

Indirect competitors include companies that sell home fitness equipment. Seminole county is serviced by a number of sporting goods stores that sell treadmills, exercise bikes, rowing machines, and other home exercise equipment. Nationwide, according to IBISWorld, the sporting good store industry has grown by an average of 3 percent over the past three years (slightly less than the fitness center industry). There are also a number of Web sites that sell exercise equipment, including eBay. According to Prime Adult Fitness's survey of 196 potential customers in Seminole county, 19 percent of the respondents indicated that they own home exercise equipment valued at $200 or more. An increase in the growth rate of the home exercise equipment market poses a threat to all fitness centers, Prime Adult Fitness included.

Future Competitors

The fitness industry should continue to grow, as indicated in the industry analysis earlier in this business plan. Seminole county will reflect this growth. Several nascent 50+ fitness chains exist, including Nifty After 50 and Club 50 (which is for people 40 years old and older). Both of these companies are selling franchises and could move into the Seminole county market. Other startups may also follow suit. Prime Adult Fitness hopes to establish a strong brand and clientele before these competitors move into the market.

Competitive Analysis Grid

Name	Prime Adult Fitness	Central Florida YMCA	LA Fitness	Gold's Gym
Geographic location	Even	Even	Even	Even
Staff	Advantage	Even	Even	Even
Fitness programs offered	Advantage	Advantage	Even	Even

FIGURE 6-3 (continued)

Name	Prime Adult Fitness	Central Florida YMCA	LA Fitness	Gold's Gym
Breadth and quality of equipment	Even	Even	Even	Even
Price	Even	Even	Even	Even
Social interaction	Advantage	Advantage	Even	Even
Tailored Services	Advantage	Disadvantage	Disadvantage	Disadvantage
Breadth of Clientele	Disadvantage	Advantage	Advantage	Advantage

Summary

The grid shows that Prime Adult Fitness will compete on par with its closest competitors on geographic location, breadth and quality of equipment, and price. It intends to establish an advantage in terms of the quality of its staff and the programs it offers. Its clearest absolute advantage is the tailored services it offers. This advantage is offset somewhat by a disadvantage in terms of breadth of clientele. Prime Adult Services feels that establishing an absolute advantage in terms of tailored services is more than worth the tradeoff.

gifts, the company is also in the gift business. If the company sees itself as in the gift business rather than just the jewelry business, it has a broader set of competitors—and opportunities—to consider.

You should list your direct competitors, indirect competitors, and future competitors; if you believe that your business will attract imitators, then future competitors are inevitable. A brief description of each type of competitor follows:

- *Direct competitors.* These are businesses that offer a product that is very similar to yours. These competitors are the most important because they are going after the same customers that you are.

- *Indirect competitors.* These competitors offer close substitutes to the product you will be offering. These firms' products are important in that they target the same basic need that will be met by your product. For example, when people told Roberto Goizueta, the late CEO of Coca-Cola, that Coke's market share was at a maximum, he countered by saying that Coke accounted for less than 2 percent of the 64 ounces of fluid that the average person drinks each day. "The enemy is coffee, milk, tea [and] water," he once said.[9]

- *Future competitors.* These are companies that are not yet direct or indirect competitors but could move into one of these roles at any time.

Normally it's impossible to identify all of your direct and indirect competitors, let alone your future competitors. As a result, you should list a handful of competitors or classes of competitors in each category. You should provide a short assessment of the scope and intensity of your competition. You'll have the opportunity to talk about your competitive advantage after you present your competitive advantage grid.

The next section focuses on your competitive analysis grid, which is a comparison of your firm to your major competitors. To complete a meaningful competitive analysis grid, you must first understand the strategies and behaviors of your competitors. This requires you to engage in **competitive intelligence,** which is the process of gathering information about your competitors. Suggestions for how to approach this task are provided in the Business Plan Insights box.

BUSINESS PLAN INSIGHTS

Sources of Competitive Intelligence

To complete a meaningful competitive analysis grid, a startup must first understand the strategies and behaviors of its competitors. The information that is gathered by a firm to learn about its competitors is referred to as **competitive intelligence.** Obtaining sound competitive intelligence is not always an easy task. If a competitor is a publicly traded firm, a description of the firm's business and its financial information is available through annual reports filed with the Securities and Exchange Commission (SEC). These reports are public records and are available at the SEC's Web site (http://www.sec.gov).

More often than not, however, a new firm will compete primarily against other private companies. In these instances, the task is more difficult. Private companies are not required to divulge information to the public. As a result, when preparing your business plan, you have to find ways to ethically obtain information about your competitors. Here are some suggestions for doing that:

- Attend conferences and trade shows. Most industries have conferences and trade shows at which firms talk about the latest trends in the industry and display their products.

- Read industry-related trade publications, magazines, and Web sites, along with general business magazines, such as *Business 2.0* and *Business Week*.

- Read industry reports via online resources such as IBISWorld, Mintel, and Standard and Poor's. For example, for each of the industries that it covers, IBISWorld has a section in its report titled "Major Competitors."

- Purchase competitor' products to understand their features, benefits, and shortcomings: The process of purchasing the product will also provide data about how the competitor treats its customers.

- Talk to customers about what motivated them to buy your product as opposed to your competitors' products. Customers can provide a wealth of information about the advantages and disadvantages of competing products.

- Study competitors' Web sites. Many companies put a lot of information on their Web sites, including their company's history, profiles of their management teams, product information, and the latest news about the company.

COMPETITIVE ANALYSIS GRID

A competitive analysis grid is a tool for organizing and presenting the information you collect about your competitors. It can help you to see how you stack up against your competitors in key areas and illustrate your primary sources of competitive advantage. To be a viable company, a new venture must have at least one clear competitive advantage over its major competitors.

The Prime Adult Fitness competitive analysis grid is shown in Figure 6-3. The way to complete the grid is to show the key success factors for firms in your target market on the vertical axis of the grid and then show your firm along with your four or five major direct competitors on the horizontal axis. In each box, you rate yourself relative to your competitors on each of the key success factors. The purpose of this exercise is to see how you stack up against your major competitors on key success factors and to illustrate the areas in which you have an advantage (and have a disadvantage). For example, Prime Adult Fitness sees itself as superior to it competitors in terms of "tailoring its activities to its target market." The process of completing a competitive analysis grid also helps a firm fine-tune its offering. For example, if your business plan is for a retail store, and one of the key success factors in your industry is "hours of operation," in most cases, you would want to make sure you're equal to or have an advantage over your competitors in this area. Completing the competitive analysis grid may reveal that you're at a disadvantage in this area, which will help you make adjustments if appropriate.

Similar to all sections of the business plan, you should draw conclusions and help your reader interpret the information you are presenting. For example, as depicted in Figure 6-3, Prime Adult Fitness uses its competitive analysis grid to illustrate its sources of competitive advantage.

The next section focuses on how to estimate the annual sales and market share for a new firm. Prime Adult's estimates are shown in Figure 6-4.

ESTIMATE OF ANNUAL SALES AND MARKET SHARE

The final section of the market analysis focuses on computing an estimate of your firm's initial annual sales and market share. In many business plans, this analysis is provided in the financial plan section, which is usually near the end of the business plan. As mentioned earlier in the chapter, the advantage of providing the estimate here is that it helps set up the remainder of the plan. For a company like Prime Adult Fitness, it must have a good handle on the type of membership and revenues to expect before the firm can plan its facility, project the number of employees it will need, plan its marketing budget, and so on.

There are four basic ways for a new firm to estimate its initial sales. All of the methods produce estimates—there is no way to precisely predict the sales of a new business. More than one method should be used if possible. The most important thing is to come up with an estimate that is based on sound assumptions and seems both realistic and attainable.

FIGURE 6-4   Estimate of Annual Sales and Market Share (Prime Adult Fitness Business Plan)

Estimate of Annual Sales

The following steps were taken to estimate the size of Prime Adult Fitness's annual sales.

Step 1: Determine the number of members Prime Adult Fitness will have.

Prime Adult Fitness's target is 2,100 membership units within 12 months of opening its doors. A "unit" is a single member or a couple paying for a couple's membership.

Step 2: Based on 2,100 membership units, what will Prime Adult Fitness's annual sales be?

Prime Adult Fitness estimates it will take 12 months to reach 2,100 membership units. It is projecting 2,100 membership units at the end of 2009 (first year of operation), 2,226 in 2010, 2,360 in 2011, and 2,502 in 2012. It will generate income in the following three ways:

Membership Fees: The membership fees will be $70 per month for a single membership and $92.50 per month for a couple's membership. Based on discussions with industry experts, the founders estimate that 70 percent of its memberships will be single members and 30 percent will be couples.

For its first year, Prime Adult Fitness projects it will obtain its 2,100 membership units in the following order (January, February, and March are the biggest months for fitness club "new" memberships):

2009 Membership Unit Enrollment Projection

Number of New Members	Single Membership	Couples Membership	Total
January	180	80	260
February	180	80	260
March	175	75	250
April	175	75	250
May	150	60	210
June	150	60	210
July	100	35	135
August	80	35	115
September	70	35	105
October	70	35	105
November	70	35	105
December	70	25	95
Total	1,470	630	2,100

Projected membership income:

2009: $1,251,275 (based on enrollment timing and projections)

2010: $2,050,146

2011: $2,173,560

2012: $2,304,342

FIGURE 6-4 (continued)

One-Time Enrollment Fees: Prime Adult Fitness's one-time enrollment fee will be $150 for both singles and couples. An attrition rate of 25 percent per year is anticipated. These numbers translate into the following projected enrollment fee income.

2009: $315,000 (2,100 membership units × $150/unit)
2010: $110,100 (734 new membership units × $150/unit)
2011: $116,700 (778 new membership units × $150/unit)
2012: $123,750 (825 new membership units × $150/unit)

Additional Sources of Income: Prime Adult Fitness will collect license fee income from massage therapists, physical therapists, and mental health professionals that will provide services in its facilities on a fee basis. It will also operate a coffee and smoothie bar. Prime Adult Fitness anticipates that its additional income will be 12.5 percent of its membership fees.

2009: $124,123*
2010: $256,268
2011: $271,695
2012: $288,042

*This number is not 12.5 percent of 2009 membership income due to the timing of when people join the center.

Total Projected Sales from All Sources:

2009: $1,690,398
2010: $2,416,514
2011: $2,561,955
2012: $2,716,134

Estimate of Annual Market Share
Prime Adult Fitness, through focus groups and a study conducted by our Customer Advisory Board, believes that 50% of our membership will come from people who already belong to other fitness centers and 50% will be new members (to the fitness center industry). If 50% of revenues come from the existing market, Prime Adult Fitness will need to capture an 11.44% share of the 50+ market for people in Seminole County, FL who currently belong to a fitness center. We feel this number is achievable.

The first way to estimate the sales for a new business is to contact the premier trade associations in your industry and ask if they track the sales numbers for businesses that are similar to the business you plan to start. If the trade association doesn't track actual sales numbers for comparable businesses, ask if there are other rules of thumb or metrics that help new companies estimate sales. For example, many industries collect statistics such as "average sales per square foot" or "average sales per employee" for the firms in their industry. These numbers may be helpful to you in estimating your initial sales. To find the trade associations in your industry, check Mintel's analysis of your industry (a list of trade associations is listed in the Appendix of each report) or check one of the three online trade association directories listed in the Internet Resources Table in Appendix 2.2 at the end of Chapter 2.

The second way to estimate a new firm's sales is to find a comparable firm, or a company that's selling a comparable product. Many financial experts feel that this is the most effective approach. For example, if you are planning to open a woman's clothing boutique, try to find a boutique that is similar to the one you are planning, and simply call the owner and ask for a chance to talk to him or her about the business. You should try to find a store out of your trade area so the owner doesn't see you as a potential competitor. As indicated in Chapter 3, even if the owner is only willing to talk in general terms (i.e., our annual sales are between $300,000 and $400,000 per year), that information is better than nothing. Of course, you'll need to use common sense to adjust the numbers based on whether your store will be smaller or larger than the comparable store, will be in a better location or a poorer location, and so on. You should report your assumptions so it's clear to the reader of your plan exactly how you arrived at your sales estimate. If you're planning to sell a product, such as a new type of iPod accessory, the same approach applies. Try to find a company that won't be a direct competitor that is selling a similar product, and try to arrange a telephone appointment or engage in an e-mail exchange. In all instances, simply tell the person you're talking to that you're working on a business plan for your startup and you're trying to arrive at a sales estimate. Ask for help regarding what types of sales to expect for the first one to three years of your business based on their experiences. Many first-time entrepreneurs are surprised at how helpful businesspeople are in freely divulging this type of information.

The third way to try to estimate sales is to conduct Internet searches to try to find magazine and newspaper articles that focus on firms in your industry. On occasion, the articles will talk about the sales experiences of a similar early stage firm. If you know of a firm that's comparable to your firm, target that firm first in your search. To find articles, you should use general search engines such as Google and Yahoo! and more powerful search directories such as LexisNexis and Pro-Quest. The latter two directories are fee-based but are normally free if accessed through a university library. Publicly traded companies report their sales number, and the numbers are available via Hoovers (http://www.hoovers.com) and through many other sources. These companies, however, are rarely good comparables because they are much larger than startups and are often multidivision firms.

The fourth way to estimate a startup's sales is to use a multiplication method to try to arrive at a reasonable number. Startups that plan to sell a product on a national basis normally use a top-down approach to arrive at this number. This typically involves trying to estimate the total number of users of the product, estimate the average price customers pay, and estimate how much of the market their business will garner. Startups that plan to sell locally, such as a restaurant or clothing boutique, normally use a more bottom-up approach. This approach involves trying to determine how many customers to expect and the average amount each customer will spend. The numbers are usually computed on a weekly, monthly, and yearly basis.

Sometimes the multiplication method gets fairly complicated, and you have to consider several industries and conduct primary research to get a good estimate. For example, if you had started H20Audio, the company that makes waterproof housing for the Apple iPod, how would you have used the multiplication method to estimate your initial sales? One way to approach this task would be to gather data on the total number of people who regularly engage in sports where they are likely to get wet, which is H20Audio's target market. These sports include swimming, surfing, snowboarding, snorkeling, and similar activities. The next step would be to locate data on the number of people who listen to an iPod while exercising or engaging in outdoor activities. Working with these numbers, you could then estimate the percentage of people who engage in water sports who are iPod users. You would then have to conduct primary research to make an estimate of the percentage of those people who would buy your product and the average amount they would spend. The primary research activities might involve distributing your concept statement and buying intentions survey to a sample of your potential customers, talking to industry experts, talking to sporting goods store owners, talking to companies who have brought a similar product or iPod accessory to the market, and pursuing similar sources of information and advice.

To estimate its initial sales using the multiplication approach, Prime Adult Fitness used a variation of the bottom-up method as shown in its business plan in Figure 6-4.

The ideal scenario for startups is to use all four methods of estimating initial sales and then compare the estimates. The key is to arrive at your estimates by following a clear rationale and to present numbers that appear to be both realistic and obtainable.

Chapter Summary

1. The marketing analysis section of a business plan is distinctly different from the marketing section. The market analysis section focuses on describing a firm's target market, customers, and competitors; how it will compete in the marketplace; and potential sales and market share. In contrast, the marketing section focuses on the classic marketing functions, including product, price, promotion, and distribution.

2. The market analysis is an extremely important section of a business plan for two reasons. First, it helps define the nature of the business and the remainder of the plan. Second, it affirms that a company has a well thought out target market, understands its customers, and can generate sales in the face of competition.

3. Market segmentation is the process of dividing a market into distinct subsets (or segments) that behave in the same way or have similar needs. An exciting element of the entrepreneurial process is that it often results in the identification of new segments of an industry that weren't previously considered.

4. After a firm segments its market, it selects a segment within the market to target. The biggest mistake that people make when selecting a target market is to define their market too broadly or to try to target more than one segment simultaneously. Startups are usually best served by zeroing in on a specific target market.

5. Estimating the size of a target market can be a tricky proposition. The first rule of thumb is to not make frivolous predictions. The key is to explain the path that leads you to your conclusions. If you are producing a product that is an enhanced version of something that is already available, the numbers will be fairly easy to get. Estimating the size of a target market for a market that doesn't exist is harder.

6. It's important to include a section in the market analysis that deals directly with the behavior of the consumers in a firm's target market. The more a startup knows about the consumers in its target market, the more it can gear products or services to accommodate their needs.

7. A competitor analysis is a detailed analysis of a firm's competition. It helps a firm understand the positions of its major competitors and the opportunities that are available to gain a competitive advantage in one or more areas.

8. A firm's competitors include direct competitors, indirect competitors, and future competitors.

9. A competitive analysis grid is a tool for organizing and presenting the information you collect about your competitors.

10. There are four basic ways for a firm to estimate its initial sales: contacting trade associations, finding comparable firms, finding sales estimates for comparable firms in magazine and newspaper articles, and using the multiplication method.

Review Questions

1. Explain the purpose of the market analysis section of a business plan.
2. Describe the difference between the market analysis section and the marketing plan section of a business plan.
3. Explain the process of market segmentation and why it's important for a firm to select a specific target market.
4. Describe the requirements for successfully segmenting a market.
5. What is the biggest mistake that people make when selecting a target market?
6. Why is estimating the size of a target market referred to as a "tricky" proposition?
7. Describe why it's important to include a section on "buyer behavior" in a business plan.
8. Explain the purpose of a competitor analysis.
9. Explain why it's important to collect competitive intelligence, and describe some of the techniques that are used to collect it.
10. Briefly describe the four separate ways of estimating the annual sales and market share of a new business.

Application Questions

1. A friend of yours just completed a 42-page business plan for a solar power company. The company will be asking for $4 million in venture capital funding to ramp up production of a new type of solar panel they have developed. While looking through the plan, you noticed that the company will be targeting three segments of the solar energy market: commercial users, residential users, and government buildings. When you asked your friend if he thought the company might be spreading itself too thin, he replied by saying, "No. In fact, we thought about targeting additional segments. We want to show the VCs that we have broad markets for our product." Do you think your friend's target market strategy is wise? Explain your answer.

2. According to the chapter, one way that markets are segmented is on psychographic variables. Explain what a psychographic variable is, and provide three examples of markets that might be segmented on one or more of these variables.

3. Recreate Prime Adult Fitness's estimate of the size of its target market, and substitute the county that your college of university is located in for Seminole County, Florida. How do your numbers compare with the numbers reported in Prime Adult Fitness's estimate?

4. Put yourself in the place of an investor listening to Prime Adult Fitness present the market analysis portion of its business plan. Think of three penetrating questions that you would ask about their market analysis.

5. Expresso Fitness is producing an exercise bike that keeps its users engaged and motivated by turning the bike into a sort of video game. Go to Expresso Fitness's Web site (http://www.expressofitness.com), and study the company. If you had been the founder of Expresso Fitness, explain how you would have estimated the company's initial sales using the multiplication method.

Endnotes

1. D. Clark, "Start-Up to Tailor Wireless Service for Seniors," *The Wall Street Journal*, April 3, 2006.
2. PricewaterhouseCoopers, *Three Keys to Obtaining Venture Capital* (New York: PricewaterhouseCoopers, 2001).
3. "Market Segment" (Wikipedia). http://en.wikipedia.org/wiki/Market_setmentation (June 13, 2007).
4. J. Kurtzman, *Startups That Work* (New York: Portfolio, 2005), 156.
5. "500 List," *Inc.*, January 2004, 64.
6. "Sporting and Athletic Manufacturing in the US" (IBISWorld Industry Report). http://www.ibisworld.com.au (2007).
7. Metro Orlando Economic Development Commission, "Demographic Detail Summary Report for Seminole County, Florida," (2007).
8. "Industry Statistics" (Fitness Management). http://www.finessmanagement.com/FM/information/statistics (2007).
9. P. Kotler, *Marketing Insights From A to Z* (Hokoken, NJ: Wiley, 2003), 23.

MARKETING PLAN

INTRODUCTION

This chapter builds on Chapter 6, which discussed the market analysis. Whereas the market analysis focused on describing a firm's target market, customers, competitors, and potential sales, this chapter focuses on how the firm will actually find customers and close sales. It deals with the nuts and bolts of marketing in terms of price, promotions, distribution, and sales. For example, Great Call (http://www.jitterbug.com), the firm that makes cell phones for older users, may have a great product, a well-defined target market, a good understanding of its customers and competitors, and a sizeable market, but it still has to find customers and persuade them to buy its product. The marketing plan section communicates your specific plans for meeting these objectives.

The best way to describe a company's marketing plan is to start by articulating its marketing strategy, positioning, and points of differentiation, and then talk about how these overall aspects of the plan will be supported by price, promotional mix and sales process, and distribution strategy. If you haven't discussed your product yet, it should be talked about here. Most business plans provide a description of their product or service in an earlier section of the plan, however.

The marketing section must lay out specifically how you plan to make your target market aware of the existence of your product or service. Many business plans do a good job of describing the size of a company's target market and the merits of its product but do a poor job of dealing with the practicalities of how the product will be sold. Obviously, it's not possible to include a full-blown marketing plan in the four to five pages permitted in a business plan for the marketing section, but you need to provide your reader a sense of how you'll market and sell your product within the confines of a reasonable budget. It's also important to reinforce how your product provides its user unique value and differs from similar products in the marketplace.

There are two things to be mindful of as you write this section. First, all of the elements of a firm's marketing plan should be developed with the customer plainly in mind. This notion extends beyond producing a product or service that accommodates your customers' needs, to knowing the amount of disposable income they have, the periodicals they read, the media they watch, and so on, depending on the type of business you have. Knowledge of these, and similar factors, helps you to find-tune your marketing strategy and lower expenses. An example of the potential benefits involved is provided by Ron Boire, the president of sales for Sony consumer electronics. In 2000, Sony (http://www.sony.com) ran an advertising campaign to try to resurrect the Sony Walkman, the original portable music player. The campaign, titled "The Walkman Has Landed," featured an alien mascot that looked like a cross between E.T. and Smurf. Sony ran its ads in print and media outlets that specifically catered to its target market—Generation Y consumers (13–30 years old). During the campaign, Boire was reminded of the value of restricting his ad dollars to media most likely to be seen by his target market:

> I think that our experience with the Walkman alien campaign that was started in 2000 best captures it. We were spending tens of millions of dollars on media and I had friends (over 30 years old) say, "You know, I've never seen the ads." It's like, "Good. That's a good thing that we've run hundreds and hundreds of slots and you've never seen one, because you're not the target. That means I'm targeting razor sharp."[1]

Although Sony is a large, multinational firm, the same logic applies to a startup. By knowing your customers and tailoring your marketing efforts specifically to them, you can deliver a sharper message and avoid the expenses associated with reaching people less likely to buy your product. The "Buyer Behavior" section in Chapter 6 contains information that, along with other insights you are able to accumulate, should inform all of your marketing-related decisions.

The second thing to be mindful of as you write this section is that you must detail exactly who will sell your product and how your sales process will work. Many business plans provide an overview of how their product will be priced and promoted but never zero in on how it will actually be sold. This is a critical issue that is often missing from business plans. You should describe your sales process and the methods that you'll use to sell your product, whether it is via a direct sales force, through distributors or wholesalers, through an alliance with companies that sell complementary products, or through some other means. If you plan to field a direct sales force, you should describe how you plan to recruit salespeople, how their jobs will be structured, and how they will be compensated. Knowing that you have thought through these issues will bolster the confidence your readers have in the plan.

This marketing chapter of the business plan contains four sections: overall marketing strategy, pricing strategy, sales process and promotions mix, and distribution and sales. The overall marketing strategy of the Prime Adult Fitness business plan is shown in Figure 7-1.

FIGURE 7-1   Overall Marketing Strategy (Prime Adult Fitness Business Plan)

Overall Marketing Strategy
The overall objective of Prime Adult Fitness's marketing strategy is to make people 50 years old and older aware of the benefits of exercise and to sell them on the idea that our fitness center is the best place for them to either start or to continue exercising. We don't plan to accomplish this objective through splashy ads. Our overall approach will be to generate grassroots support and word-of-mouth referrals through a series of marketing tactics that will demonstrate how exercise and membership in Prime Adult Fitness enhances the lives of our members.

Our marketing strategy is also based on the notion that marketing is everyone's responsibility—our staff, our employees, our directors, our advisory board members, and even our members. Every program, every class, every piece of equipment we buy, and every interaction with our members will be based on the goal of fulfilling our mission, which is expressed through our tagline "Meet Your Dreams." We so strongly believe that people 50 years and older want to be fit and lead healthy lives that we've created a fitness center just for them. We want our target market to know how much we care. That sentiment will be reflected through our marketing strategy and tactics.

We are also keenly aware that we must reach our membership goals. The number 2,100 is our membership goal for 2010. That number will be a motivational tool and will be the central metric we use to hold ourselves accountable for translating our caring attitudes into business results. The slogan "Let's Care Enough to Reach 2,100" will appear on all our internal documents and will be a central part of our employee motivation program.

Positioning
Prime Adult Fitness's target market is the health and fitness club market for people 50 years old and older. Its position in the market is to offer a tailored offering (meaning its facilities and programs will be specifically geared to people 50 years old and older) at the high end of the market, in terms of amenities and price.

Points of Differentiation

- Only fitness center in our target market exclusively for people 50 years old and older
- Strong emphasis placed on the social aspect of belonging to a fitness center
- Well-trained staff that cares about the needs and lives of older people

Product Attribute Map
Prime Adult Fitness's positioning strategy and its primary point of differentiation are illustrated in the product attribute map shown below. As shown, Prime Adult Fitness will be the only fitness center in its trade area that ranks high on both (1) the degree to which it is tailored specifically to the needs of its clientele and (2) the extent to which it offers a high range of amenities for its members. It ranks slightly lower than generic fitness centers in terms of range of amenities. There are several aspects of general fitness centers, like large weight rooms (for free weights), that will be scaled down by Prime Adult Fitness given our clientele.

FIGURE 7-1 (continued)

Prime Adult Fitness's second and third points of differentiation, a strong emphasis on socialization and a trained and caring staff, brings its positioning strategy and primary point of differentiation to life (and makes them sustainable). Its objective is to not only open and run a fitness center for 50+ individuals, but also to open and run a center that makes them feel safe, secure, welcome, and at home.

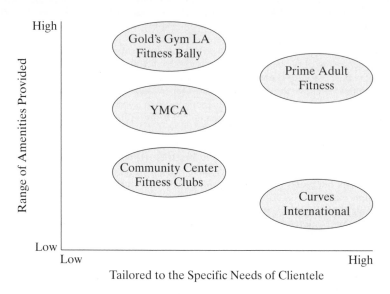

OVERALL MARKETING STRATEGY

Marketing strategy refers to a firm's approach to marketing its products and services stated in broad terms, which forms the basis of all of its marketing-related activities. It's a good idea to begin the marketing plan section of a business plan by articulating your marketing strategy because it sets the tone for the entire section. It also reassures your reader that your various marketing activities are part of an overall approach or plan. All firms have constraints regarding the resources they have to devote to their marketing and sales efforts. As a result, it's extremely important that a firm have an overall philosophy or approach to marketing that enables it to deploy resources in a purposeful and consistent manner.

Another important reason for having a marketing strategy and for articulating it in a business plan is to make sure that a firm's marketing efforts are consistent with its overall mission and understanding of the market. This desired congruence is clearly seen in Prime Adult Fitness's marketing strategy, which is shown in Figure 7-1. The company's marketing strategy is clearly a reflection of how the company feels about its target market (which is reflective of its mission) and what it learned in completing its industry analysis and market analysis.

There are two additional parts to this section: positioning strategy and points of differentiation.

POSITIONING STRATEGY

After selecting a target market, the next step is for a firm to select a "position" in the market. **Position** is concerned with how a firm is situated relative to its rivals (or potential rivals). In a sense, a position is the part of a specific target market that a firm is claiming for its own. To understand a firm's market position, you need to study the features of its goods or services. For example, BMW's position (luxury) in the automobile market differs from Chevrolet's position (functional). Clearly, these products differ from one another in substantial ways. Even within the luxury automobile market, BMW's position (more sports-driving oriented) differs from that of Infinity (more luxury-features oriented).

As shown earlier in Figure 7-1, Prime Adult Fitness has positioned itself at the top end of the fitness market, in terms of the range of amenities offered, for its target market (people 50 years old and older). It will offer its members access to a premier selection of exercise equipment, fitness classes, and other programs, in a modern, comfortable 21,600 square foot facility. In exchange for these amenities, Prime Adult Fitness will charge a monthly membership fee that is also at the top end of the market. This is Prime Adult Fitness's position. There are other positions in its target market that it could have occupied. For instance, Prime Adult Fitness could offer a much more limited set of amenities to its members and charge a lower monthly fee, as Curves has done in its target market. Both positions may be viable and profitable. Determining which position to occupy and compete in is simply a judgment call on the part of a company based on its mission, its overall approach to the marketplace, and its competitive landscape.

POINTS OF DIFFERENTIATION

You should also clearly articulate your specific points of differentiation early in the marketing plan section of your business plan. These points were illustrated in your competitive analysis grid in Chapter 6. It's typically best to limit the points of differentiation that you talk about to two or three points, to make them memorable and distinct. Also, make sure that the value of these points is easy for your reader to see. For example, ZUCA (http://www.zuca.com), the backpack on rollers, has two distinct points of differentiation: it relieves back pain by putting the backpack on rollers, and it's sturdy enough for either a child or an adult to sit on. Laura Udall, ZUCA's founder, confirmed the meaningfulness of these points of differentiation through focus groups.[2] She even has a picture of her teenage son sitting on the ZUCA's seat, which anyone could imagine might be handy for kids waiting for the school bus. You should also make sure your points of differentiation aren't liabilities, if a discerning reader starts playing devil's advocate. For instance, if Udall said that the ZUCA will be offered in 20 different colors, on the face of it, that sounds good. But think about the ramifications of offering 20 different colors: complicated production process, limited channels through which the product is sold, and few retailers with enough shelf space to carry 20 different colors of a backpack. This type of disconnect or naivety undermines the credibility of a business plan.

There are many other potential sources of differentiation. Noel Capon, a marketing expert and author of the book *Marketing Mavens,* makes the point that the most compelling forms of differentiation are created through innovations that are difficult to imitate because they are created by competencies unique to a firm. Starbucks creates this type of differentiation through the ambiance of its restaurants. Apple does it through product design. Dave Roberts, the CEO of PopCap Games (http://www.popcap.com), a company introduced earlier in the book, explains this point about Apple as follows:

> An example I use (to describe a product that's hard to copy) is the iPod. What is it about the iPod that makes it work? Some of it is Apple's branding, but a lot of it is that it simply feels good. You pick up an iPod and it feels exactly right. You know how to use it, and you can't say that for a lot of the other MP3 players.[3]

The point of Roberts' statement is that there is something about Apple that enables it to excel at design in a manner that no other firm can. If you feel that your startup has a set of competencies that might provide this type of advantage, you should mention that in this portion of your product description.

A useful way for a startup to visually depict its primary point of differentiation is through a product attribute map. A **product attribute map** is created by articulating two of a product's most important attributes, one on the x-axis of the map and the other on the y-axis. A firm then simply plots itself relative to its major competitors. Prime Adult Fitness's product attribute map is shown in Figure 7-1. The map clearly illustrate that Prime Adult Fitness is the only fitness center in its trade that ranks high on both the degree to which it is tailored specifically to the needs of its clientele and the extent to which it offers a high range of amenities for its members. In the product attribute map assessment, the firm makes the further point that it plans to protect its primary source of differentiation (highly tailored service/high level of amenities) through its two other sources of differentiation—a strong emphasis on socialization and a trained and caring staff.

PRICING STRATEGY

This section should explain how you plan to price your product or service. Price is an important issue because it determines how much money a company can earn. The price a company charges for its products also sends a clear message to its target customers. For example, Oakley (http://www.oakley.com) positions its sunglasses as innovative, state-of-the art products that are both high quality and visually appealing. This position in the market suggests the premium price that Oakley charges. If Oakley advertised innovative, state-of-the art products but charged a bargain basement price, it would send confusing signals to its customers. Its customers would wonder, "Are Oakley sunglasses high quality or

FIGURE 7-2 Pricing Strategy (Prime Adult Fitness Business Plan)

Pricing Strategy
Prime Adult Fitness will adopt a policy of value-based (opposed to cost-based) pricing and will price its initial enrollment fee and monthly membership fee on two criteria:

- Current prices charged by director competitors in its trade area
- The perceived value of its service by its target clientele

Prime Adult Fitness's Prices vs. Direct Competitors and National Averages

	Prime Adult Fitness	*Direct Competitors in Trade Area*	*National Average*
Initial (One-Time)	Single: $150	Single: $145	Single: $150
Membership Fee	Couples: $150	Couples: $165	Couples: $199
	Family: n/a	Family: $165	Family: $199
Monthly	Single: $70	Single: $72.50	Single: $55
Membership Fee	Couples: $92.50	Couples: $87.50	Couples: $89
	Family: n/a	Family: $87.50	Family: $89

Sources: Direct Competitors, Prime Adult Fitness Survey

National Averages: International Health, Racquet & Sportsclub Association

Summary
The pricing schedule shown above demonstrates that Prime Adult Fitness's prices are on par with its direct competitors and national averages. The schedule was subjected to scrutiny in three focus groups, and no serious objections were raised.

aren't they?" In addition, the lower price wouldn't generate the sales revenue Oakley needs to continuously differentiate its sunglasses from competitors' products in ways that create value for its customers.

In this section, you should state how you plan to price your product or service and provide a brief rationale for your pricing philosophy. The Prime Adult Fitness business plan, shown in Figure 7-2, plainly states its pricing policy and then shows a comparison of the pricing structure to direct competitors and national averages. Although at first glance, price seems like a straightforward topic, it is actually quite complex. There are different methods for determining a product's price, and a variety of other issues are involved.

This part of the marketing plan includes two sections: cost-based vs. value-based pricing and other pricing-related issues.

COST-BASED PRICING VS. VALUE-BASED PRICING

The two methods for determining the price of a product or service are cost-based pricing and value-based pricing. In **cost-based pricing,** the list price is determined by adding a markup percentage to a product's cost. The markup percentage may be standard for the industry or may be arbitrarily determined by you. The advantage of this method is that it's straightforward, and it's relatively easy to justify the price of a good or service. For this reason, many regulated utilities use cost-based pricing.

The disadvantage is that it's not always easy to estimate what the costs of a product will be, particularly for a startup. After a price is set, raising the price is difficult, even if a company's costs increase. In addition, cost-based pricing is based on what a company thinks it should receive rather than what the market thinks a good or service is worth. Companies are finding it increasingly difficult to dictate prices to their customers, given customers' ability to comparison shop, even for industrial goods, on the Internet to find what they believe is the best price.[4]

In **value-based pricing,** the list price is determined by estimating what consumers are willing to pay for a product and then backing off a bit to provide a cushion. What a customer is willing to pay is determined by the perceived value of the product and by the number of choices available in the marketplace. Sometimes, to make this determination, a company has to conduct focus groups or try different pricing options in test markets. A firm influences its customers' perception of value through positioning, branding, promotions, and the other elements of its marketing plan.

Whether you choose cost-based pricing or value-based pricing is an important call. Most experts recommend value-based pricing because it hinges on the perceived value of a product or service rather than cost plus markup, which is a formula that ignores the customer. Value-based pricing also frequently produces a higher gross margin. A **gross margin** (a company's net sales minus its cost of goods sold) of 60 percent to 80 percent is not uncommon in high-tech industries. An Intel chip that sells for $300 may cost $50 to produce. This type of markup reflects the perceived value of the chip. If Intel had used a cost-based pricing method instead of a value-based approach, it would probably charge much less for its chip.

Of course, regardless of whether you choose cost-based or value-based pricing, your price must make sense given the realities of your market. Prime Adult Fitness included the table that compares its price to its direct competitors and national averages to reassure its readers that the target market will see the price as fair and reasonable given the alternatives.

OTHER PRICING-RELATED ISSUES

Most experts warn startups to resist the temptation to charge a low price for their products in the hopes of capturing market share. This approach can win a sale but generates little profit. In addition, most consumers make a **price-quality attribution** when looking at the price of a product. This means that consumers naturally assume that the high-priced product is also the better-quality product. If a firm charges a low price for its products, it sends a signal to customers that the product is low quality regardless of whether it really is.

A vivid example of the association between price and quality is provided by SmugMug (http://www.smugmug.com), an online photo-sharing site that charges a $40 per year base subscription fee. SmugMug, which is growing rapidly, has 200,000 paying customers and more than 100,000,000 million photos stored. What's interesting about the company is that most of its competitors, including Shutterfly (http://www.shutterfly.com), Flickr (http://www.flickr.com), and WebShots (http://www.webshots.com), offer a similar service for free. Ostensibly, the reason SmugMug is able to charge a fee is that it offers higher levels of customer service and has a more user-friendly interface (in terms of how you view your photos online) than its competitors. But the owners of SmugMug feel that its ability to charge goes beyond these obvious points. Some of the free sites have closed abruptly, and their users have lost photos. SmugMug, because it charges, is seen as more reliable and dependable for the long term. (Who wants to lose their photos?) In addition, the owners believe that when people pay for something, they innately assign a higher value to it. As a result, SmugMug users tend to treat the site with respect, by posting attractive, high-quality photos that are in good taste. SumgMug's users appreciate this facet of the site, compared to the free sites, where unseemly photos often creep in.[5]

The overarching point of this example and the preceding discussion is that the price you're able to charge is largely a function of (1) the objective quality of your product or service and (2) the perception of value that you create in the minds of your customers relative to completing products in the marketplace. You should carefully assess each of these criteria as you set your prices and develop your pricing philosophy.

The next section focuses on a firm's sales process and its promotional mix. This section of Prime Adult Fitness's business plan is shown in Figure 7-3.

FIGURE 7-3   Sales Process and Promotional Mix (Prime Adult Fitness Business Plan)

Sales Process (or Cycle)
A foundational aspect of Prime Adult Fitness's sales and promotional strategy is its sales process. This is the process the company will use to recruit members and is the process that the in-house staff will follow when people walk into the center and inquire about membership. At times, the process will takes weeks to unfold, if Prime Adult Fitness personnel have multiple contacts with a prospect, and at times the process will unfold in a few minutes, as an employee provides a prospect a tour of the facility and answers questions.

The company has devised specific marketing tactics to support each step in the sales process. These tactics are a work-in-process and will invariably be enhanced and revised as Prime Adult Fitness learns more about the characteristics of its target market.

Stage in Process	Ways Prime Adult Fitness Will Support Each Phase of the Process
1. Prospecting (or sales lead)	• Referrals from current members. • Direct mail (targeting households that meet Prime Adult Fitness's demographic profile). • Partnership with Central Florida Health Food*. • Partnership with Oviedo Doctor's and Surgeon's Medical Practice*. • Downloads from company Web site*. • Responses from the company's radio and print advertisements.

FIGURE 7-3 (continued)

2. The initial contact	• All employees will be provided training in building rapport with prospects.
	• Prospects are provided an information packet about Prime Adult Fitness.
	• Radio and print ads will direct prospects to Prime Adult Fitness's Web site, which contains a short video and other promotional material.
3. Qualifying the lead	• All employees will be trained to assess whether a prospect represents a qualified lead. Prospects that are qualified as good leads will be offered a tour of Prime Adult Fitness's facilities.
	• If a qualified lead does not join initially, he or she will be contacted by phone as a follow-up three days after the visit.
4. Sales presentation	• Qualified leads will be provided a facility tour.
	• Qualified leads will be shown a short film (nine minutes) featuring Prime Adult Fitness's facility and programs and the benefits of fitness for older people.
	• A packet of testimonials will be developed over time and provided to prospects as part of the sales presentation process.
5. Meeting objections and concerns	• Employees will be trained on how to meet the most common and obvious objections and concerns.
	• In regard to price objections, a brochure has been prepared that compares (1) Prime Adult Fitness's initial (one-time) enrollment fee and monthly membership fee to other fitness centers and (2) the cost of joining and belonging to a fitness center as opposed to other forms of recreation and entertainment (i.e., boating, golfing).
	• A similar brochure has been prepared to compare Prime Adult Fitness's amenities to the amenities of other fitness centers.
6. Closing the sale	• All employees will be trained to ask qualified prospects to join.
7. Follow-up	• Each new member will be contacted by phone 30 days after they join as a courtesy to see how things are going. After that, they will be contacted by phone once a year. Each phone call will also be used to ask for names of referrals.
	• Prime Adult Fitness will produce a monthly newsletter that will be mailed to each member.
	• Prime Adult Fitness's staff and employees will be trained to engage members and to thank them for their membership and solicit suggestions for improvement on a continual basis.

*Described under promotional activities.

FIGURE 7-3 (continued)

Promotional Activities

Other promotional activities and tactics are planned as follows:

- *Partnership with Central Florida Health Food.* Prime Adult Fitness has entered into a cobranding relationship with Central Florida Health Food. Central Florida Health Food will periodically place coupons in its shopping bags that provide access to premiums for taking a tour of Prime Adult Fitness's facilities.
- *Partnership with Oviedo Doctor's and Surgeon's Medical Practice.* Prime Adult Fitness has entered into a cobranding relationship with Oviedo Doctor's and Surgeon's medical practice, which will cover a range of activities. For example, the practice will periodically show a film that features Prime Adult Fitness and the benefits of exercise for older people in the waiting room of its facility.
- *Downloads from Web Site.* Prime Adult Fitness will place information on its Web site that can be downloaded. Some of the richest information will require a free registration prior to the download. The names and addresses taken from the registrations will be used as sales leads.
- *Radio Advertising.* Prime Adult Fitness will create radio ads that will be periodically run on WMFE, the public radio station that services Prime Adult Fitness's trade area.
- *Print Advertising.* Select print advertisements will be run.
- *Membership Drive.* Prime Adult Fitness will execute a membership drive in January and February of each year. January, February, and March are the three biggest months for new memberships in fitness clubs.

Annual Marketing Budget

Item	*Budget*
Promotional material (brochures, handouts)	$ 12,000
Radio advertising	$ 16,000
Print advertising	$ 12,000
Web site material, updating, and support (50% of cost of supporting site)	$ 6,000
Updating film portraying Prime Adult Fitness and the benefit of fitness for older people	$ 4,000
Other (including local sponsorships and community support)	$ 6,000
Total	$ 56,000

SALES PROCESS AND PROMOTIONS MIX

A firm's sales process (or cycle) depicts the steps it goes through to identify prospects and close sales. A firm's promotions mix refers to the specific tactics it uses, such as advertising and public relations, to support the sales process and enhance its overall brand. The entirety of this process is typically scrutinized carefully by discerning readers of a business plan. Sales and promotions is one area where hard work and ingenuity can make up for a lack of funds. It is also an area where money can be easily wasted if the sales process is not carefully thought through and executed, and promotional tactics, such as print and media advertising campaigns, are poorly conceived or badly implemented.

This section includes two subsections: sales process and promotions mix.

SALES PROCESS

A firm's **sales process** (or cycle) refers to the steps it goes through to establish relationships with customers and close sales. The process varies by firm, but normally includes the following steps:

1. Prospect for (or gather) sales leads.
2. Make the initial contact.
3. Qualify the lead.
4. Make the sales presentation.
5. Meet objections and concerns.
6. Close the sale.
7. Follow up.

Ostensibly, following a structured process to generate and close sales benefits a firm in two ways. First, it enables a firm to fine-tune its approach to sales and build uniformity into the process. Second, it helps a firm qualify leads, so the firm can spend its time and money pursuing the most likely buyers of the product or service. Most well-managed firms have a formal sales process, similar to the one shown previously, and train their employees accordingly.

Prime Adult Fitness articulates its sales process in its business plan (refer to Figure 7-3), which mirrors the process shown in the preceding list. The business plan also indicates Prime's general plans for supporting each stage in the process. As indicated in the plan, the sales process is an early prototype of what it will most likely become because Prime Adult Fitness will invariably tweak the process as it gains experience in the marketplace. Still, the process shown in the business plan is an important starting point for developing a customized and effective sales process for the company.

PROMOTIONS MIX

A firm's promotions mix includes the specific tactics that a firm uses to communicate with potential customers. The approaches to promotions discussed here include advertising, public relations, and other promotions-related activities.

ADVERTISING

Advertising is making people aware of a product in hopes of persuading them to buy it. The major goals of advertising are to raise customer awareness of a product, explain a product's comparative features and benefits, and create an association between a product and a certain lifestyle (or a certain objective in a business-to-business context). These goals can be accomplished through a number of media, including direct mail, magazines, newspapers, radio, the Internet, television, and billboard advertising. The media used normally depends on a firm's target market. For example, a new piece of industrial equipment typically would be advertised through an industry trade magazine, whereas a consumer product would be advertised through the medium most likely to be viewed by the company's target audience.

Although selective forms of advertising may be appropriate for your business, there are many downsides to conventional forms of advertising, which steers most startups away from advertising on a broad basis. The major weaknesses include the following:

- Low credibility
- The possibility that a high percentage of the people who see the ad will not be interested
- Message clutter (meaning that after hearing or reading so many ads, people simply tune out)
- Relative costliness compared to other forms of promotions
- The perception that advertising is intrusive
- The possibility that a poorly crafted ad runs the risk of irritating the firm's target market

Because of these weaknesses, most startups do not advertise broadly.[6] Instead, they tend to be very frugal and selective in their advertising efforts, such as limiting their print ads to industry trade journals or using highly focused pay-per-click advertising provided by Google, Yahoo!, Ask.com, or another online firm.

Despite the potential downsides, you shouldn't be reluctant to use advertising if it makes sense given your target market, and you can clearly explain its rationale. For example, if you launched a Web site to sell plus-sized clothing for children, the only way to reach a specific audience and achieve the sales volume you desire may be via targeted pay-per-click advertising on the Internet. Many of the better pay-per-click programs, such as Google AdWords (http://adwords.google.com), also helps businesses strictly control the amount of money they spend through the program.

PUBLIC RELATIONS

Public relations refers to efforts to establish and maintain a company's image with the public. The major difference between public relations and advertising is that public relations isn't paid for. As a result, many startups emphasize public relations over advertising because it's free and helps build the firm's credibility. Many techniques fit the definition of public relations. Some of the more common techniques are as follows:

- Press release
- Media coverage
- Articles about the firm in local newspapers, national magazines, or industry press
- Blogging
- Monthly newsletter
- Civic, social, and community involvement

In most cases, firms believe that generating favorable public relations about their company is better than advertising because it is more grassroots and doesn't seem to be as self-serving. The key to getting public relations that's created by others, such as a newspaper or magazine article written about your company, is to create a human-interest story that's associated with your firm. It also helps to be proactive in regard to speaking out on behalf of your industry and talking to trade groups and civic groups about your industry or area of expertise.

Lisa Druxman, the founder of Stroller Strides (http://www.strollerstrides .com), a franchise organization for new mothers, provides an example of how these efforts come together to create positive public relations for a firm. Stroller Strides is a concept that Druxman created to get herself back in shape after she had her first baby. It is an organized workout class where women push strollers, power-walk, and exercise outdoors to meet their fitness goals and socialize with other new mothers. Prior to starting Stroller Strides, Druxman was the general manager of a health club. Druxman's story is a classic illustration of how public relations works and the potential payoffs involved:

> When I (was) the general manager at the health club, I would regularly go on the news promoting new workouts. One day the TV station called me and asked, "Would you mind coming in with your baby and giving (some) tips on how to get back in shape?" So I did, and I promoted my class as if it were this big business—I gave out my home e-mail and personal cell phone number. By the time I got home from the station, I had 75 calls and e-mails from all over San Diego from people who were interested in taking my class. I had my grand opening class 3 weeks after that, with 40 people there and more news coverage.[7]

The key to Druxman's success, in this instance, was that she was able to tell her story through an unbiased third party, the TV program. Her story was compelling enough that it drew more free publicity, in the form of news coverage of her grand opening. Many startups seek similar types of public relations through stories in local newspapers or business journals or through national publications such as *Inc.* or *Business 2.0*. The key to getting this type of coverage is to have an interesting story to tell, rather than simply extolling the value of your product or service. If you think your company has the potential to generate good public relations, you should make that part of your promotions strategy.

OTHER PROMOTIONS-RELATED ACTIVITIES

Many other activities can help a firm promote and sell its products. Some firms, for example, give away free sample or trial memberships as a way of exposing potential customers to their product or service. SmugMug, for example, gives away a free 14-day trial to its photo-sharing service, with a conversation rate in excess of 80 percent. Many food companies distribute free samples in grocery stores and discount centers. Red Bull (http://www.redbull.com), the highly successful energy drink company, created interest in its product by initially offering free samples through sports clubs and other places in which athletes congregated.

BUSINESS PLAN INSIGHT

Selling Benefits Rather Than Features

Many startups make the mistake of promoting the features rather than the benefits of their product or service. A promotional strategy that focuses on the features of a product, such as its technical merits, is usually much less effective than a campaign focusing on the merits of what the product can do. Consider an ad for Prime Adult Fitness that reads something like this, "Our fitness center, which is just for adults, has 16 exercises classes, a pool that is available for water aerobics and open swims, and a full spa and massage service." These are all features, and while features are nice, they typically don't entice someone to join a health club. A better way for Prime Adult Fitness to promote itself would be to say, "Our fitness center, which is just for adults, will feature classes and exercise equipment that help adults maintain their fitness, avoid the onset of certain alignment, and lead healthier lives." This statement focuses on benefits by telling prospects how joining Prime Adult Fitness will enhance their lives.

As a general rule of thumb, it's more effective to tote the benefits of a product or service rather than the features.

This type of initiative is often pursued to try to create "buzz" or word-of-mouth advertising for a product or service. Creating **buzz** means creating awareness and a sense of anticipation about a company and its offerings. This process can start during feasibility analysis, when a company shows its concept statement or product prototype to prospective buyers or industry experts. Unless a company wants all activities kept secret (to preserve its proprietary technology or its first-mover advantage), the goal is to get people talking about the company and the exciting new product or service. You should investigate the many techniques for creating buzz or word-of-mouth marketing at a low cost.[8]

One issue that is particularly important in executing a promotions plan is to focus on the benefits of a product or service rather than the features. The importance of this issue is explained in the Business Plan Insights box.

In most cases, putting together a specific budget for promotional activities is helpful. Prime Adult Fitness includes a promotional budget in its business plan as shown earlier in Figure 7-3.

The next section of this portion of the business plan focuses on distribution.

DISTRIBUTION AND SALES

Distribution encompasses all the activities that move a firm's product from its place of origin to the consumer. For a company like Prime Adult Fitness, distribution is not a major issue because it's a service business that provides for its own sales functions. As a result, the company relies on working through the sales process and on promotional activities to gain memberships to its fitness center—so there is no separate distribution and sales section in this business plan. The landscape is much different for other companies. When Laura Udall first invented the ZUCA (back-pack on wheels), she had to decide how the product would be distributed and sold. There were many choices. ZUCA could hire and field its own sales force, or work through intermediaries, such as wholesalers, distributors, or manufacturing repre-sentatives, as will be explained in more detail later in this chapter.

This section of your business plan should clearly identify your distribution and sales plan, in terms of who will make the sales. To assist you with thinking through these issues, this part of the chapter includes two sections: distribution and sales alternatives, and sales strategy and related issues.

DISTRIBUTION AND SALES ALTERNATIVES

The first step in determining a distribution and sales strategy, for a firm that is more complex that Prime Adult Fitness on this dimension, is to sort through the choices. For example, imagine you are starting a firm that sells an electronics product to consumers. You could opt to field a sales force that approaches com-panies such as Circuit City and Best Buy to persuade them to carry your product. You could also sell direct to consumers without the need for salespeople, through catalogue or Internet sales. Another option is to sell through an intermediary, such as a distributor, a wholesaler, or a manufacturer's representative. If you de-cided to go this route, your intermediary would call on Circuit City and Best Buy to try to persuade them to carry your product on your behalf.

A similar set of choices would apply if you were selling a service rather than an electronics product. Hotels, for example, sell their services (typically rooms) directly through their Web sites and telephone reservation services, and also through intermediaries, such as travel agents, tour operators, airlines, and so forth. For ex-ample, if you were planning a trip to Disney World in Orlando, Florida, you could book your flight, rental car, and hotel through Orbitz (http://www.orbitz.com), Travelocity (http://www.travelocity.com), or many other similar services. In this instance, Orbitz and the others are acting as intermediaries for the service providers.

The key to making the right choices among these alternatives is to think care-fully first about where people in your target market shop, and then about the most effective and economical ways to get your products some shelf space in those outlets. You also need to think about the operational ramifications of your choices. Although it might sound good to get your product placed in Wal-Mart or Costco from the outset, few startups are prepared to ramp up production fast enough to satisfy these types of retailers. In addition, you need to carefully weigh the choice of retail outlets and other resellers (such as Orbitz and Travelocity) with your brand and the image you want to convey to your target market.

Timbuk2 (http://www.timbuk2.com), a company that makes urban shoulder bags, provides an example of the types of dilemmas companies face as the result of the intersection of these factors. In early 2003, the company was on the top of the world because it had just inked a deal with CompUSA (http://www.compusa.com)

to carry its bags. Three months later, Timbuk2 backed out of the deal. Why? Although sales were booming, it was being squeezed by CompUSA's thin margins and high volume demand. In addition, Mike Dwight, Timbuk2's CEO, became increasingly concerned that selling through a mainstream retailer like CompUSA would change the way consumers viewed the company. He wanted to see his company increase sales but didn't want it to lose its quirkiness and unique appeal either. In refocusing the company, and backing out of the CompUSA deal, he compared Timbuk2 to Coach (http://www.coach.com), which is a billion-dollar company, but sells primarily through specialty stores. Specialty stores, such as the Sharper Image and upscale boutiques, appeal to consumers who prioritize quality and brand image over price. This attribute of specialty stores allows vendors such as Timbuk2 to earn higher margins than they would at a big box retailer such as CompUSA, which compensates for the lower-volume sales. Selling simultaneously through specialty stores and big-box retailers is difficult for a firm such as Timbuk2. The larger retailers invariably insist on a lower price point than the specialty retailer, which forces the vendor to either undercut the sales price of the specialty retailers or enhance the product sold through the specialty retailer in some way to increase the price.[9]

This overall discussion indicates that selecting the manner to distribute and sell a product or service is not a trivial issue. Instead, this critical issue lies at the heart of a firm's overall marketing plan and its ability to effectively reach its target market, which should be clearly spelled out in the business plan.

SALES STRATEGY AND RELATED ISSUES

The description of your distribution and sales plan should make it clear whether you plan to field your own sales force. If you do decide to employ sales personnel, you should describe how many salespeople you will initially need, how their numbers will be ramped up as your company grows, and how they will be compensated. You will probably need to talk to industry experts and study industry trade journals and reports to make these calls. You'll also rely heavily on the sales projections for your firm created in Chapter 6 to assess your needs.

If you plan to distribute your products through intermediaries, you should briefly explain how the intermediaries will be chosen, and the ways in which the intermediaries will interface with the sales outlets in your industry. In most cases, you will have to support your distributors and other intermediaries with training, technical support, shipping, point-of-sale advertising material, and other forms of sales support. If any out-of-the ordinary levels of support apply in your case, they should be identified.

An exciting element of distribution and sales strategy for new firms is that the conventional forms of distribution and sales don't always have to be followed. One way a new firm can innovate and provide unique value in the marketplace is via distribution and sales. For example, Dell (http://www.dell.com) revolutionized the computer industry by deciding to sell directly to the consumer, first over the phone and later via the Internet, rather than through retail stores, which was the conventional method for selling computers in 1984 when Dell was founded. Similarly, IKEA (http://www.ikea.com), the Swedish furniture company, introduced a new concept in the furniture industry by opening retail outlets that are essentially display stores, and after an item is selected, the purchaser is directed to a loading dock where a boxed and unassembled version of the item is provided. Both of these companies have succeeded, in part, because their approach to distribution and sales were novel and fit their respective target markets. Dell's target market is the business customer who doesn't need help from a salesperson in a retail store to buy a computer and who are glad to avoid a trip to the store. IKEA's target market is singles and young families who don't mind trading off some home assembly work for a lower price.

Again, if any of these special circumstances apply in regard to your distribution and sales strategy, they should be discussed in this portion of your business plan.

Chapter Summary

1. The best way to describe a company's marketing plan is to start by articulating marketing strategy, positioning, and points of differentiation, and then talk about how these overall aspects of the plan will be supported by price, promotional mix and sales process, and distribution strategy. If you haven't discussed your product yet, it should be talked about here.

2. There are two things to be particularly mindful of as you write the marketing section of your business plan. First, all the elements of a firm's marketing plan should be developed with the customer plainly in mind. Second, you must detail exactly who will sell your product or service.

3. This marketing section of the business plan contains four subsections: overall marketing strategy, pricing strategy, sales process and promotions mix, and distribution and sales.

4. A firm's marketing strategy is its approach to marketing products or services stated in broad terms, which forms the basis of all of its marketing-related activities.

5. After selecting a target market, the next step is for a firm to select a "position" in the market. Position is concerned with how a firm is situated relative to its rivals. In a sense, a position is a part of the market or a specific target market that a firm is claiming for its own.

6. Price is an important issue because it determines how much money a company can earn. The price a company charges for its products also sends a clear message to its target customers.

7. The two methods for determining the price of a product or service are cost-based pricing and value-based pricing. In cost-based pricing, the list price is determined by adding a markup percentage to a product's cost. In value-based pricing, the list price is determined by estimating what consumers are willing to pay for a product and then backing off a bit to provide a cushion. Most experts recommend value-based pricing because it hinges on the perceived value of a

product or service rather than cost plus markup, which is a formula that ignores the customer.

8. A firm's sales process (or cycle) refers to the steps it goes through to establish relationships with customers and to close sales.

9. Advertising is making people aware of a product in hopes of persuading them to buy it. The major difference between public relations and advertising is that public relations isn't paid for. As a result, many startups emphasize public relations over advertising because it's free and helps build the firm's credibility.

10. One issue that is particularly important in executing a promotions plan is to focus on the benefits of a product or service rather than the features.

11. Distribution encompasses all the activities that move a firm's product from its place of origin to the consumer.

Review Questions

1. Describe the difference between the market analysis section of a business plan and the marketing section.
2. Why is it important for the marketing plan to be developed with the customer plainly in mind?
3. What is a company's marketing strategy, and why is it important?
4. What is meant by a company's "positioning" strategy?
5. What is the purpose of a product attribute map?
6. Describe the difference between cost-based pricing and value-based pricing.
7. What is the price-quality attribution?
8. Describe the differences between advertising and public relations? Which of the two alternatives do startups tend to prefer?
9. Provide several examples of public relations strategies.
10. Describe how firms should approach the topic of distribution and sales.

Application Questions

1. Spend some time looking at ZUCA's Web site (http://www.zuca.com). Comment on each element of ZUCA's marketing plan (product, price, promotion, and distribution and sales). On a scale of 1 to 10 (10 is high), rate the strength of ZUCA's overall marketing plan. Justify your rating.

2. Kathy has developed a new type of smoke detector that is much more sensitive than previous generations of smoke detectors and is particularly geared to people who live in small spaces, such as apartments or dorm rooms. Kathy doesn't know how to price this product. Describe to Kathy the two most common methods of pricing, and give her your recommendation for how to price the product.

3. Study the Web site of Velocity Sports Performance (http://www.velocitysp .com), a franchise organization that helps athletes in every sport, at all ages

and skill levels, realize their athletic potential. Make a list of the types of public relations activities that the owners of Velocity Sports Performance and their franchisees could engage in to promote the company.

4. Beth Andrews has developed a new line of women's clothing that has created some positive buzz among friends and some business stores in her local community. When asked by a reporter, "Where do you plan to sell your clothing?" Beth said, "Hopefully everywhere—Costco, Wal-Mart, Sacks, Nordstroms, the Internet, and specialty clothing boutiques." Write a critique of Beth's distribution and sales strategy. Provide her recommendations for a more appropriate distribution and sales strategy.

5. Think of a company, other than Dell or IKEA, which has innovated in a very meaningful way in regard to how it distributes and sells its product or service. Write a short critique of how this innovative distribution or sales strategy has contributed to the company's success.

Endnotes

1. N. Capon, *The Marketing Mavens* (New York: Crown Business, 2007), 131.
2. "Laura Udall" (Mom Inventor's Inc.). http://www.mominventors.com (June 25, 2007).
3. Dave Roberts, CEO of PopCap Games (nPost). http://www.npost.com (June 26, 2007).
4. M.J. Silverstein, *Treasure Hunt* (New York: Portfolio, 2006).
5. Don MacAskill, CEO of SmugMug (nPost). http://www.npost.com (June 27, 2007).
6. R. A. Nykiel, *Marketing Your Business: A Guide to Developing a Strategic Marketing Plan* (New York: Best Business Books, 2003).
7. Ladies Who Launch homepage, http://www.ladieswholaunch.com (June 27, 2007).
8. E. Rosen, *The Anatomy of Buzz* (New York: Doubleday, 2000).
9. A. Tilin, "Bagging the Right Customers," *Business 2.0,* May 25, 2005, 56–57.

CHAPTER 8

MANAGEMENT TEAM AND COMPANY STRUCTURE

INTRODUCTION

This pivotal chapter describes a startup's management team and company structure. Many investors and others who read business plans look first at the executive summary, and then go directly to the management team section to assess the strength of the people starting the firm. This practice stems from the prevalent belief that unless a proposed new venture has a strong management team, little else matters. Affirming this sentiment, Joel Kurtzman, the author and business consultant introduced in Chapter 6, said:

> In my own view, business is about people first and everything else second. Strategies, processes, structures, and systems are only as good as the people implementing them. Good ideas never succeed on their own.[1]

This view, which is widespread in startup circles, illustrates the importance of carefully constructing the management team section of the business plan, particularly for startups that are seeking funding. Investors read more business plans with interesting ideas and exciting markets than they are able to finance. As a result, it's often not the idea or market that wins funding among competing plans, but the perception that one management team is better prepared to execute their idea than the others.

In their evaluation of management teams, investors and others tend to evaluate management teams in the context of the type of business they're proposing

TABLE 8-1 Combinations of Ideas and Management Teams		
	Untested Management Team	*Tested Management Team*
Untested Idea	1	1
Tested Idea	3	4

Key:

1. Untested idea, untested management team. Untested ideas are exciting, though risky. In this case, the management team will need to build a convincing case that it's up to the challenge of bringing an untested idea to market.

2. Untested idea, tested management team. This is the strongest combination. Untested ideas, which typically have the largest upside potential, are best launched by a tested management team.

3. Tested idea, untested management team. This is potentially the weakest combination. Tested ideas normally compete in crowded fields with stiff combination. This is a high-risk environment for an untested management team.

4. Tested idea, tested management team. This is an okay combination, but typically will not produce impressive returns. Tested ideas tend to compete in crowded markets with stiff competition. In this environment, even a tested team may produce only average returns.

and the type of funding or financing they're seeking. The 2 × 2 matrix shown in Table 8-1 illustrates this point. The matrix shows four types of new ventures, defined by whether the initial management team is untested or tested and by whether the business idea is tested or untested. As shown, the best candidates for investment reside in Box 2—untested idea and tested management team. In this instance, the tested management team must prove that it is tested (in this portion of the business plan) to have the best chance of attracting investment dollars. Untested ideas typically have more upside potential because they do not reside in crowded markets. Firms that occupy the other boxes are less likely to obtain funding, at least initially, but it depends on the investor or the lender. Many bankers, for example, confine their startup investments to tested ideas and tested management teams to minimize the risk in their loans.

This part of the business plan is divided into five sections: Management Team, Board of Directors, Board of Advisors, Other Professionals, and Company Structure. The sections should be crisp and to the point, and weighty material, such as the resumes of the key employees, should be placed in an appendix to the entire plan. There are two issues that you should be particularly sensitive to as you write these sections of the plan.

First, the way your management team is assembled provides an indication of the extent to which you're open to advice and you're able to generate enthusiasm for your firm. For example, along with a description of the management team, Prime Adult Fitness's business plan shows that it already has a 5-member board of directors, a 4-member general advisory board, and a 10-member customer advisory board. Prime also reports that it has received advice from several unpaid consultants. These types of efforts are impressive. They show that the people behind Prime Adult Fitness are open to advice, are willing to share power, and are able to garner support for their business idea. The initiatives may also cause a reader of their business plan to think, "If these people are able to fill three volunteer boards in a short period of time, I bet they'll have no trouble selling their business concept to paying customers."

The second thing to be sensitive to as you write the management team section of your business plan is to clearly describe how the team will evolve. Almost all new ventures have gaps in their management teams at the business plan stage. That's normal. What's important is to describe where the gaps are and how they'll be filled. In addition, you want to avoid the impression that you're naive or are unsure about the order in which to fill the gaps. For example, during the various stages of product development, a company such as H20Audio (http://www.h20audio.com), the maker of waterproof housing for the Apple iPod, needs expertise in marketing and sales to make sure the product it's developing is saleable after it's produced. In the context of this example, for a startup to say that a marketing and sales person will be hired after the product is developed shows a lack of understanding of the proper upfront role of marketing input. If the startup can't afford to hire a marketing person during its product development stage, that's understandable, but evidence should then be provided that shows where the firm is getting access to marketing expertise. Similarly, if a company is proposing a product that it will manufacture but has no manufacturing expertise on its management team, that's a serious concern. Leaving issues like these unaddressed or unresolved gives the impression that the founders of the firm don't really know what they're doing and erodes the credibility of a business plan.

Now, let's look at each individual section of the management team and company structure of a business plan.

MANAGEMENT TEAM

The management team of a new firm typically consists of the founder or founders and a handful of key management personnel. Early stage firms may have only the founder or founders and plans to add additional personnel. The description of a firm's management team should be largely factual but should be presented in a way that makes it easy to visualize where the firm is today and where it plans to be in the foreseeable future in regard to key management team personnel.

The introduction to this section should cover the basics. Indicate the name or names of the founders, how many employees the company has, where the major gaps are, and how quickly the company will be adding personnel. Keep the introduction brief—you'll have chances to fill in the details later.

The three major parts to this section are management team personnel, management team ownership and compensation, and common mistakes to avoid. This section of Prime Adult Fitness's business plan is shown in Figure 8-1.

FIGURE 8-1 Management Team and Company Structure (Prime Adult Fitness Business Plan)

Introduction

Prime Adult Fitness's management philosophy focuses on integrity, teamwork, enthusiasm, and providing a stimulating environment for both the company's employees and its members. Employees will be selected based on their qualifications for the job and their commitment to serving the physical and mental health needs of our 50+-year-old members.

Management Team

Jeremy Ryan, Cofounder and CEO, Age 46

Responsible for strategy formulation and the overall success of the company. Jeremy started a successful fitness franchise in South Florida and grew it to 38 units in 3 years before selling to a larger company. Prior to that, he spent 11 years as VP of operations and 3 years as VP of sales for a privately held Miami fitness center that grew to 5,500 members. Jeremy has an MBA from Miami University and has published more than 30 articles in fitness trade journals and national magazines regarding the fitness needs of older people. Jeremy's passion for fitness is drawn largely from his father who, after surviving a heart attack at age 49, pledged to improve his quality of life by joining a fitness center and exercising regularly. Today, Jeremy's father is an active 73-year-old retiree.

Elizabeth Sims, Cofounder and CFO, Age 49

Responsible for raising capital and for the financial management of the company. Elizabeth served as the CFO of Jeremy Ryan's fitness franchise in South Florida and left the company when it was sold. Prior to that, Elizabeth, who is a CPA, spent 9 years with a big 5 accounting company, and 10 years as a cost accountant for a Fortune 500 company. While with the big 5 accounting company, she supervised the accounting practices of 3 publicly traded fitness franchises and 11 privately owned fitness chains.

Sarah Peterson, COO, Age 51

Responsible for the day-to-day operations of the company, the maintenance of the company's facilities, and the acquisition and installation of new equipment. Sarah has 9 years of experience as the COO of a 250-bed nursing home and 17 years as a public school teacher and principal. Sarah is the cofounder of a nonprofit organization named *Healthy After 50*, which disseminates information to aged 50+ individuals about nutrition, physical fitness, and mental health. Sarah has a master's degree in education from the University of Virginia.

Jill Campbell, Program Manager, Age 52

Responsible for all the fitness and related classes that will be offered by the company. Jill is an exercise physiologist and has spent the past 12 years practicing in a private wellness/exercise center in Jacksonville, FL. Prior to that, she was a registered nurse, assigned to the trauma center of an urban hospital. Jill has a master's degree in exercise physiology from the University of Missouri and a nursing degree from Creighton University in Omaha, Nebraska.

Alex Jackson, Marketing and Sales, Age 57

Responsible for marketing, sales, and membership growth for the company. Alex has 11 years experience as a senior marketing executive for a major fitness machine manufacturer, where he won several "salesperson of the year" awards. Prior to that, he spent 25 years in the U.S. Marine Corps (11 years as a recruiter). Alex is a world-class triathlete for his age group.

Skill Profile and Gaps in Management Team

The following skill profile depicts the most important skills required at the top management team level of the company and where the gaps exist.

FIGURE 8-1   (continued)

	Executive Leadership	Finance	Operations	Marketing & Sales	HR/Recruiting	Member Care & Relations	Program Management	Information Systems	Accounting
Jeremy Ryan	X								
Elizabeth Sims		X							X
Sarah Peterson			X					X	
Jill Campbell							X		
Alex Jackson				X					
Gap 1					O				
Gap 2						O			

X = position filled, O = position vacant

Summary: Two significant gaps exist in the management team: the director of HR/Recruiting and the director of Member Care and Relations. Both positions will be recruited and filled within six months. Currently, the HR/Recruiting position is being filled on a volunteer basis by Timothy Kemp, a Prime Adult Fitness board member and angel investor. The Member Care and Relations position is not currently open. It will become a functioning position when Prime Adult Fitness begins actively recruiting members.

Ownership and Compensation

Name	Position/Affiliation	Base Compensation	Percent Ownership in Company	Personal Investment in Company
Jeremy Ryan	Cofounder and CEO	$68,500	20.0%	$100,000
Elizabeth Sims	Co-founder and CFO	$62,000	20.0%	$100,000
Sarah Peterson	Chief Operations Officer	$60,000	10.0%	$50,000
Jill Campbell	Program Manager	$60,000	7.5%	$37,500
Alex Jackson	Marketing and Sales	$58,500	7.5%	$37,500
Timothy Kemp	Board Member and Angel Investor	N/A	15.0%	$175,000
Options Pool			20.0%	
Total		$309,000	100.0%	$500,000

MANAGEMENT TEAM PERSONNEL

A brief profile of each member of the management team should be provided, starting with the founder or founders of the firm. Each profile should include the following information:

- Title of the position.
- Duties and responsibility of the position. This item should explain specifically what the individual will do and how the individual's work will contribute to the development of the firm.
- Previous industry and related experience. This item should explain who the individual has worked for and how the individual's past experiences relate to the new firm.
- Previous successes. This item should highlight the individual's past successes and accomplishments, particularly as they relate to the challenges of helping launch a new firm. For example, has the individual been involved in previous startups, launched divisions within larger firms, spearheaded successful teams and projects, and so forth.
- Education background.

Although they should be kept brief, the profiles should illustrate why each individual is qualified and will uniquely contribute to the success of the firm. Certain attributes of a management team should also be highlighted if they apply in your case. Investors and others tend to prefer team members who've worked together before. The thinking here is that if people have worked together before and have decided to partner to start a new firm, it usually means that they get along personally and trust one another.[2] This scenario helps relieve a persistent worry—that the initial managers of a firm won't get along with one another. In Prime Adult Fitness's business plan, Elizabeth Sims' short bio indicates that she worked with Jeremy Ryan, Prime Adult Fitness's CEO, in his previous venture. In addition, the skills and ability of the members of the team should complement one another rather than reinforce a single skill or competency. Many companies initially develop around a single competency, such as writing software code, producing music, managing logistics, and so on. This factor often defines the nature of the initial management team, and the management team gets stacked with people from the same discipline. A startup that resists this tendency and develops a more well-rounded management team from the beginning has a leg up on others. It's also appropriate to include personal information about the members of the management team, if it's pertinent. For example, Jeremy Ryan's bio indicates that his passion for fitness is drawn largely from his father who, after suffering a heart attack at the age of 49, pledged to improve his quality of life by joining a fitness center and exercising regularly.

The next step in describing the management team is to identify the gaps that exist. A good way to do this, and simultaneously depict the skills that exist in the initial team, is to develop a management team skill profile. This is what Prime Adult Fitness did, as depicted in its business plan shown earlier in Figure 8-1. A management team skill profile is a grid that lists the major skills needed in a firm on the horizontal axis (marketing, finance, manufacturing, IT, etc.) and the current members of the management team on the vertical axis. The grid is completed by indicating which skills are satisfied by each management team member. The skills with no coverage represent gaps in the management team. The best way to draw attention to the gaps is to list under the current management team member's names Gap 1, Gap 2, Gap 3, and so forth, depending on the number of gaps that exist. This procedure illustrated the skills or competencies that currently have no coverage and roughly the number of people who need to be hired. You can then briefly discuss the nature of the gaps and your plans for rectifying them. Some of the gaps may currently be filled through access to expertise other than a full-time employee. For example, a particular gap may be filled by an advisory team member, a part-time nonmanagement employee, or an outsource provided. Simply explain how you are dealing with each of these individual situations. In Prime Adult Fitness's case, its gap in HR/Recruiting is currently being filled by Timothy Kemp, one of its board members and investors, as shown in Figure 8-1.

MANAGEMENT TEAM OWNERSHIP AND COMPENSATION

You must also fully disclose the ownership structure of the new venture and the compensation of the members of the management team. This should be done in a table format because it's easier to quickly assess the information. The owners of the firm may include management team members and outside investors. Prime Adult Fitness, as show in Figure 8-1, listed each owners, their percent ownership in the company, and their base compensation, if they are employed by the firm. The ownership percentages may not always add up to 100 percent, if the firm has established an options pool for future hires, as in the case with Prime Adult Fitness. An **options pool** is an inventory of company stock, usually in the neighborhood of 15 percent to 20 percent of the total stock, which is set aside for future employees. Having an options pool is particularly important if a firm is looking for investors. Attracting high-quality people to a startup often necessitates the granting of stock options as an incentive form of compensation. Investors know this and will be reassured if the owners of the firm also realize this and have made provisions to make stock options available to future key hires.

Finally, it should be clear, in the table or in another part of this section, how the money for the firm has been raised so far. As explained earlier in this book, most investors like to see that the founders, at a minimum, have "skin in the game," meaning they have invested their own money. If the founders don't have enough confidence in the venture to invest their own money, why should anyone else invest?

COMMON MISTAKES TO AVOID

There is a common set of mistakes to avoid when putting together your initial management team and writing this section of the business plan. These mistakes raise red flags and undermine the credibility of your plan. The most common mistakes are as follows:

• Placing unqualified friends or family members in key management positions
• Assuming that previous success in other industries automatically translates to your industry
• Presenting a "one-man team" philosophy—meaning that one person (or a small group of people) is wearing all hats with no plans to bolster the team
• Hiring top managers without sharing ownership in the firm
• Not disclosing management team skill or competency gaps
• Vague or unclear plans for filling the skill or competency gaps that are disclosed or clearly exist

If any of these items are present in your management team and your business plan, you should review them to contemplate if they should be revised or corrected.

The next section of the plan focuses on the role of a new firm's board of directors in regard to its management team. This section of Prime Adult Fitness's business plan is shown in Figure 8-2.

FIGURE 8-2   Board of Directors (Prime Adult Fitness Business Plan)

Prime Adult Fitness's Board of Directors was formed when the company was incorporated. All board members serve on a volunteer basis. There are three outside directors and two inside directors. There are no plans to compensate board members. All of the board members live in Central Florida. The board meets monthly. Individual board members interact with Prime Adult Fitness's top management team frequently.

Outside Directors

Dr. Kenneth Jamison, Family Practice Physician, Age 62

Dr. Jamison practices medicine in Oviedo, Florida, the home of Prime Adult Fitness, and is an outspoken advocate of fitness and preventive health care for people 50 years old and older. Dr. Jamison received his MD from Duke University and is board certified in family practice medicine. Dr. Jamison writes a widely read column for a local paper on health-related issues.

Martha Ford, Attorney, Age 52

Ms. Ford is a partner in the law company Campbell, Campbell & Ford. She specializes in providing legal advice to startups and small businesses. Ms. Ford received her law degree from the University of Iowa.

Timothy Kemp, Retired Entrepreneur, Angel Investor, Age 64

Mr. Kemp is a retired entrepreneur, having started and sold five successful companies. He has won several "entrepreneur of the year" awards. Mr. Kemp's last startup, K9 Medical Services, was purchased by a large pharmaceutical company and is still in business under its original name.

Inside Directors

Jeremy Ryan, Cofounder and CEO, Prime Adult Fitness

Elizabeth Sims, Cofounder and CFO, Prime Adult Fitness

BOARD OF DIRECTORS

The importance of this section varies by plan. If a new venture organizes as a corporation, it is legally required to have a board of directors. A **board of directors** is a panel of individuals elected by a corporation's shareholders to oversee the management of the firm. In a very early stage firm, or a small firm, the board may be restricted to the principles running the firm. In these instances, the board serves little more than a legal function. In other instances, however, the board plays an active role in the management and oversight of the firm.

If your firm has a board of directors, and it plays an active role in the management of your firm, it should be included as part of your management team. Technically, a board of directors has three responsibilities: (1) appoint the firm's officers, (2) declare dividends, and (3) oversee the affairs of the corporation. The optimal size of a board of directors for a startup is three to five people.[3] A board is typically made up of both inside and outside members. An **inside director** is a person who is also an officer of the firm. An **outside director** is someone who is not employed by the firm. A three-member board of directors normally consists of one inside director and two outside directors, and a five-member board has two inside directors and three outside directors. A list of the most desirable qualities in a board of directors and the most desirable qualities in individual board members is provided in Table 8-2.

TABLE 8-2   Attributes of an Effective Board of Directors

- Strong communication with the CEO
- Customer-focused point of view
- Complementary mix of talents
- Decisiveness
- Mutual respect and regard for each other and the top managers of the firm
- Ability and willingness to stand up to the CEO and the top managers of the firm
- Ability to focus
- Strong ethics

Attributes of Strong Board Members
- Strong personal and professional networks
- Willingness to make personal introductions on behalf of the firm
- Emotional stability
- Strong interpersonal communication skills
- Pattern recognition skills
- Ability to partner
- Investment and operating experience
- Ability and willingness to mentor the CEO and top managers of the firm

---

Source: Adapted from D. Jaffe and P. Levensohn, "After the Term Sheet: How Venture Boards Influence the Success or Failure of Technology Companies," White paper, Levensohn Venture Partners (http://www.levp.com), November, 2003.

If you include this section in your plan, you should list your board members and provide a very brief bio for each member. You don't need to provide a separate bio for the inside directors (i.e., members of the management team) who were discussed earlier. An active board of directors provides guidance and lends legitimacy to a firm. These attributes are discussed next.

PROVIDE GUIDANCE

Although a board of directors has formal oversight responsibilities, its most useful role is to provide guidance and support to the managers of the firm. Many well-intended entrepreneurs and management teams simply "don't know what they don't know," which often results in missteps early in the life of a startup. Experienced board members often see these potential missteps before they occur and help management teams avoid them. Many CEOs interact with their board members frequently and obtain important input. The key to making this happen is to select board members with needed skills and useful experiences who are willing to give advice and ask insightful and probing questions. The extent to which an effective board can help shape a firm and provide it a competitive advantage in the marketplace is expressed by Ram Charan, an expert on the role of boards of directors in corporations:

> They (effective boards) listen, probe, debate, and become engaged in the company's most pressing issues. Directors share their expertise and wisdom as a matter of course. As they do, management and the board learn together, a collective wisdom emerges, and managerial judgment improves. The on-site coaching and consulting expand the mental capacity of the CEO and the top management team and give the company a competitive edge out there in the marketplace.[4]

Boards can also help fill competency gaps at the time a company is started and on an ongoing basis. It's not uncommon for a company to shift the emphasis of its board to match its stage of development. For example, startups that are focused primarily on product development at the outset may include several product development experts on their board and replace these individuals with marketing specialists when their product comes to market. If a firm gets investment capital, the investor will normally occupy a seat on its board of directors. Investors do this to not only protect their investment but also to assume a formal role in lending advice and assistance to the firm.

LEND LEGITIMACY

Providing legitimacy for a firm is another important function of a board of directors. Well-known and respected board members bring instant credibility to the firm. For example, just imagine the positive buzz a firm could generate if it could say that Mark Cuban, the chairman of HDNet (an HDTV cable network) and the owner of the Dallas Mavericks, joined its board. This phenomenon is referred to as **signaling.** Presumably, a high-quality individual would be reluctant to serve on the board of a low-quality firm because that would put his or her reputation at risk. So when a high-quality individual does agree to serve on a board of a new firm, the individual is in essence "signaling" that the company has the potential to be successful.[5]

Achieving legitimacy through high-quality board members can result in other positive outcomes. Investors and others like to see management teams, including the board of directors, that have people with enough clout to get their foot in the door with potential suppliers and customers. Board members are also often instrumental in helping young firms arrange financing or funding.

FIGURE 8-3   Board of Advisors (Prime Adult Fitness Business Plan)

Prime Adult Fitness has two active boards of advisors. The general advisory board consists of 4 members, and the customer advisory board consists of 10 members.

General Advisory Board

Dr. Jason Steele, Sports Medicine Specialist, Age 37

Dr. Steele is a sports medicine specialist practicing at a local clinic. He has a passion for the care of older people and attracts many active older adults to his practice. Dr. Steel's passion for the care of older adults stems partially from personal experience. He and his wife are the primary caregivers to his maternal grandfather and his wife's paternal grandmother.

Primary role: To provide medical advice on the selection of exercise equipment and classes, and to provide training to Prime Adult Fitness's instructors regarding how to help older people (particularly those who have not been exercising) establish an appropriate and safe exercise regime.

Cynthia Rains, Public School Teacher, Age 66

Ms. Rains is a lifelong resident of Central Florida and has taught at Oviedo High School for 26 years. She is active and has belonged to fitness clubs for many years.

Primary role: To provide a layperson's advice on the selection of exercise equipment and classes, and to provide tours, on a volunteer basis, of Prime Adult Fitness's facility.

Rosa Torres, Clinical Psychologist, Age 46

Ms. Torres is a clinical psychologist, having spent the last 10 years of her career working in the wellness field for older adults. Her particular specialty is neurobics, which is a relatively new field that focuses on mental exercise. Prime Adult Fitness will have several classes focused on neurobics and will feature a neurobics center in its facility.

Primary role: To help shape Prime Adult's Fitness's approach to neurobics.

Bradley Manning, Retired Fundraiser, Age 66

Mr. Manning spent the majority of his professional life in various fundraising roles, primarily for nonprofit organizations.

Primary role: To provide advice for building membership.

Customer Advisory Board

Prime Adult Fitness maintains a 10-member customer advisory board. The board members participate in focus groups, serve on committees that are helping shape the activities of the company, and participate in related activities. Board members serve on a volunteer basis for a one-year term.

These guidance and legitimacy issues should be woven into the short descriptions of the board members provided in the business plan, as appropriate. A final point is that the majority of firms will have an active board of directors at some point if they grow to any appreciable size. As a result, if a company currently doesn't have a board of directors, it may be prudent for the business plan to indicate that it anticipates having a board of directors at some point in the future and will make the board part of its overall management team.

The next section focuses on the Board of Advisors, a source of counsel and advice that all firms, regardless of size, can take advantage of. This section of Prime Adult Fitness's business plan is shown in Figure 8-3.

BOARD OF ADVISORS

A **board of advisors** is a panel of experts asked by a firm's managers to provide counsel and advice on an ongoing basis. Unlike a board of directors, a board of advisors possesses no legal responsibility for the firm and gives nonbinding advice.[6] As a result, many people are more willing to serve on a company's board of advisors than on its board of directors because it requires less time and no legal liability is involved. A board of advisors can be established for general purposes or can be set up to address a specific issue or need. For example, some startups set up customer advisory boards shortly after they are founded to help them fine-tune their initial offerings. Prime Adult Fitness, as noted earlier, has a 10-member customer advisory board to help select exercise equipment and decide on the schedule of fitness classes and activities. Similar to a board of directors, the main purposes of a board of advisors is to provide guidance and lend legitimacy to a firm. Both of these attributes are seen in the advisory board set up by Laura Udall, the entrepreneur who started ZUCA backpack on rollers company (http://www.zuca.com). When asked about the types of advice and support she gets from people outside her immediate management team, Udall said:

> The company has a board of directors, but I also have created a wonderful board of volunteer advisors that has been very helpful with tactical and strategic decisions. The advisory board has evolved over the years as a result of my network. I asked each of the members to join as a result of their specific expertise. It now includes a CFO/COO of a prominent corporation, an executive in the luggage industry, a mom inventor who has founded several successful companies, a product designer, and a manufacturing expert.[7]

Imagine the type of advice and support Udall gleans from this group of advisors. An example of a firm that set up a customer advisory board for a different reason, to help develop its initial product, is highlighted in the Business Plan Insight box.

Most boards of advisors have between 5 and 15 members and interact with each other and with a firm's managers in several ways. Some advisory boards

---

BUSINESS PLAN INSIGHTS

Struggling with Product Development?: Consider Setting Up a Customer Advisory Board

Although most firms that have a customer advisory board set them up after their firm is started, primarily to assess customer satisfaction and brainstorm new product ideas, customer advisory boards can be useful before a firm has customers as well. An example of a firm that did this is iConclude (http://www.opsware.com), an IT solutions company that was recently acquired by Opsware. iConclude was founded to help other companies troubleshoot mission-critical software and hardware problems, but when it came to producing an actual product, the company wasn't exactly sure what the product should look like. To make sure it didn't stumble and produce a product that didn't meet client needs, the company decided to form a customer advisory board to dig deep into its future customers' problems and discern the exact features the product should include. Reflecting on the nature of the customer advisory board that was set up and what the effort accomplished, Sunny Gupta, iConclude's founder, recalls:

> We were very upfront with all of the companies we spoke with. We realized we needed real customer input in order for us to really get the right product into the market. That led us to form a customer advisory board of 7 to 8 of these (firms with large IT departments) companies mostly out of Seattle. They met with us every second week and really tried to hone down on exactly what their problems were and what would be the ideal solution from their perspective. This got them on board much, much earlier with us, which was pretty instrumental because we identified real requirements that enabled us to build the right product.

Ultimately, iConclude built a successful product and was bought out shortly after by a much larger firm. This illustration is an instructive example of an innovative way that a customer advisory board can be used.

Source: "Sunny Gupta, CEO of iConclude" (nPost). http://www.npost.com, (June 22, 2007).

---

meet three or four times a year at the company's offices or in another location. Other advisory boards meet in an online environment. In some cases, a firm's board of advisors will be scattered across the country, making it more cost-effective for a firm's managers to interact with the members of the board on the telephone or via e-mail rather than bring them together physically. In these situations, board members don't interact with each other at all on a face-to-face basis, yet they still provide high levels of counsel and advice. The fact that a startup has a board of directors does not preclude it from establishing one or more advisory boards. For example, Coolibar (http://www.coolibar.com), a maker of sun protective clothing, has a board of directors and a medical advisory board. According to Coolibar, its medical advisory board "provides advice to the company regarding UV radiation, sunburn, and the science of detecting, preventing, and treating skin cancer and other UV-related medical disorders, such as lupus."[8] The board currently consists of six medical doctors, all with impressive credentials. Similarly, Intouch

---

FIGURE 8-4 Other Professionals (Prime Adult Fitness Business Plan)

Prime Adult Fitness relies on the advice, counsel, and encouragement of professionals in our community on an as-needed basis. None of our professional advisors are paid a regular retainer.

Other Professionals

Attorney, Cameron Campbell, partner in the law firm of Campbell, Campbell & Ford. Mr. Campbell is a well-known Orlando, FL attorney with 23 years of experience. Mr. Campbell is the partner of Prime Adult Fitness board member Martha Ford.

CPA, Katherine Chen, Private Practice. Ms. Chen has 19 years of auditing and general accounting experience.

SBDC, SCORE, and the Central Florida Technology Incubator. Prime Adult Fitness has sought the advice from counselors associated with each of these agencies.

Technologies (http://www.intouchhealth.com), a medical robotics company, has a board of directors along with a business and strategy advisory board, an applications and clinical advisory board, and a scientific and technical advisory board.[9]

Although having a board of advisors is widely recommended in startup circles, most startups do not have one. As a result, one way you can make your startup stand out is to have one or more boards of advisors. In terms of your business plan, you should identify your boards of advisors and provide a brief bio for each member. A description of Prime Adult Fitness's general advisory board and its customer advisory board is provided in its business plan as shown previously in Figure 8-3.

The next section of this part of the business plan focuses on the role of "other professionals" in rounding out a company's management team. This portion of Prime Adult Fitness's business plan is shown in Figure 8-4.

OTHER PROFESSIONALS

At times, other professional assume important roles in a new venture's success. If this applies in your case, a separate heading should be included in the management team section of your business plan to make note of these individuals or their firms. The other professionals that are often mentioned include attorneys, bankers, investors, and business consultants.

Briefly identify the professionals, including attorneys and accountants, that apply in your case and provide a short bio if appropriate. The objective is to not only disclose who you're working with but also to assure the readers of your plan that you're getting good quality advice. Similarly, if you have a relationship with a banker or investor, that should be disclosed. Other potentially key relationships, such as a relationship with the director of a university-sponsored or city-sponsored business incubator, should be mentioned. Often, the substance of a particular relationship isn't as important to the reader of your plan as the fact that the relationship exists. There is an oft-repeated story about the early days of eBay that illustrates this point. During its beginning stages, eBay's partners, Pierre Omidyar and Jeff Skoll, decided to recruit a CEO. They wanted someone who was not only experienced but also had the types of credentials that Wall Street investors' value. They soon discovered that every experienced manager they tried to recruit asked if they had venture capital backing, which at the time they did not. For a firm trying to recruit a seasoned executive, at least at that time, venture capital backing was a sort of seal of legitimacy. To get this valuable seal, Omidyar and Skoll obtained funding from Benchmark Venture Capital, even though eBay didn't really need the money. Writer Randall Stross recalls this event as follows:

> eBay was an anomaly: a profitable company that was able to self-fund its growth and that turned to venture capital solely for contacts and counsel. No larger lesson can be drawn. When Benchmark wired the first millions to eBay's bank account, the figurative check was tossed into the vault—and there it would sit, unneeded and undisturbed.[10]

This strategy worked for eBay. Soon after affiliating with Benchmark, Bob Kagle, one of Benchmark's general partners, led eBay to Meg Whitman, an executive who had experience working for several top firms, including Procter & Gamble, Disney, and Hasbro. Meg Whitman remains eBay's chairman today.

FIGURE 8-5   Organizational Chart (Prime Adult Fitness Business Plan)

Prime Adult Fitness Organizational Chart
The senior staff reports to CEO Jeremy Ryan as shown below. Finance & Accounting is a Senior Vice President position. COO, Program Manager, Marketing & Sales, HR/Recruiting, and Member Care & Relations are Vice President positions. Each VP will be responsible for their respective employees.

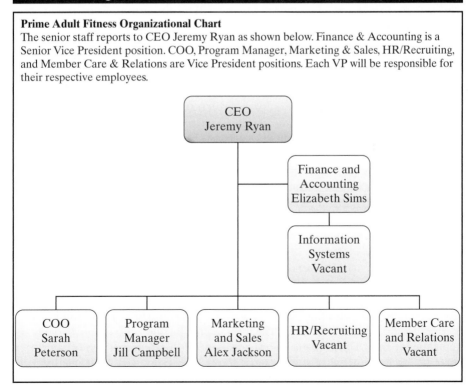

Consultants make up another important source of advice for many startup firms. A **consultant** is an individual who gives professional or expert advice. Consultants fall into two categories: paid consultants and unpaid consultants. Unpaid consultants include organizations such as the Small Business Development Center (http://www.sba.gov/sbdc) and SCORE (http://www.score.org). These sources often prove to be very useful. Startups generally use paid consultants sparingly because of the costs involved. An exception might be a startup that needs help in a specialized area, such as building a product prototype or providing independent certification of the technical merits or safety of a particular product. In addition, some startups use services of consulting companies such as Bain & Company (http://www.bain.com) and Accenture (http://www.accenture.com) but usually on a limited basis. In all cases, sources of advice should be noted in the business plan if they are substantive and worth mention. Again, the impression you want to give is that you are actively engaged and are seeking advice regarding your business venture.

The next section of this part of the business plan focuses on company structure. This section of Prime Adult Fitness's business plan is shown in Figure 8-5.

COMPANY STRUCTURE

This section focuses on how your company will be structured. Even if you are a small firm, you should outline how the company is currently structured and how it will be structured as it grows. It's important that the internal structure of a company makes sense and that the lines of communication and accountability are clear. Including a description of your company's structure also reassures the people who read the plan that you know how to translate your business idea into a functioning firm. Company structure is a "nuts-and-bolts" type of issue that deals within the interworkings of a firm. It's exactly this type of issue, however, that entrepreneurs must take seriously to develop smoothly functioning firms.

The most effective way to illustrate how a company will be structured and the lines of authority and accountability that will be in place is to include an organizational chart in the plan. An **organizational chart** is a graphic representation of how authority and responsibility are distributed within a company.[11] The organizational chart should be presented in a graphical format, similar to the manner in which Prime Adult Fitness's organizational chart is shown in its business plan in Figure 8-5. If you're unable to display your organizational chart in a graphical format, a narrative discussion of the key reporting relationships in your firm should be provided. Companies are generally organized along functional, product, or geographical lines. If you're not familiar with these distinctions, you should consult an organizational behavior or a principles of management textbook, so your organizational chart conforms to the norms your readers expect. The organization chart needs to show what the business looks like today and what it intends to become in the short-term or intermediate-term future. As a result, there may be some unfilled boxes on the organizational chart, consistent with the "gaps" in management personnel shown in the skill profile discussed earlier. In all cases, you should provide a brief interpretation of the organizational chart and discuss the most signification relationships that are displayed.

If your firm has more than one founder, you should comment on the specific role that each founder will take on as the firm moves forward. A frequent source of tension in new ventures, particularly if two or more founders start out as "equals," is a failure to delineate the specific roles they will fill. The organization chart is an effective tool for showing that the founders have worked out which of the "boxes" each will fill. Knowing that this issue has been resolved will be reassuring to the readers of your plan.

Some business plans complement their discussion of company structure with a brief analysis of how the firm will be managed from a leadership, motivational, and corporate culture point of view. If you feel it is appropriate, you should include a short section in your plan that covers these topics.

Chapter Summary

1. The management team and company structure section is pivotal in a business plan. Many investors and others who read business plans look first at the executive summary and then go directly to the management team section to assess the strengths of the people who will be starting the firm.

2. There are two issues that you should be particularly sensitive to as you write the management team and company structure section of your business plan. First, the way your management team is assembled provides an indication of the extent to which you're open to advice and are able to generate enthusiasm for your firm. Second, as you write the management team section of your business plan, you should clearly describe how the management team will evolve.

3. The three major parts to the "management team" portion of this section of the business plan are management team personnel, management team ownership and compensation, and common mistakes to avoid.

4. A good way to describe the gaps that exist in a management team is to develop a management team skill profile.

5. You must fully disclose the ownership structure of the new venture and the compensation of the members of the management team in the business plan. A table that shows the names of each of the owners of the firm, along with their age, their percent ownership in the company, and their compensation if they work for the firm is the best method.

6. There are a set of common mistakes to avoid when putting together your initial management team and writing your business plan. These common mistakes include placing unqualified friends or family members in key management positions, assuming that previous success in other industries automatically translates to your industry, presenting a "one-man team" philosophy, hiring top managers without sharing ownership in the firm, not disclosing management

team skill or competency gaps, and having vague or unclear plans for filling the skill or competency gaps that are disclosed or clearly exist.

7. A board of directors is a panel of individuals elected by a corporation's shareholders to oversee the management of the firm. Many firms have active boards of directors that provide guidance and lend legitimacy to the firm.

8. An advisory board is a panel of experts asked by a firm's managers to provide counsel and advice on an ongoing basis.

9. At times, professional, such as attorneys, bankers, investors, and consultants, assume important roles in a new venture's success. These individuals and firms should be identified and included as part of a firm's overall management team in its business plan.

10. The most effective way to illustrate how a company will be structured and the lines of authority and accountability that will be in place is to include an organizational chart in the business plan.

Review Questions

1. Why is the "management team and company structure" section referred to as pivotal in a business plan?

2. To what degree does the way a firm assembles its management team provide an indication of the extent to which the managers of the firm are open to advice and are able to generate enthusiasm for their firm?

3. Why is it important to show how a company will evolve in regard to the composition of its management team?

4. Why do investors tend to prefer management teams members who have worked together before?

5. Describe what a management team skill profile is and how it is set up.

6. Why is it important to fully disclose the ownership structure of a new venture and the compensation of the members of its management team in the business plan?

7. What are some of the common mistakes to avoid in putting together an initial management team?

8. What role does a company's board of directors play in its overall management team?

9. What is a board of advisors? What role does a board of advisors play in the management of a firm?

10. Describe the purpose of an organizational chart.

Application Questions

1. Kathy Jones, a friend of yours, just finished a business plan for a quick printing service she plans to open. When you looked over Kathy's plan, you noticed that the "management team and company structure" portion of the plan was only one page long. It provided a short bio of Kathy and of her business partner Kay, and briefly mentioned that the firm plans to set up an advisory

board at some point in the future. When you said to Kathy that this section of the plan looked like it was incomplete, Kathy seemed surprised, and asked you what she left out. What would you tell her?

2. Melanie Ford has read several books on how to write a business plan. All of the books explained the importance of the management team section, stressing the number one thing that investors focus on is the strength of a new venture's management team. Melanie can't figure out why this is true. Recently, she wrote a letter to the editor of *Inc.* magazine and asked, "Why do investors put so much stock in the portion of a business plan that deals with the strength of the management team? If a startup's product doesn't do well in the marketplace, what's the value of having a top notch management team?" If you were the editor of *Inc.* how would you reply to Melanie's letter?

3. If you were one of the founders of Prime Adult Fitness, make a list of the activities that your 4-member general advisory board and your 10-member customer advisory board could help you with.

4. Find an example of a firm, not mentioned in the chapter, that has a board of advisors. Describe each of the members of the board of advisors and speculate regarding the roles they each play in providing advice and lending legitimacy to the firm.

5. Imagine you are starting a firm with two partners, and you are all college seniors with limited work experience. You don't have impressive credentials to include in the management team section of your business plan. How can you construct this section of your plan, and the company itself, in a way that reassures the readers of the plan that you know what you're doing and will get the advice you need to launch a successful company?

Endnotes

1. J. Kurtzman, *Startups That Work* (New York: Portfolio, 2005), 6.
2. K. Eisenhardt and C. Schoonhoven, "Organizational Growth: Linking Founding Team Strategy, Environment, and Growth among U.S. Semiconductor Ventures, 1978-1988," *Administrative Science Quarterly* 35 (1990): 504–529.
3. D. Jaffe and P. Levensohn, "After the Term Sheet: How Venture Boards Influence the Success or Failure of Technology Companies," White paper, (Levensohn Venture Partners, November, 2003). http://www.levp.com.
4. R. Charan, *Boards at Work* (San Francisco: Jossey-Bass Publishers, 1998), 3.
5. L. W. Busenitz, J. O. Fiet, and D. D. Mosel, "Signaling in Venture Capitalist-New Venture Team Funding Decisions: Does It Indicate Long-Term Venture Outcomes?" *Entrepreneurship Theory and Practice* 29 (2005): 1–12.
6. A. Sherman, *Fast-Track Business Growth* (Washington, DC: Kiplinger Books, 2001).
7. "Featured Mom Inventors: Laura Udall" (Mom Inventors). http://www.mominventors.com, (June 22, 2007).
8. Coolibar homepage, http://www.coolibar.com (July 10, 2007).
9. Intouch Health hompage, http://www.intouchhealth.com (July 10, 2007).
10. R. Stross, *eBoys* (New York: Crown Books, 2000), 29.
11. Investorwords.com homepage, http://www.investorwords.com (June 22, 2007).

CHAPTER 9

OPERATIONS PLAN AND PRODUCT (OR SERVICE) DEVELOPMENT PLAN

INTRODUCTION

This chapter is divided into two parts. The first part of the chapter describes the operations section of a business plan, which focuses on how you will produce your product or service and run your business. This is an important section that should appear in every business plan. The second half of this chapter focuses on a topic that is singled out in some business plans and is not in others—the status of the development of a product or service. If you are developing a nonexistent product, such as Laura Udall did when she developed the ZUCA (backpack on rollers for kids), you'll need to include a chapter that describes the design and development of the product. If you're opening a more traditional business, such as a restaurant or a woman's clothing boutique, then you don't normally need a chapter on product design and development. In these instances, you can include product-relevant information in the operations section. For purposes of illustration, we'll show both the operations plan and the product design and development plan for Prime Adult Fitness.

Both of the topics discussed in this chapter require you to strike a careful balance between adequately describing the topic and not going into too much detail. Your readers will want an overall sense of how the business will be run and how your product will be developed, but they generally will not be looking for detailed explanations. It is best to keep each section short and crisp. If you provide too much information, the reader may believe that you are too immersed in the details of running your business to see the bigger picture.

The most important rule of thumb for writing the operations section and the product design and development section of your business plan is to focus on the aspects of each of these areas that are either essential to the success of your business or that set you apart from your competitors. Routine topics should be dealt with lightly and quickly. For example, anyone reading the operations section of Laura Udall's business plan for the ZUCA (http://www.zuca.com) would have wanted to know, in particular, how her product (backpack on rollers) was going to be manufactured, how they would be stored, how long they would held in inventory before they were sold, and how the products would be shipped to distributors, retailers, or consumers if they were sold through ZUCA's Web site. These issues, due to their importance to ZUCA's success, should have been discussed in sufficient detail. Less critical issues, such as the physical location of ZUCA's office and warehouse and the type of insurance its needs, could have been dealt with more briefly and quickly. Obviously, the critical issues will vary from plan to plan. The important thing is to identify the critical operational and product development issues facing your business and devote the majority of your available space to discussing these issues.

Now, let's look at the operations plan section of a business plan.

OPERATIONS PLAN

The **operations plan section** of the business plan outlines how your business will be run and how your product or service will be produced. The topics that are generally included are operating model and procedures, business location, facilities and equipment, and operations strategy and plans. Other topics may be included depending on the nature of the business.

The degree of importance that the reader of your plan will place on the operations plan varies dramatically by plan. For example, if you plan to open a sporting goods store and have a substantial amount of retail experience on your management team, your reader probably wouldn't delve deeply into this part of your plan. The most important operational issues may be store location and layout, and your reader, because of the amount of retail experience on your team, may trust you to figure out the rest. In contrast, if you're taking on the challenge of producing an entirely new product, the operations section may be pivotal, even if you have experienced product-development people on your team. There is a vast difference between thinking up a new product idea and actually designing a business to manufacture, market, and sell it. Savvy readers know this and will be looking for convincing evidence that the product can actually be built and that the founders have a handle on the operational aspects of the business.

The first section of the operations plan focuses on the operating model and procedures. This section of Prime Adult Fitness's business plan is shown in Figure 9-1.

**FIGURE 9-1 Operations Model and Procedures
(Prime Adult Fitness Business Plan)**

Introduction

Prime Adult Fitness will operate a full-service fitness center for people 50 years old or older. The operating model and procedures for the center are explained in the following sections.

General Approach to Operations

Operating a fitness center for people 50 years and older is a unique situation. It requires a careful balance of not drawing undo attention to the age of the members while at the same time tailoring all the activities of the center for an older clientele. It also requires an extreme sensitivity to the needs of older members. Fitness centers that cater to older people have found that the upper end of the age range is normally well represented. As a result, our operations plans and procedures must fully anticipate providing services to members in their 70s, 80s, and even 90s.

The biggest challenge in operating a fitness center is to motivate people to join and make exercise a part of their daily or weekly routine. People will find many reasons to not exercise. As a result, the operations of the center will be geared to (1) providing an uplifting environment for the members, (2) providing high-quality classes and equipment, (3) encouraging people to socialize and make Prime Adult Fitness one of the centerpieces of their life, and (4) establishing a rapport between Prime Adult Fitness staff and employees and our members. Both back stage (behind the scenes) and front stage (what the members see and experience) operational issues are critical.

Back Stage (Behind the Scenes Operations Activities)

- *Staff Selection.* The staff and employees will be carefully selected. Along with the skills they need to perform their job, staff members must be able to relate to older adults, their families, and guests in a professional, thoughtful, and caring manner.
- *Operations Manual.* An operations manual has been prepared to document and articulate the day-to-day operational procedures of the center.
- *Exercise Classes and Programs.* The exercise classes and programs will be the backbone of the center's offerings. All the classes will have special names, such as "Sunrisers," "Water Dynamics," or "Bones in Motion." This tactic helps members' identify the classes and teachers.
- *Exercise Machines.* The exercise machines will be modern and up-to-date. Specific employees will be trained to maintain the machines.
- *Member Motivation.* One of the most important ingredients to our success will be to make our members feel safe, secure, and successful. Older exercises need to feel that the staff cares and will respond if they need assistance. Staff at all levels will be trained to offer this type of service and attention. In addition, gentle follow-up and encouragement is needed to keep people coming to a fitness center. The staff will be encouraged to remember the names of the participants in their classes and devise a system for letting people know they are missed when they miss a class or quit coming for a while. It is often the personal connection to teachers, classmates, and staff that keeps people motivated to come back to exercise.
- *Employee Orientation.* All employees will go through a three-hour orientation before they begin work, where they will become acquainted with the operations manual and the philosophy of the center.

FIGURE 9-1   (continued)

- *Employee Education.* Staff members and teachers will routinely attend workshops and conferences to understand current trends in fitness, obtain certifications, and tap into other resources.
- *Emergency Plans.* Emergency action plans, policies, procedures, and rules have been established and are documented in the operations manual. All employees will be trained in the procedures. There will be no ambiguity or indecision when an emergency occurs. If a member is injured or needs medical attention, all employees will know the procedure to follow.
- *Waivers.* After a member finishes orientation (which is required for all new members), he or she will be asked to sign a waiver. The waiver acknowledges that the individual has gone through the orientation, understands the risks of exercise, has checked with a doctor about starting an exercise regime, and holds Prime Adult Fitness harmless if any type of medical problem occurs.

Front Stage (What the Members See and Experience)

- *Member Tours.* A prospective member will be provided a tour of the facility, and offered a free 10-day trial period to try the facilities and classes. (Facilities that use this approach normally experience an 80% to 85% conversion rate.)
- *Orientation.* After an individual decides to join, he or she will go through a 30-minute orientation before being are allowed to start using the facility.
- *Operating Hours.* The center will be open from 6:30 am until 9:00 pm Monday through Saturday and will be closed on Sundays.
- *Staff Assistance.* Fitness center staff will be available to teach members how to use the equipment, encourage them with tips on form, and help them track their efforts.
- *Fitness Classes and Programs.* The fitness classes and programs will be offered at various times during the day. Most classes will run either 30 or 60 minutes. Nontraditional classes will also be offered, such as outdoor "walking" classes where members will walk in groups through neighborhoods near the center.
- *Workshops.* Along with fitness classes, workshops on nutrition, sleep, dance movements, and neurobics (brain exercises) will be provided.
- *Family Swims.* There will be two scheduled "family swims" per week where members can invite their families as guests to use the larger pool. Guests will not be permitted at other times during the week. Other fitness centers have found that establishing a "guest policy" alleviates potential conflicts regarding the use of facilities.
- *Multipurpose Room Rental.* The multipurpose rooms will be available for rent, by members only, for special occasions such as birthday parties and anniversary parties. Part of the reason for doing this is to make the center a central place in our member's lives.
- *Game Room.* A well-stocked game room will be available for members to pay mind-stimulating games, such as Sudoku, and socially stimulating games, such as bridge.
- *Monthly Newsletter.* Members will receive a monthly newsletter.

Inventory
Because of the nature of its operations, Prime Adult Fitness will not be required to carry a significant amount of inventory.

Schedule of Classes and Management of Peak Times
To make maximum use of our proposed facility, the classes and programs will be scheduled throughout the day, to relieve congestion in the center at obvious peak times of the day, which are before and after work. Prime Adult Fitness anticipates that 50% of its clientele will be retirees. As a result, Prime Adult Fitness should not experience the early morning and late afternoon bottlenecks experienced by most fitness centers.

OPERATIONS MODEL AND PROCEDURE

The primary objective of this section is to show that you have a firm grasp on the operational details of launching and running your business. It is usually not necessary to include a step-by-step description of how the business will be run, but major items should be covered. As mentioned previously, in many instances the operations section of a business plan will not be carefully dissected, but in some instances, the information that's included represents make-or-break issues for a firm. For example, a company such as H20Audio (http://www.h20audio.com), which makes waterproof housings for the Apple iPod, will ultimately be judged by consumers by whether its product works, which is an operations issue. If its waterproof housings leak allowing users' iPods to get wet, or if its headphones don't work well under water, the company will have no chance of being successful.

A useful way to illustrate how your business will be run is to first articulate your general approach to operations in terms of what's most important and what the make-or-break issues are. You can then frame the discussion in terms of "back stage," or behind the scenes activities, and "front stage," or what the customer sees and experiences. As an alternative, some business plans frame the discussion of their operations in the context of a "day in the life of a business." The Prime Adult Fitness business plan, as shown in Figure 9-1, is framed using the back stage/front stage metaphor.

Another useful way to illustrate how a product or service is produced is to include an operations flow diagram in your business plan.[1] An **operations flow diagram** shows the key steps in the production of a product or the delivery of a service. Many manufacturing startups, in particular, include an operations flow diagram to illustrate the participants in their value chain. Often, the operations flow diagram also depicts how the company intends to improve the flow of activities in its operations compared to industry norms; for example, IKEA (http://www.ikea.com) is the Swedish furniture company known for its brightly colored furniture and its approach of requiring customers to assemble their furniture (in exchange for a lower price). Figure 9-2 demonstrates IKEA's operations flow. Traditional furniture manufacturers tend to complete more of the activities themselves, whereas IKEA has opted to outsource the manufacturer of its parts to contract manufacturers and outsource the assembly and delivery of its furniture to its customers. In IKEA's case, its operations flow diagram paints a fairly clear picture of how the company operates.

Although the approaches explained previously help describe how a company's operations work, issues usually need to be singled out and discussed in more detail in this section. Examples of issues that fall into this category include the following:

- An explanation of how your inventory will be stored and how frequently it will be turned over
- A description of the length and nature of your product or service's production cycle (when do you pay for inputs?, how long does it take to produce the product?, when does the customer buy the product?, when do you get paid?)
- An explanation of where bottlenecks are likely to occur in your manufacturing process or service delivery and how these will be handled

FIGURE 9-2   IKEA's Operations Flow Diagram (IKEA only performs design, ship and warehouse, and sale)

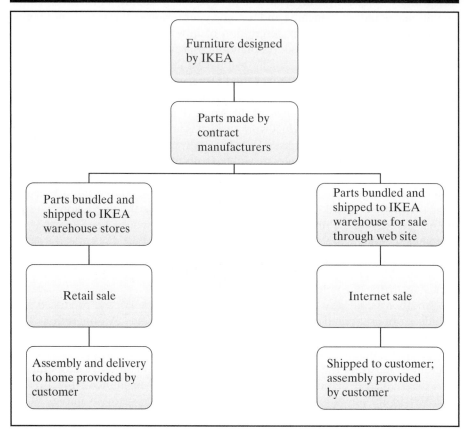

- An explanation of how seasonal production loads will be handled without service disruption (normally accomplished by building up inventory and using part-time help during peak periods)
- An explanation of how your quality control will be managed
- An explanation of how your after-sale service, if applicable, will be handled

An example of how these issues come into play is provided by Oopsy Daisy (http://www.oopsydaisy.com), a company that makes murals and other high-quality artwork for children's bedrooms and playrooms, schools, and doctor's offices. The company contracts with independent artists for original designs and converts the designs into murals and similar artwork in its manufacturing facility in San Diego. Its artwork is then sold through channels set up and maintained by others, including The Land of Nod catalog, Magic Cabin catalog, Neiman Marcus catalog, and a host of individually owned stores and boutiques.[2] Although Oopsy

Daisy's operations flow is well designed and easy to envision, it doesn't tell the whole story. There are additional issues, represented in the bullet point shown previously, that are equally critical to its operations and its ultimate success, and should be explained, either through one of the general discussion formats described earlier or under a separate heading. For example, how long does it take to produce a mural or similar piece of art? Is each product hand made, or is the process automated? How long is the average piece of art held in inventory before it is sold? If an Oopsy Daisy product doesn't sell in a store or boutique, can it be returned? If so, who pays for the shipping and what happens to the product then? How long does it take, on average, between when a product is shipped to a store or boutique and when Oopsy Daisy is paid? What happens if Oopsy Daisy increases its inventory for Christmas or another peak period, and its products don't sell well? These are the types of operations-oriented questions that would immediately occur to a discerning reader of Oopsy Daisy's business plan.

The next section of the operations plan deals with a business's location. This portion of the Prime Adult Fitness business plan is shown in Figure 9-3.

FIGURE 9-3   Business Location (Prime Adult Fitness Business Plan)

Prime Adult Fitness is proposing to operate a single facility at 201 Oak Drive in Oviedo, FL. This location is considered to be ideal for Prime Adult Fitness for the following reasons:

Advantages of Location

- *Ideal Community.* Oviedo has a higher percentage of older people and people with a higher income than national averages. Both of these metrics are important to support a full-service fitness center for people 50 years old and older.

- *Suburb of Orlando.* Oviedo is a suburb of Orlando. Although Oviedo's population is only 30,000, it is part of a densely populated suburban area adjacent to a city. Prime Adult Fitness's trade area, Seminole County, FL (the county in which Oviedo is located), has approximately 65,420 people 50 years old or older. Oviedo, and its surrounding area, continues to grow, with new neighborhoods and more multifamily complexes, such as apartment building and townhouses, being built on a continual basis.

- *Visibility and Parking.* The Prime Adult Fitness location will be on a busy thoroughfare, with two lanes in each direction divided by a grassy medium. The road was widened in 2005, so no new road construction is anticipated in the immediate future. This fact was confirmed by the Oviedo City Engineer. Adequate access is provided into and out of the facility's parking from Oak Street or from Blackstone Blvd. Blackstone Blvd. runs adjacent to the Prime Adult Fitness parking lot to the east.

- *Proximity to Suppliers.* Locating in an urban area provides the company easy access to suppliers.

- *Proximity to University.* Prime Adult Fitness will be 12 miles from the University of Central Florida, which is a large university. The proximity to the university provides the company access to a labor pool of young people who enjoy working in a fitness environment and have a passion for working with older people. Prime Adult Fitness plans to work with the university to arrange work-study internships for students.

BUSINESS LOCATION

This section of your plan describes the geographic location of your business. In some instances, location is an extremely important issue, and in other instances, it isn't. For example, one of the reasons Jeff Bezos located Amazon.com in Seattle is that Seattle is a major distribution hub for several large book publishers. By locating near these distribution facilities, Amazon.com has enjoyed a cost advantage that it wouldn't have had otherwise.

There are several specific instances in which a business's location is a critical factor in its capability to operate efficiently and effectively:

- Proximity to a qualified labor force
- Closeness to suppliers
- Access to transportation, such as a major airport or an interstate highway
- Access to international shipping alternatives, such as a major airport, a rail hub, and/or a seaport
- Proximity to customers with a profile conducive to a firm's business, such as a high income neighborhood for an upscale clothing boutique or a certain ethnic population for an ethic restaurant
- Access to favorable state and local tax rates
- Access to economic incentives for locating in a certain area, such as tax abatements and/or low-priced land or labor
- Proximity to a high-quality community, in terms of public education, recreational opportunities, health care, and the arts, to attract a high-quality workforce

On a more fine-grained level, for restaurants and retail businesses, the specific location within a mall or shopping center, or a certain side of a busy street, may make a dramatic difference. For example, restaurants that feature breakfast food, such as a doughnut shop or a coffee shop, typically want to be on the side of a street that has the heaviest amount of traffic in the mornings. A miscue in a strategic area like this could cost a firm a substantial amount of business.

You should describe the rationale for your location in this portion of your business plan. For example, as shown previously in its business plan in Figure 9-3, Prime Adult Fitness decided to locate in Oviedo, Florida (a suburb of Orlando) because it is an upper-income community in an area with a relative heavy concentration of people 50 years old and older—its target market. It would have made much less sense for Prime Adult Fitness to locate in an area with opposite demographic characteristics.

The next section of a startup's operations plan focuses on its facilities and equipment. This section of Prime Adult's business plan is shown in Figure 9-4.

FIGURE 9-4 Facilities and Equipment (Prime Adult Fitness Business Plan)

How the Equipment and Programs Are Being Chosen

An overarching objective of Prime Adult Fitness is to manage a fitness facility that has programs, classes, and equipment specifically tailored for our target audience—people 50 years old and older. To accomplish that goal, the following steps have been completed and are currently underway to guide our selection of facilities, programs, and equipment.

- *Visits to Other Fitness Centers.* Although there is not another facility exactly like the one Prime Adult Fitness envisions, there are a number of fitness facilities (sponsored primarily by retirement communities and health care organizations) that have been built and equipped specifically with an older clientele in mind. A committee comprising two members of the Prime Adult Fitness management team, two general advisory board members, and two customer advisory board members visited six facilities to collect information and meet with their staffs. The committee also visited two all-purpose fitness facilities in the Orlando area and two in Jacksonville, FL, which were gracious enough to provide tours and talk about their efforts to accommodate older patrons.
- *Focus Groups.* Prime Adult Fitness has conducted three focus groups with prospective members in Seminole county to solicit their input regarding facilities and equipment. Two more focus groups are scheduled.
- *Attendance at Industry Trade Shows.* The Prime Adult Fitness initial management team has attended three industry trade shows that display fitness equipment and program material.
- *Advisory Boards.* Both the Prime Adult Fitness General Advisory Board and the Customer Advisory Board have been actively involved in providing input on important topics.

Building and Future Growth

Prime Adult Fitness has identified a 21,600 square foot, two-story facility (201 Oak Drive, Oviedo, FL) that is available for lease. The company has signed an option to lease the property for seven years, pending funding, with an option to buy the property at the end of the seven-year lease. The facility was built by a real estate investment trust in 1998 and was leased to a major fitness chain, which occupied the facility and used it as a fitness center until the chain retrenched and closed all of its fitness centers in the Southeast United States. For purpose of comparison, the average Bally Total Fitness or Gold's Gym is in the 30,000 square foot range.

Prime Adult Fitness is projecting 2,502 membership units by 2012. A total of 2,202 membership units (a membership unit is a single or a couple's account) translates into 3,250 people that will be using the facility (one couples account means two people will be using the facility). The building's capacity is 3,500. If Prime Adult Fitness grows its membership unit base beyond 2,502, it will do it by opening a facility in a new location, to tap into a new trade area. The building will take some retrofitting to suite Prime Adult Fitness's needs. The process to complete this work and the costs involved are discussed in a later part of the plan. The building, after the retrofitting is complete, will feature the following:

- A four lane fitness pool (83 degrees)
- A therapy pool (93 degrees)
- A general exercise room that includes the fitness equipment
- Four rooms for exercise classes and programs
- One multipurpose
- A game room

FIGURE 9-4 (continued)

- Men's and women's locker room
- A reception area designed to encourage people to gather and linger
- A suite specially equipped for massage and physical therapy
- A kitchen
- A coffee and juice bar
- A small movie theater
- Office space for the staff
- Three small janitorial rooms
- A mechanical service area (i.e., water heater, furnace, etc.)
- Guest restrooms

Equipment

Prime Adult Fitness is in the process of selecting fitness equipment that will facilitate the specific needs of our clientele. Generally, lower intensity equipment will be chosen than that offered by a traditional fitness center, and weights and resistance equipment specifically designed for older people will be obtained. The selection of the specific equipment is a work in progress. A committee that is comprised of Sarah Peterson (COO), Jim Campbell (Program Manager), Dr. Kenneth Jamison, (Director and Family Practice Physician), and Dr. Jason Steele (Advisory Board Member and Sports Medicine Specialist) is in the process of researching options and will make a formal recommendation to the Prime Adult Fitness management team and board.

Government Codes and Regulations

A committee comprised of Elizabeth Sims (CFO), Sarah Peterson (COO), and Martha Ford (Advisory Board Member) has investigated and determined the government codes and regulations that Prime Adult Fitness must comply with if it occupies the Oak Drive facility. The committee has also been in regular contact with the city of Oviedo and Seminole county FL to anticipate all zoning, parking, and neighbored impact issues that will be associated with opening the center. There are no issues that are anticipated to be of concern.

FACILITIES AND EQUIPMENT

This section describes a firm's facilities and equipment. You should list your most important facilities and equipment and briefly describe how they will be (or have been) acquired, in terms of whether they will be purchased, leased, or acquired through some other means. If you will be producing your own product, you should describe the production facility that you have or are looking for. This is a particularly important consideration for a business-to-business startup, especially if you are an OEM (original equipment manufacturer). An **OEM** is a company that sells parts to larger companies that use the parts in products they sell. Most manufacturers are very discerning about the OEMs they do business with and regularly visit and inspect their facilities. As a result, if you are an OEM and plan to maintain your own production facilities, you will need to convince the reader of your plan that your facility (or the one you hope to acquire) will pass muster with discerning customers.

If you will be producing a product and will contract or outsource your production, you should comment on the facilities of your business partners. If the contracting or outsourcing will be done in a foreign country, you should explain how you located your contracting or outsource partner and how you know that its facilities are suitable for your purposes. You may also want to comment on the degree to which you will hold your foreign partners accountable for the working conditions in their factories and for their environmental standards.

If your facilities are nondescript, such as generic workspace for computer programmers, a lot of explanation is not required. If your business plan is for a restaurant or retail store, and you already have a facility, it may be helpful to include a floor plan and interior and exterior photos. If you're still in the process of locating a facility, or plan to build, a tentative floor plan and an artist or architect's rendition of the facility you want to have is appropriate. If your facility is subject to any special zoning or OSHA regulations, those should be disclosed. In terms of equipment, you should comment on any especially critical or expensive equipment you will require.

If your business is projecting fairly rapid growth, you should comment on how you'll be able to grow within your existing facilities or how you plan to transition from your existing facility to a larger one. You don't necessarily have to have all the answers at this point. It's important, however, to show your reader that you're aware of this issue and that it's part of your ongoing planning process.

The next section of your operations plan focuses on operations strategy and plans. This section of Prime Adult's business plan is shown in Figure 9-5.

FIGURE 9-5   Operations Strategy and Plans (Prime Adult Fitness Business Plan)

Relationship Between Business Strategy and Operations Strategy

The Prime Adult Fitness business strategy and competitive advantage hinge on two things:

(1) meetings the needs of our 50+ year old clientele in a manner that is specifically tailored to them, and (2) reaching our annual membership goals through new members and member retention. Our operations strategy, described previously, is specifically geared to meeting these objectives, and will be updated on an ongoing basis. Our overarching objective is to fully understand the needs of our clientele and to serve them in an efficient and caring manner.

In-House vs. Contract Activities

To maintain consistency for our members, full-time and part-time employees will conduct the vast majority of our operations. Contract employees will be used occasionally to teach specialized classes. There are two exceptions to this general rule:

- *Massage Service.* A massage service will be offered in our facility on a fee basis. The service will be offered by a local massage company, which is fully certified and has been carefully selected. Prime Adult Fitness will receive a licensing income representing a percentage of the fees collected.
- *Physical Therapy.* A physical therapy service will also be offered and will be staffed by personnel from an Orlando area hospital. Prime Adult Fitness will receive a licensing income representing a percentage of the fees collected.

OPERATIONS STRATEGY AND PLANS

This section deals with strategic and longer-term issues pertaining to your operations strategy. An important issue that is normally covered is the portion of your production process (or service delivery process) that you'll perform in-house as opposed to the activities that will be done by others. You may want to refer to your operations flow diagram to explain the choices you've made or plan to make. The model that many firms use in constructing their operations flow (or supply chain) is to perform the activities in-house that they are particularly good at and find partners to do the rest. Although this approach sounds simple, the task of actually finding reliable partners and managing the operations flow can be complex. As a result, if you will rely heavily on partners to help you produce your product or deliver your service, you should provide an explanation of how the entire process will work.

An example of how complex and managerially taxing selecting partners and managing an operations flow or supply chain can be is provided in the Business Plan Insights box. The feature focuses on Patagonia (http://www.patagonia.com), a company that sells rugged clothing and gear to mountain climbers, skiers, and other extreme-sport enthusiasts.

BUSINESS PLAN INSIGHT

Outsourcing the Manufacturing of a Product: A Practice That Requires More Work Than You Might Think

Many startups that plan to produce a product indicate in their business plan that the actual production of the product will be "outsourced" or produced by a contract manufacturer. Although this approach sounds good and is often successfully implemented, it requires more work and explaining than you might think. Often, companies are not able to find a partner that can build its entire product. In these instances, several outsource partners or contract manufacturers must be located, and the company must coordinate the work among its partners. In addition, in most cases, the production of a company's product isn't simply handed over to another company with no further work involved. A company must constantly monitor the quality of goods it is receiving from its outside partners and must interact with its partners on a continual basis.

An illustration of the amount of work that's involved with managing two or more contract manufacturers is provided by Patagonia (http://www.patagonia.com), a company that sells clothing to extreme sports enthusiasts. Patagonia has never owned a fabric mill or a sewing shop. Instead, to make a ski jacket, for example, it buys fabric from a mill, buys zippers and facings from other manufacturers, and then hires a sewing shop to complete the garment. To meet its own environmental standards and ensure product quality, it works closely with each partner to make sure the jacket meets its rigid standards.

> As a result of these standards, Patagonia does as much business as it can with as few partners as possible and chooses its relationships carefully. Once a relationship is established, Patagonia doesn't leave adherence to its principles to chance. Its production department monitors its partners on a consistent basis. Although Patagonia avoids the work of actually producing its products, a substantial amount of work is involved in managing those that do.

Another operational issue with strategic implications is the extent to which a firm's operations are clearly supportive of its business strategy. For example, if you plan to sell a high-quality product, then your approach to operations should reflect that in everything you do (i.e., partner selection, manufacturing process, customer service, quality control). It may be helpful to include a sentence or two in this part of your plan that clearly makes the link between your business strategy and your operations strategy. For example, Silpada Designs (http://www.silpada.com), a company that sells high-end jewelry through in-home parties, emphasizes quality in the products it sells. Its products are made by skilled artisans in more than 10 countries around the world. To ensure that the products meet Silpada's quality standards, they are inspected twice—at their point of manufacture and when they arrive at Silpada's distribution center in the United States.[3] This level of diligence is an example of how a company backs up its business strategy (i.e., high quality) with an appropriate operational response (i.e., two quality inspections).

Other issues that are discussed in this section include a firm's overall approach to quality control, production control, inventory control, and similar issues, depending on the nature of the business.

PRODUCT (OR SERVICE) DEVELOPMENT PLAN

As indicated at the outset of this chapter, if you are developing a completely new product or service, you need to include a section in your business plan that focuses on the status of your development efforts. Many seemingly promising startups never get off the ground because their product development efforts stall or the actual development of a product or service turns out to be more difficult than anticipated. In addition, in many cases, building a working prototype of a product is not enough. A startup must also have a credible plan for ramping up the production of a product to satisfy the sales estimates in its financial projections.

This section of your business plan has four parts: development status and tasks, challenges and risks, costs, and intellectual property. The portion of the Prime Adult Fitness business plan that focuses on development status and tasks is shown in Figure 9-6.

DEVELOPMENT STATUS AND TASKS

The purpose of this section is to describe the present state of the development of your product or service. Most products follow a logical path of development that

---

FIGURE 9-6 Development Status and Tasks (Prime Adult Fitness Business Plan)

Timeline

If funding is obtained, Prime Adult Fitness will open at 201 Oak Drive in Oviedo, FL on January 1, 2009. The following milestones have been completed and remain to be completed to open the center.

Completed Milestones

November—December, 2007	• Completed feasibility analysis
January, 2008	• Incorporated business
	• Selected board of directors and advisory boards
	• Applied for trademarks and copyrights
February—March, 2008	• Signed seven-year lease on building (subject to funding)
	• Hired architect to plan building retrofitting
	• Hired, by two founders, three other members of initial management team
	• Conducted a series of focus groups, visits to other fitness centers, and special meetings of the advisory boards to plan the retrofitting of the building, begin selecting fitness equipment, and start planning the initial classes for the center

Milestones to Be Completed

April—June, 2008	• Obtain commitment for funding
	• Begin retrofitting of building when funding is obtained
July—October, 2008	• Supervise retrofitting of building
	• Make final decisions on fitness equipment, complete planning of initial classes and programs
November—December, 2008	• Begin hiring and training staff and employees to open business
	• Ramp up marketing and public relations initiatives
	• Begin offering "pilot" exercise classes to solicit feedback
	• Host three open houses
January 1, 2009*	• Have grand opening and begin operations

Retrofitting of Building

The 21,600 square foot building Prime Adult Fitness will occupy will require approximately $1 million of retrofitting to make suitable for the company's purposes. Prime Adult Fitness will pay for 75% of the retrofitting, and the building owners will pay 25%. An architectural firm, experienced in designing facilities for older people, will provide plans for the retrofitting. The following special issues have been considered in drawing up plans to retrofit the facility:

- Maximum use of natural light through installing additional skylights and windows
- Reduction in noise throughout the facility through the installation of special noise reduction material

FIGURE 9-6   (continued)

- An improvement of the ventilation system throughout the building so that the locker rooms can be warmer than the exercise areas
- Resurface the areas adjacent to the swimming pools with special material to alleviate concerns about slipping on the surface
- Installation of ramps for entering and exiting both pools (to accommodate people who have trouble navigating stairs to walk into the pool on an even surface)
- Installation of special assistance locker room space in both the men's and women's locker room to accommodate physical therapy patients (who may need assistance dressing before and after pool treatments)
- Installation of additional grab bars throughout the facility
- Updating the color schemes and general décor of the facility
- Installation of updated information systems

includes product conception, prototyping, initial production, and full production. Depending on the sophistication of your product- or service-development process, products and services typically pass tests that probe their performance and technical merits as they pass from one step in the development process to the next. You should explain the process you'll follow to move your product from one stage to the next.

You should describe specifically the point that your product or service is at and provide a timeline that describes the remaining steps. Prime Adult Fitness, as shown in Figure 9-6, framed its timeline in the context of milestones. You should also describe how the process of completing the development of your product or service will unfold, in terms of the steps that need to be completed and the people who will be involved. Many startups, for example, involve prospective customers in testing early versions of their products and services to obtain feedback. If these types of tests have already been conducted, you should briefly comment on the process you've used and your results to date.

If you are a very early stage firm and only have an idea, you should carefully explain how a prototype of your product will be made. A **prototype** is the first physical depiction of a new product.[4] For a new product, such as ZUCA's backpack on rollers or H20Audio's waterproof housing for the Apple iPod, a prototype is needed to test the merits of the product and get substantive feedback from others. For example, regardless of how good H20Audio's product looked on paper, the only way for the founders of the company to ensure themselves and others that the product worked was to build one or more prototypes of the product and test them under various conditions. It's one thing for a company such as H20Audio to say that its waterproof housings will keep an Apple iPod dry while swimming and that its headphones will work in water. It's another thing to show convincing evidence that swimmers have used prototypes of the product repeatedly without a single failure in terms of keeping their iPod's dry and the performance of the headphones in water.

For a company like Prime Adult Fitness, which will not produce a physical product, a prototype can take the form of a "sample daily schedule" of the fitness center's activities and a booklet that provides illustrations of what the exterior and interior of the center will look like. Short descriptions of the classes that will be offered and the programs that will be available, along with short bios of some are the instructors, are also helpful. If this information can be put together in a tight, attractive package, it can serve the role of a prototype and can be distributed to people for feedback.

There are many ways to get a product prototype made if the process requires specialized equipment or expertise. For example, the Thomas Register (http://www.thomasnet.com), a directory of all the manufacturers in the United States, has a listing of rapid prototyping services. Similarly, the American Institute of Graphic Arts (http://www.aiga.org) lists designers and prototype engineers looking for work. Individual projects can also be listed on more general job sites such as Craigslist.com and Monster.com. In some instances, a virtual prototype, which is less expensive than a physical prototype, is sufficient. A **virtual prototype** is a computer-generated 3D image of an idea. It displays an invention as a 3D model that can be viewed from all sides and rotated 360 degrees.

If your product or service is beyond the prototype stage, explain the stage of development of your product. After a company has a working prototype of its product, usability testing often takes place. **Usability testing** is a form of product/service feasibility analysis, which measures a product's ease of use and the user's perception of the experience. Usability tests are sometimes called user tests, beta tests, or field trials, depending on the circumstances involved. Usability testing is particularly important for software and Web site design. According to one survey, 36 percent of all Web site owners in the United States conduct usability research.[5]

As you write this section of your overall product or service development plan, be aware that there is typically a direct correlation between how far away you are from having an actual product or service that can be sold in quantity to how risky the reader of your plan will perceive your business to be. A helpful illustration of this point is made by Stanley Rich and David Gumpert, the authors of *Business Plans That Win.*[6] Rich and Gumpert place companies into four distinct categories, in terms of how ready their products or services are to being sold:

- *Level 4: Going Concern.* In these companies, the product or service has not only been developed, but it is being produced and sold to customers who are satisfied.

- *Level 3: Ready to Go.* Companies at this stage have completed development and engineering of their product or service (the product actually exists). It is ready to be introduced to the market and ready for aggressive marketing and sales efforts.

- *Level 2: Almost There.* Companies at this stage have built a prototype, which works but isn't ready for marketing and production because it still needs additional evaluation and engineering. It also needs additional input from prospective customers to verify user benefits.

• *Level 1: A Great Idea, But . . . .* Companies have an idea for a product or service but haven't moved beyond the idea stage. No prototype of the product exists.

According to Rich and Gumpert it's tough for Level 1 companies to get funding, unless they have an exceptionally highly qualified management team (that can be depended on to develop the product) or a product or service idea that is an obvious winner. Because most startups do not meet either of these criteria, Rich and Gumpert urge companies to move beyond Level 1 and put some development work into their products or services before they present their business plans to investors or others. If they don't, according to Rich and Gumpert's logic, in most cases, the business will be seen as too risky to merit funding. This stipulation requires a startup to basically self-fund or bootstrap its early product-development efforts. If your company fits this description, you should briefly mention how you have funded your product development efforts to date.

One nice touch that dresses up a business plan is to provide a picture of your product if it exists or an artist's rendition of what the product (or service setting) will look like after it's developed. It's normally easier for readers to relate to a product (or service setting) that they have a good visual image of.

The next section of your product or service design and development plan deals with the challenges and risks involved. The portion of the Prime Adult Fitness business plan is shown in Figure 9-7.

CHALLENGES AND RISKS

This section should disclose any major anticipated design and development challenges (and risks) that will be involved in bringing your product or service to

---

FIGURE 9-7 Challenges and Risks (Prime Adult Fitness Business Plan)

The following challenges and risks are associated with the design, maintenance, and use of Prime Adult Fitness's facilities.

• *Completion of Retrofitting.* Any delay in completing the retrofitting of the building, according to the "milestones to be completed" schedule would severely impact the scheduled opening of the facility on January 1, 2008.
• *Purchase and Installation of Fitness Equipment.* The final decisions for purchasing and leasing fitness equipment are currently underway and will ramp up once funding is obtained. Any delays in the proper shipping and installation of equipment would severely impact the scheduled opening date.
• *Exceeding Costs of Budgeted Items.* The initial opening and staffing of the facility has been carefully budgeted, as shown in the financial section of this plan. Exceeding the budget would be problematic for the firm financially.
• *Final Clearances from the City of Oviedo and Seminole County, FL.* Final clearances regarding city and county regulations pertaining to the opening of our facility cannot be completed until the building retrofitting initiative is complete.

Prime Adult Fitness is confident that the risks inherent in these four items have been minimized.

market. You should be very candid and transparent in identifying these issues for two reasons. First, your reader will anticipate that challenges and risks exist and will want to know what they are. Second, your reader will want to see evidence that you are aware of the risks and challenges that exist. The last thing you want to do is paint an overly rosy picture of how quickly and effortlessly your design and development process will unfold. Experienced readers know that product and service development is an inherently bumpy and challenging process and will want insight into the challenges and risks you anticipate with your particular offering. If you omit this section, gloss over it, or provide an overly optimistic outlook, the credibility of your business plan will be undermined.

You should discuss the possible effects the challenges and risks you disclose could have on the development of your product or service, the costs involved, and your timeline for bringing the product or service to market. You should also discuss how you plan to avoid or deal with the challenges and risks involved if they occur.

The next section of your product or service design and development plan deals with the costs involved. The corresponding section of the Prime Adult Fitness business plan is shown in Figure 9-8.

Costs

This section should provide a budget for the remaining design and development work that needs to be done to bring your product or service to market. The budget should include the costs of labor, material, consulting fees, prototyping, usability testing, and so on. You will probably need to talk to experienced people

---

FIGURE 9-8 Costs (Prime Adult Fitness Business Plan)

Design and Development Budget
The budget associated with the building and facilities, to bring Prime Adult Fitness to its opening date, is as follows:

Item	Cost
Retrofitting Building	$ 750,000
Exercise Equipment *	$ 150,000
Office and Computer Equipment	$ 60,000
Furniture	$ 30,000
Sales and Marketing Materials	$ 40,000
Other	$ 15,000
Total	$1,045,000

*Special Note—Exercise Equipment

A total of $150,000 of exercise equipment will be obtained as follows:

Method Used to Obtain Equipment	
Purchase	$ 50,000
Lease	$ 50,000
Financed by vendors	$ 50,000

FIGURE 9-9   Intellectual Property (Prime Adult Fitness Business Plan)

Patents	Due to the nature of its operations, Prime Adult Fitness does not anticipate filing for any patents.
Trademarks	All of Prime Adult Fitness's distinctive marks, including its name, its logo, and its tagline, have been trademarked. Its Internet domain name (http://www.primeadultfitness.com) has been obtained.
Copyrights	The company will routinely copyright appropriate material.
Trade Secrets	Prime Adult Fitness considers the following material to be trade secrets: operating manuals, employee orientation material, membership lists, prospects lists, business plan, results of membership surveys, and financial records. This material is not allowed to leave Prime Adult Fitness's premises, nor is it allowed to be copied without the permission of an officer of the firm.

in your industry to arrive at accurate estimates, particularly if you're not far along in your design and development efforts.

In most cases, exceeding your design and development budget will be one of the risks disclosed in the challenges and risks section shown previously. You should discuss the impact that exceeding your budget could have on your startup's overall cash flow and financial stability.

The last section of the product (or service) design and development portion of your business plan focuses on intellectual property. This portion of the Prime Adult Fitness business plan is shown in Figure 9-9.

INTELLECTUAL PROPERTY

This section should describe any patents, trademarks, copyrights, or trade secrets that you have secured or plan to secure relative to the products or services you are developing. If your startup is still an early stage company, and you have not taken action on intellectual property issues yet, you should get legal advice so you can at a minimum discuss your plans in this area.

The four forms of intellectual property that should be discussed in this section are patents, trademarks, copyrights, and trade secrets. **Intellectual property** is any product of human intellect that is intangible but has value in the marketplace. It is called "intellectual" property because it is the product of human imagination, creativity, and inventiveness. Traditionally, businesses have thought of their physical assets, such as land, buildings, and equipment, as their most important assets. Increasingly, however, a company's intellectual assets are the most valuable. Prime Adult Fitness's intellectual assets and the forms of intellectual property protection used to secure them, are shown in its business plan in Figure 9-9.

Prime Adult Fitness has moved quickly to protect its intellectual assets, particularly its trademarks. It has also established a firm policy to protect its trade secrets. A **trade secret** is any formula, pattern, physical device, idea, process, or other information that provides the owners of the information with a competitive advantage in the marketplace. Trade secrets include marketing plans, product formulas, financial forecasts, employee rosters, logs of sales calls, laboratory notebooks, operations manuals, and similar material. Unlike patents, trademarks, and copyrights, no single government agency regulates trade secret laws. Instead, trade secrets are governed by a patchwork of state laws. The federal **Economic Espionage Act,** passed in 1996, does criminalize the theft of trade secrets.

The key to protecting trade secrets is to keep them confidential and reveal them only on a need to know basis to employees within the firm. In general, information that is known to the public or that competitors can discover through legal means (like looking at a company's Web site) doesn't qualify for trade secret information. It is also prudent to safeguard information that you deem as a trade secret through simple common sense means. For example, a company's membership list should be available only through a password-protected computer file and only to employees who have a legitimate reason to use it.

The primary rule of thumb for deciding if intellectual property should be protected is to determine whether it's related to a firm's competitive advantage. If it is, then legal protection should be pursued. Trademarks and copyrights can be obtained fairly inexpensively. Patents are expensive to obtain, which poses a challenge for many startups. The total cost of applying for a patent ranges from $5,000 to $50,000, depending on the nature of the patent. In addition, a patent must be applied for within one year of when a product or process is first offered for sale, put into public use, or is described in any printed publication (such as a concept statement) or the right to file a patent application for the product or process is forfeited. Thus, the decision regarding whether to spend the money to apply for a patent on a product or process must been made soon in the life of a new firm. One provision of the patent law that is particularly important for entrepreneurs is that the U.S. Patent and Trademark Office allows inventors to file a **provisional patent application,** pending the preparation and filing of a complete application. This part of the law grants "provisional rights" to an inventor for up to one year, pending the filing of a complete and final application. This provision of the law allows a startup to stake a claim to a particular invention for up to a year while it's deciding whether to move forward with a complete patent application. As of July 2007, the fee for filing a provisional patent application for a small firm (which receives a discount) was $100. You usually need to employ an attorney, however, to help prepare the application.

One sticky point in business plans is to decide how much to reveal about a company's potential intellectual property, knowing that the plan will be read by people who ultimately won't be involved with the venture. Although a company wants the readers of its business plan to fully grasp its potential, the fear is that by revealing too much, a startup risks losing the confidential nature of its plans, particularly as it relates to products that may be patented and trade names that will eventually be legally protected. There is no good answer to this conundrum, so you must make a judgment call. The vast majority of business ideas are not unique enough that this issue becomes a problem, but that isn't always the case. To resolve this dilemma, some startups provide just enough information in their business plans to entice their readers to want to know more and then reveal more information to interested parties on a case-by-case basis.

A full discussion on intellectual property and its importance is beyond the scope of this book. If you feel that patents, trademarks, copyrights, and trade secrets will be important to your startup, you should locate a credible publication to further acquaint yourself with the pluses and minuses of paying for intellectual property protection before you complete this portion of your business plan.

Chapter Summary

1. This chapter is divided into two parts. The first part of the chapter describes the operations section of a business plan, which focuses on how you will produce your product or service and run your business. This is an important section that should appear in every business plan. The second half of the chapter focuses on a topic that is singled out in some business plans and is not in others—the status of the development of a product or service.

2. The most important rule of thumb for writing the operations section and the product design and development section of your business plan is to focus on the aspects of each of these areas that are either essential to the success of your business or that sets you apart from your competitors. Routine topics should be dealt with lightly and quickly.

3. The operations plan section of the business plan outlines how your business will be run and how your product or service will be produced. The topics generally included are operating model and procedures, business location, facilities and equipment, and operations strategy and plans. Other topics may be included depending on the nature of the business.

4. A useful way to illustrate how a product or service will be produced is to include an operations flow diagram in your business plan. An operations flow diagram shows the key steps in the production of a product or the delivery of a service.

5. Although the operations flow diagram explains how a product or service is produced, there are other issues that are relevant for this section. These issues include an explanation of how your inventory will be stored and how frequently it will be turned over, a description of the length and nature of your product or service's production cycle, an explanation of where bottlenecks are likely to occur in your manufacturing process or service delivery and how these will be handled, an explanation of how seasonal production loads will be handled without service disruption, an explanation of how your quality control will be managed, and an explanation of how your after-sale service, if applicable, will be handled.

6. This product design and development section of your business plan has four parts: development status and tasks, difficulties and risks, costs, and intellectual property. Many seemingly promising startups never get off the ground because their product development efforts stall or the actual development of a product or service turned out to be more difficult than anticipated.

7. Most products follow a logical path of development that includes product conception, prototyping, initial production, and full production. Depending on the sophistication of your product- or service-development process, products and services typically pass tests that probe their performance and technical merits as they pass from one step in the development process to the next. You should explain the process you followed to move your product from one stage to the next.

8. If you are a very early stage firm and only have an idea, you should carefully explain how a prototype of your product will be made. A prototype is the first physical depiction of a new product.

9. One sticky point in business plans is to decide how much to reveal about a company's potential intellectual property, knowing that the plan will be read by people who ultimately won't be involved with the venture. Although a company wants the readers of its business plan to fully grasp its potential, the fear is that by revealing too much, a startup risks losing the confidential nature of its plans, particularly as it relates to products that may be patented and trade names that will eventually be legally protected. The vast majority of business ideas are not unique enough that this issue becomes a problem, but that isn't always the case.

Review Questions

1. Why is it important to include an operations plan in a business plan?
2. When writing the operations plan and the product (and service) design and development plan sections of a business plan, why is it important to strike a careful balance between adequately describing the topics and not going into too much detail?
3. What is the most important rule of thumb for writing the operations and the product design and development sections of your business plan?
4. According to the chapter, there is a vast difference between thinking up a new product idea and actually designing and manufacturing the product. Explain the nature and importance of this difference.
5. What is an operations flow diagram, and why is it important?
6. Identify three specific instances in which a business's location is a critical factor in its capability to operate efficiently and effectively.
7. What is a product prototype, and why it is important?
8. Describe what usability testing is and why it is important.
9. To what extent should a startup be candid and transparent regarding the challenges and risks associated with its product development process?
10. What are the four types of intellectual property, and why is it important to address intellectual property issues in a business plan?

Application Questions

1. Radar Golf (http://www.radargolf.com) is the name of a company that places tiny electronic tags inside golf balls to make them easy to find when lost.

Spend some time looking at Radar Golf's Web site to get acquainted with its product offerings. What do you think were the major "operational" issues that Radar Golf included in its business plan?

2. Gene Patterson, a professional acquaintance of yours, asked you to review his business plan. Gene's plan is for a new iPhone accessory, which will allow people to use their iPhone as a karaoke machine. Gene is particularly proud of the operations section of the plan, which describes in painstaking detail the technology behind converting an iPhone into a karaoke machine and explains in a step-by-step manner how the business will be run. In total, the operations section of Gene's plan comprises 11 of the 29 pages of the plan. Give Gene some feedback regarding the scope and length of the operations section of his plan.

3. Imagine that you have invented a new type of backpack for students to carry their books on campus. As part of your business plan, you have decided to "outsource" the actual manufacture of the backpack to a company in China. Do some research to determine how you would locate a company in China to manufacture your backpack. After you locate an appropriate company, how much information should you include in your business plan about the company that will manufacture your backpack?

4. Suppose you launched a new social networking Web site for college students to compete against Facebook and MySpace. What factors should you consider in selecting the physical location of your business? How would you determine how much attention to devote to this issue in your business plan?

5. Suppose you were the founder of Slingbox (http://www.slingmedia.com), the company that produces a device that allows people who are away from home to tap into their home television cable box or satellite receiver and watch any program that is being played at home on their remote computer. (Spend some time looking at Slingbox's Web site and its product.) How would you have put together the product design and development section of your business plan? What portions in the product design and development section would you have particularly emphasized?

Endnotes

1. A. Zacharakis, "The Business Plan," in *The Portable MBA in Finance and Accounting*, ed. John L. Livingstone and T. Grossman (New York: John Wiley & Sons, Inc., 2002), 260–290.
2. Mom Inventor's Network homepage, http://www.mominventors.com (July 5, 2007).
3. Silpada Design's homepage, http://www.silpada.com (July 5, 2007).
4. American Marketing Association Dictionary of Marketing Terms, http://www.marketingpower.com (July 6, 2007).
5. The Usability Company homepage, http://www.theusabilitycompany.com (July 9, 2007).
6. S. Rich and D. Gumpert, *Business Plans That Win* (Cambridge, MA: Harper & Row, 1985).

CHAPTER 10

FINANCIAL PROJECTIONS

INTRODUCTION

The final section of a business plan presents a firm's pro forma (or projected) financial projections. Having completed the previous sections of the plan, it's easy to see why the financial projections come last. They take the plans you've developed and express them in financial terms. As a result, you'll find yourself referring to earlier sections in your business plan frequently while you prepare your financial projections. For example, you prepared your sales forecasts in Chapter 6, a marketing budget in Chapter 7, and a schedule of the salaries of your initial management team in Chapter 8. These numbers, along with others, flow directly to the financial projections you develop in this chapter.

There are three things to be particularly mindful of as you approach this chapter. First, although you may be very passionate about a particular business idea, like starting a fitness center for people 50 years old and older, the people who read your plan will be primarily interested in your business's potential financial results. Investors are normally interested in the size of the returns and how quickly a company can grow, whereas bankers are more interested in the predictability and stability of a company's financial results and how it will minimize risk. As a result, it's important to provide these folks the financial information they need to make their judgments. If your plan is beautifully written, but the financial section is lacking, investors and bankers simply won't have the information they need to offer you financing or funding.

The second thing to be mindful of as you approach this chapter is that your financial statements show whether your business can get up and running successfully. There are many businesses that once started, represent viable ongoing businesses. The trick is to get them started. Unless your business is cash flow positive from the beginning, which is rare, there will be a period of time that you'll lose money while you're ramping up the business. For example, as you'll see later in the chapter, Prime Adult Fitness's financial projections look very promising for 2010 and beyond. But its startup year, 2009, is projected to be challenging. Its 2009 income statement projects a $94,570 loss, and its 2009 cash flow statement show that the company will need to rely on a prearranged line of credit from a bank to avoid running seriously low on cash. The main reason that Prime Adult Fitness's first year will be so tough is that it will open its doors on January 1, 2009 with a fully equipped building and staff (and all the related expenses), but only a handful of members. It will take the entire year for the company to reach its goal of 2,100 membership units. In the meantime, all of its fixed expenses (and most of its variable expenses) march on. In 2010 and beyond, its cash flow improves dramatically because its membership goals are projected to be met. The challenge for Prime Adult Fitness will be to survive 2009 (the year it is building its membership) to get to 2010 and beyond.

Most startups are similar to Prime Adult Fitness—there will be a startup period during which they lose money until they are fully up to speed and reach profitability. A firm's pro forma financial statements, in particular its initial balance sheets and cash flows, show how this period will unfold. Discerning readers will be looking for this information. Very few, if any, investors or bankers will finance a firm that doesn't demonstrate that it has thought through this critical issue. If the statements are missing, or if they are done poorly or incorrectly, the entire plan will be compromised.

The third thing to be mindful of as you approach this chapter is that most students and entrepreneurs are not familiar with how to complete pro forma financial projections. If you fall into this category (as most people do), don't wing it. Get help. The financial statements are too important to not be completed carefully and accurately. A good source for one-on-one help is SCORE (http://www.score.org), an organization of retired business people who will normally provide assistance for free. Small Business Develop Centers frequently hold classes and workshops on how to complete financial statements. Approaching an accounting professor in your own college or university to ask for assistance may be another viable option.

This chapter consists of six parts that cover the information normally included in the financial section of a business plan: sources and uses of funds statement, assumptions sheet, income statements, balance sheets, cash flows, and ratio analysis.

Now let's look at the first section in this chapter, the sources and uses of funds statement. The Prime Adult Fitness sources and uses of funds statement is shown in Figure 10-1.

SOURCE AND USE OF FUNDS STATEMENT

The **source and use of funds statement** is a document that lays out specifically how much money a firm needs (if the intention of the business plan is to raise money), where the money will come from, and what the money will be used for. Normally, a portion of the startup funds is provided by the founders or the initial

FIGURE 10-1	Source and Use of Funds Statement (Prime Adult Fitness Business Plan)

Sources of Funds

Source	Amount
Management Team Investment	$ 325,000
Angel Investor—Timothy Kemp	$ 175,000
Grant from *Healthy After 50*	$ 60,000
Line of Credit with Oviedo Security Bank ($100,000 LOC; $50,000 to be disbursed when business opens)	$ 50,000
Total Funds Committed	$ 610,000
Total Funds Required	$ 1,125,000
Total Funds Needed from an Equity Investor	$ 515,000

Uses of Funds

Cost	Item
Retrofit Building (including architect)	$ 750,000
Exercise Equipment—Purchase Outright	$ 50,000
Office and Computer Equipment	$ 60,000
Furniture	$ 30,000
Sales and Marketing	$ 40,000
Attorney Fees	$ 10,000
Initial Inventory	$ 20,000
Other	$ 15,000
Cash (working capital and reserve to cover 2009 losses)	$ 150,000
Total Required Funds	$ 1,125,000

*Approximately $25,000 in additional startup costs have been bootstrapped by founders.

management team; a portion is contributed by an early investor, such as an angel investor, a friend, or a family member of one of the founders; and the remainder is what's still needed. The level of detail, regarding both sources and uses of funds, shown in the Prime Adult Fitness sources and uses of funds statement in Figure 10-1 is appropriate for most new ventures. The items from the sources and uses of funds statement normally become the initial assets and liabilities of the firm. As explained later in this chapter, only certain items qualify to be reflected on a firm's balance sheet. Still, the sources and uses of funds statement is an important starting point in preparing the initial balance sheet for the firm.

If any of the funds you will be receiving come from an unusual source, you should substantiate the source of funding. For example, one of Prime Adult Fitness's sources of funds, as shown in Figure 10-1, is a grant from a nonprofit agency called Healthy After 50. This organization believes in Prime Adult Fitness's overall mission and has committed $60,000 to help the company get

FIGURE 10-2   Assumptions Sheet (Prime Adult Fitness Business Plan)

The financial statements depend on important assumptions. The key underlying assumptions are as follows:

General (Assumptions)

1. Interest in fitness and exercise will remain strong.
   Sources: Mintel, IBISWorld, International Health, Racquet & Sportsclub Association
2. We assume access to equity capital in the amount of $515,000, consistent with the Sources and Uses of Funds statement in this business plan.

Financial Statements (Assumptions)

Income Statements

1. Sales forecasts are based on the analysis presented in the "market analysis" section of this business plan. Sales are projected to increase 6% per year.
2. Cost of Goods Sold (COGS): 27.5% of net sales
   Sources: Results of a survey of 88 fitness centers, in the same sales range as Prime Adult Fitness, conducted by BizMiner (http://www.bizminer.com)
3. We assume that our receivables, which will primarily consist of overdue monthly membership fees, will take 30 days (on average) to collect.
4. Officer's compensation based on "Ownership and Compensation" table shown in the "management team" section of this business plan.
5. COGS for each month includes direct labor costs associated with delivering fitness classes and maintaining fitness machines.
6. Employees' benefits figured at 17.5% of salary.
7. Marketing expenses based on annual marketing budget in "marketing plan" section of this business plan.

Balance Sheets

1. Accumulation of accounts receivable is consistent with industry norms.
2. The retrofitting of the building and the leasing of fitness equipment are "off the balance sheet" transactions consistent with normal accounting practices.

started. Placing a letter from the director or president of Healthy After 50 in the Appendix to the business plan to verify that the grant is forthcoming would be appropriate.

The next section of this portion of the business plan presents the assumptions sheet. This section of the Prime Adult Fitness business plan is shown in Figure 10-2.

ASSUMPTIONS SHEET

An **assumptions sheet** is an explanation of the most critical assumptions that your financial statements are based on. Some assumptions will be based on general information, and no specific sources will be cited to substantiate the assumption.

For example, if you believe that the U.S. economy will remain strong, and that's an underlying assumption driving your sales projections, then you should state that assumption. In this instance, you wouldn't cite a specific source—you're reflecting a consensus view. (It's then up to your reader to agree or disagree.) Other assumptions will be based on very specific information, and you should cite the source for your assumption. For example, on its pro forma income statements, Prime Adult Fitness computes its cost of good sold (COGS) at 27.5 percent of sales. A BizMiner (http://www.bizminer.com) survey of 88 fitness centers, in the same sales range as Prime Adult Fitness, reported COGS from 24 to 32 percent. As shown in Figure 10-1, Prime Adult Fitness cites BizMiner as a source in making this assumption.

In many instances, the assumption sheet references earlier portions of the business plan. For example, Prime Adult Fitness computed its sales projections in the market analysis section of the plan, where a full explanation of where the numbers came from was provided. The explanation doesn't need to be repeated here. Although the assumption sheet is only meant to comment on the most critical numbers used to prepare the financial statements, it's impossible to overemphasize the importance of conveying to your reader that your statements are built on good data. The online resources shown in Appendix 2.2 at the end of Chapter 2 provide an excellent starting point to look for industry norms and other data. There are two reference books that are also helpful in computing financial statements: *Dun & Bradstreet Industry Norms and Key Business Ratios*[1] and the *Almanac of Business and Industrial Financial Ratios*.[2] Both of these books are usually available in the reference section of a university or major city library. The *Almanac of Business and Industrial Financial Ratios*, for example, reports the average operating costs (for line items such as cost of operations and employee benefits) as a percent of net sales for many lines of business at different sales levels.

In many instances, simple gumshoe labor and inquisitiveness is all that's needed to obtain and report an important financial number. For example, if your business will be occupying a building, a simple call to the electric company or a rental company that manages buildings may be all that's needed to get a good handle on anticipated utility costs. It's fully appropriate to cite these types of sources, as long as you're convinced that they're credible, in the assumptions sheet.

PRO FORMA FINANCIAL STATEMENTS

The **pro forma (or projected) financial statements** are the heart of the financial section of a business plan. Although at first glance preparing financial statements appears to be a tedious exercise, it's a fairly straightforward process if the preceding sections of your plan are thorough. If your plan has been built in the manner described in this book, most of the hard work, such as projecting sales and creating a marketing budget, has already been done. The financial statements also represent the culmination or finale of the entire plan. As a result, it's interesting to see how they turn out.

A firm's pro forma financial statements are similar to the historical statements an established firm would normally prepare, except they look forward rather than track the past. Pro forma financial statements include the income statement, balance sheet, and cash flow statement. The statements are usually prepared in this order because information flows logically from one to the next. Most experts recommend three to five years of statements, with the first two years for the income statement and the cash flow statement complete on a monthly basis. If the company you're writing your plan for already exists, you should also include three years of historic financial statements.

The first statements that are normally prepared are the pro forma income statements. The Prime Adult Fitness pro forma income statements for 2009, 2010, 2011, and 2012 are shown in Figure 10-3.

PRO FORMA INCOME STATEMENT

The **pro forma income statement** reflects the projected results of the operations for a firm for a given period of time. It records all the projected sales and expenses for the given period and shows whether the firms will be making a profit or experiencing a loss (which is why the income statement is often referred to as the "profit and loss"). Income statements are typically prepared on a monthly, quarterly, or annual basis. For a startup, it's important to complete the statements on a monthly basis, at least for the first two years. Most pro forma income statements are prepared in a multiyear format, making it easy to spot trends.

The pro forma income statements for Prime Adult Fitness are shown in Figure 10-3. The value of the multiyear format is clear. After a loss in 2009 (its startup year), the company is projected to experience healthy increases in sales and net income for 2010, 2011, and 2012. An income statement also exposes a company's risks. For example, even though Prime Adult Fitness shows a $317,740 net income in 2010, a 15 percent drop in projected sales would turn the $317,740 gain into a $44,736 loss. This scenario illustrates in part why projecting sales as accurately as possible is such a critical issue.

The three numbers that receive the most attention when evaluating an income statement are the following:

- *Net sales.* **Net sales** consist of total sales minus allowances for returned goods and discounts.
- *Cost of goods sold (COGS).* **COGS** includes all the direct costs associated with producing or delivering a product or service, including the material costs and direct labor. For Prime Adult Fitness, this includes the direct labor needed to teach the center's classes, run its programs, and maintain the fitness equipment, as well as the materials disbursed to members in classes.
- *Operating expenses.* **Operating expenses** include marketing, utilities, and administrative costs not directly related to producing a product or service.

In regard to increases in net sales from one year to the next in the pro forma statements, these numbers are normally determined in the "market analysis"

FIGURE 10-3   Pro Forma Income Statements 2009, 2010, 2011, 2012 (Prime Adult Fitness Business Plan)

Pro Forma Income Statement 2009 (First Year of Business)

	January	February	March	April	May	June
Gross Sales	60,890	83,000	102,600	123,710	135,360	152,020
(Returned Goods and Discounts)						
Net Sales	60,890	83,000	102,600	123,710	135,360	152,020
(Cost of Goods Sold)	16,740	22,820	28,210	34,020	37,220	41,800
Gross Profit	44,150	60,180	74,390	89,690	98,140	110,220
Expenses—General and Administrative						
Officers Compensation	25,750	25,750	25,750	25,750	25,750	25,750
Salaries and Wages	16,000	16,000	16,000	17,000	17,000	17,000
Payroll Taxes	3,820	3,820	3,820	3,890	3,890	3,890
Employee Benefits	10,800	10,800	10,800	10,980	10,980	10,980
Professional Services	1,000	1,000	1,000	1,000	1,000	1,000
Building Rent	27,000	27,000	27,000	27,000	27,000	27,000
Utilities	5,850	5,850	5,850	5,850	5,850	5,850
Telephone, Internet, and Web Site	1,300	1,300	1,300	1,300	1,300	1,300
Office Equipment Lease	1,400	1,400	1,400	1,400	1,400	1,400
Insurance	3,000	3,000	3,000	3,000	3,000	3,000
Marketing	10,000	9,000	7,000	4,000	3,000	3,000
Supplies	1,500	1,500	1,500	1,500	1,500	1,500
Interest	500	500	500	500	500	500
Taxes						
Other General and Admin Expenses	3,500	3,500	3,500	3,500	3,500	3,500
Depreciation and Amortization	1,500	1,500	1,500	1,500	1,500	1,500
Total Expenses	112,920	111,920	109,920	108,170	107,170	107,170
Net Income	(68,770)	(51,740)	(35,530)	(18,480)	(9,030)	3,050

	July	August	September	October	November	December	Total
Gross Sales	153,030	159,750	167,200	176,150	185,100	191,540	1,690,350
(Returned Goods and Discounts)							
Net Sales	153,030	159,750	167,200	176,150	185,100	191,540	1,690,350
(Cost of Goods Sold)	42,080	43,930	45,980	48,440	50,900	52,670	464,810
Gross Profit	110,950	115,820	121,220	127,710	134,200	138,870	1,225,540
Expenses—General and Administrative							
Officers Compensation	25,750	25,750	25,750	25,750	25,750	25,750	309,000
Salaries and Wages	18,000	18,000	18,000	19,000	19,000	19,000	210,000
Payroll Taxes	3,940	3,940	3,940	3,990	3,990	3,990	46,920
Employee Benefits	11,160	11,160	11,160	11,340	11,340	11,340	132,840
Professional Services	1,000	1,000	1,000	1,000	1,000	1,000	12,000
Building Rent	27,000	27,000	27,000	27,000	27,000	27,000	324,000
Utilities	5,850	5,850	5,850	5,850	5,850	5,850	70,200

FIGURE 10-3 (continued)

	July	August	September	October	November	December	Total
Telephone, Internet, and Web Site	1,300	1,300	1,300	1,300	1,300	1,300	15,600
Fitness Equipment Lease	1,400	1,400	1,400	1,400	1,400	1,400	16,800
Insurance	3,000	3,000	3,000	3,000	3,000	3,000	36,000
Marketing	2,000	2,000	2,000	2,000	6,000	6,000	56,000
Supplies	1,500	1,500	1,500	1,500	1,500	1,500	18,000
Interest	500	500	500	500	500	7,250	12,750
Taxes							
Other General and Admin Expenses	3,500	3,500	3,500	3,500	3,500	3,500	42,000
Depreciation and Amortization	1,500	1,500	1,500	1,500	1,500	1,500	18,000
Total Expenses	107,400	107,400	107,400	108,630	112,630	119,380	1,320,110
Net Income	3,550	8,420	13,820	19,080	21,570	19,490	(94,570)
Income as a Percent of Gross Sales							

Pro Forma Income Statement 2010 (Second Year of Business)

	January	February	March	April	May	June
Gross Sales	201,400	201,400	201,400	201,400	201,400	201,400
(Returned Goods and Discounts)						
Net Sales	201,400	201,400	201,400	201,400	201,400	201,400
(Cost of Goods Sold)	55,380	55,380	55,380	55,380	55,380	55,380
Gross Profit	146,020	146,020	146,020	146,020	146,020	146,020
Expenses—General and Administrative						
Officers Compensation	25,750	25,750	25,750	25,750	25,750	25,750
Salaries and Wages	20,000	20,000	20,000	20,000	20,000	20,000
Payroll Taxes	4,070	4,070	4,070	4,070	4,070	4,070
Employee Benefits	11,500	11,500	11,500	11,500	11,500	11,500
Professional Services	1,000	1,000	1,000	7,000	1,000	1,000
Building Rent	27,000	27,000	27,000	27,000	27,000	27,000
Utilities	6,150	6,150	6,150	6,150	6,150	6,150
Telephone, Internet, and Web Site	1,400	1,400	1,400	1,400	1,400	1,400
Office Equipment Lease	1,400	1,400	1,400	1,400	1,400	1,400
Insurance	3,150	3,150	3,150	3,150	3,150	3,150
Marketing	10,000	9,000	7,000	4,000	3,000	3,000
Supplies	1,500	1,500	1,500	1,500	1,500	1,500
Interest	500	500	500	500	500	500
Taxes	5,200	5,200	5,200	5,200	5,200	5,200
Other General and Admin Expenses	3,670	3,670	3,670	3,670	3,670	3,670
Depreciation and Amortization	1,500	1,500	1,500	1,500	1,500	1,500
Total Expenses	123,790	122,790	120,790	123,790	116,790	116,790
Net Income	22,230	23,230	25,230	22,230	29,230	29,230

FIGURE 10-3   (continued)

	July	August	September	October	November	December	Total
Gross Sales	201,400	201,400	201,400	201,400	201,400	201,110	2,416,510
(Returned Goods and Discounts)	-	-	-	-	-	-	-
Net Sales	201,400	201,400	201,400	201,400	201,400	201,110	2,416,510
(Cost of Goods Sold)	55,380	55,380	55,380	55,380	55,380	55,360	664,540
Gross Profit	146,020	146,020	146,020	146,020	146,020	144,750	1,751,970
Expenses—General and Administrative							
Officers Compensation	25,750	25,750	25,750	25,750	25,750	25,750	309,000
Salaries and Wages	20,000	20,000	20,000	20,000	20,000	20,000	240,000
Payroll Taxes	4,070	4,070	4,070	4,070	4,070	4,070	48,840
Employee Benefits	11,500	11,500	11,500	11,500	11,500	11,500	138,000
Professional Services	1,000	1,000	1,000	1,000	1,000	1,000	18,000
Building Rent	27,000	27,000	27,000	27,000	27,000	27,000	324,000
Utilities	6,150	6,150	6,150	6,150	6,150	6,150	73,800
Telephone, Internet, and Web Site	1,400	1,400	1,400	1,400	1,400	1,400	16,800
Fitness Equipment Lease	1,400	1,400	1,400	1,400	1,400	1,400	16,800
Insurance	3,150	3,150	3,150	3,150	3,150	3,150	37,800
Marketing	2,000	2,000	2,000	2,000	6,000	6,000	56,000
Supplies	1,500	1,500	1,500	1,500	1,500	1,500	18,000
Interest	500	500	500	500	500	7,250	12,750
Taxes	5,200	5,200	5,200	5,200	5,200	5,200	62,400
Other General and Admin Expenses	3,670	3,670	3,670	3,670	3,670	3,670	44,040
Depreciation and Amortization	1,500	1,500	1,500	1,500	1,500	1,500	18,000
Total Expenses	115,790	115,790	115,790	115,790	119,790	126,540	1,434,230
Net Income	30,230	30,230	30,230	30,230	26,230	19,210	317,740
Income as a Percent of Gross Sales							13.1

Pro Forma Income Statement 2011 (Third Year of Business)

Gross Sales	2,561,290
(Returned Goods and Discounts)	
Net Sales	2,561,290
(Cost of Goods Sold)	704,350
Gross Profit	1,856,940
Expenses—General and Administrative	
Officers Compensation	397,540
Salaries and Wages	254,400
Payroll Taxes	56,110
Employee Benefits	158,560
Professional Services	19,080
Building Rent	324,000
Utilities	78,220
Telephone, Internet, and Web Site	17,800
Fitness Equipment Lease	16,800

FIGURE 10-3 (continued)

Insurance	40,070
Marketing	59,360
Supplies	19,080
Interest	12,750
Taxes	68,820
Other General and Admin Expenses	46,680
Depreciation and Amortization	18,000
Total Expenses	1,587,270
Net Income	269,670
Income as a Percent of Gross Sales	10.5%

Pro Forma Income Statement 2012 (Fourth Year of Business)

Gross Sales	2,716,130
(Returned Goods and Discounts)	
Net Sales	2,716,130
(Cost of Goods Sold)	746,930
Gross Profit	1,969,200
Expenses—General and Administrative	
Officers Compensation	421,390
Salaries and Wages	269,660
Payroll Taxes	59,470
Employee Benefits	168,070
Professional Services	20,240
Building Rent	324,000
Utilities	82,910
Telephone, Internet, and Web Site	18,860
Fitness Equipment Lease	16,800
Insurance	42,470
Marketing	62,920
Supplies	20,220
Interest	12,750
Taxes	72,950
Other General and Admin Expenses	49,480
Depreciation and Amortization	18,000
Total Expenses	1,660,190
Net Income	309,010
Income as a Percent of Gross Sales	11.3

portion of a firm's business plan and are simply transferred to the pro forma statements. There are two ways to handle year-to-year increases in projected expenses. Some increase in expenses will be known. For example, in 2011, Prime Adult Fitness projects adding a Senior Vice President of Strategic Planning to its management team. The salary range for this position is known, so a direct number can be added to the category "officers compensation," and appropriate adjustments can be made to payroll taxes and employee benefits to reflect the change. For general expense items, many firms use the **constant ratio method** of forecasting—which increases expense items at the same rate as sales. Prime

Adult Fitness used this method in preparing the expenses portion of its pro forma income statements.

One ratio of particular importance in evaluating a firm's pro forma income statements is a firm's projected profit margins, or return on sales (ROS). This number is computed by dividing net income by net sales. Beyond 2009, its startup year, Prime Adult Fitness's ROS is projected to be 13.1 percent, 10.5 percent, and 11.3 percent for the years 2010, 2011, and 2012, respectively. These are healthy numbers. IBISWorld, as reported in the "industry analysis" section of this business plan, reported that the average ROS for a sample of 196 fitness centers was 9 percent. Prime Adult Fitness's higher percentages likely reflect the greater scale of its operations than many of the fitness centers in the survey. Any time an apparent discrepancy appears in financial ratios, you should be prepared to explain the discrepancy at a minute's notice. For example, Prime Adult Fitness's projected drop from a 13.1 percent ROS in 2010 to a 10.5 percent ROS in 2011 may require an explanation in an investor presentation. The projected drop is due to the company's plans to add a VP of Strategic Planning position to its top management team in January 2010, as mentioned previously, at a cost of $70,000 a year plus benefits. The salary and benefits are reflected as a 70,000+ increase in expenses, without a corresponding increase in sales. This is what's causing the drop in 2010 ROS.

Pro forma income statements are useful in envisioning a firm's overall earnings potential and prospective changes from year to year. They don't, however, provide an indication of a firm's cash position. A firm can show excellent sales numbers, but if the sales accumulate as accounts receivable (or are used to build inventory), a firm can run out of cash despite glowing income statements. As a result, enthusiasm for impressive sales and net income figures on pro forma income statements are usually tempered. The sales still have to be realized and the money has to be collected for the results to be meaningful.

Still, Prime Adult Fitness's growth in net sales and net income during the period projected demonstrates the upside potential of the opportunity. If everything goes right, and the company launches as planned, the numbers appear to be realistic and feasible. The key phrase, however, is that everything must go as planned. Ultimately, your reader must have confidence that you and your team have the ability to execute the opportunity.

The second set of pro forma financial statements that are normally prepared are the pro forma balance sheets. Prime Adult Fitness's pro balances sheets for 2009, 2010, 2011, and 2012 are shown in Figure 10-4.

BALANCE SHEET

Unlike the pro forma income statement, which covers a specific period of time, a **pro forma balance sheet** is a projection of a firm's assets, liabilities, and owner's equity at a specific point in time. The top of a balance sheet (or the left-hand side, depending on how it is displayed), shows a firm's assets, whereas the bottom (or right-hand side) shows its liabilities and owner's equity. The assets are listed in order of their "liquidity," or the length of time it takes to convert them to cash.

FIGURE 10-4 Pro Forma Balance Sheets 2009, 2010, 2011, 2012 (Prime Adult Fitness Business Plan)

	1/1/2009 Start of business	12/31/2009 End of first year	12/31/2010 End of second year	12/31/2011 End of third year	12/31/2012 End of fourth year
Assets					
Current Assets					
Cash and Cash Equivalents	200,000	140,930	317,170	426,840	748,850
Accounts Receivable		50,000	100,000	150,000	150,000
Inventory	20,000	35,000	45,000	50,000	50,000
Other Current Assets	10,000	17,500		25,000	25,000
Total Current Assets	230,000	243,430	462,170	651,840	973,850
Fixed Assets					
Fitness Equipment	100,000	125,000	175,000	185,000	185,000
Vehicles				35,000	70,000
Furniture	30,000	35,000	35,000	55,000	60,000
Office Equipment	60,000	70,000	72,000	100,000	100,000
Less Accumulated					
Depreciation		(18,000)	(36,000)	(54,000)	(72,000)
Total Noncurrent Assets	190,000	212,000	246,000	321,000	343,000
Other Assets					
Total Assets	420,000	455,430	708,170	972,840	1,316,850
Liabilities					
Current Liabilities					
Accounts Payable		75,000	100,000	125,000	150,000
Accrued Expenses		25,000	25,000	35,000	45,000
Short-Term Notes Payable	50,000	90,000	10,000		
Total Current Liabilities	50,000	190,000	135,000	160,000	195,000
Long-Term Liabilities					
Long-Term Notes Payable	50,000	40,000	30,000		
Mortgages Payable					
Total Long-Term Liabilities	50,000	40,000	30,000		
Total Liabilities	100,000	230,000	165,000	160,000	195,000
Contributed Capital	320,000	320,000	320,000	320,000	320,000
Retained Earnings	0	(94,570)	223,170	492,840	801,850
Total Liabilities and					
Shareholder's Equity	420,000	455,430	708,170	972,840	1,316,850

The liabilities are listed in the order in which they must be paid. A balance sheet must always "balance," meaning a firm's assets must always equal its liabilities plus owner's equity.

Most startups create a projected opening, or base, balance sheet that shows what the business will look like at a beginning point in time. The Prime Adult Fitness base balance sheet is January 1, 2009, which coincides with the start date for its pro forma income statements and cash flows. The major categories of assets listed on a pro forma balance sheet are the following:

- *Current assets.* **Current assets** include cash plus items that are readily convertible to cash. It also includes items such as accounts receivable and inventory.

- *Fixed assets.* **Fixed assets** are assets used over a longer time frame, such as real estate, buildings, equipment, and furniture.

  The major categories of liabilities listed on a balance sheet are the following:

- *Current liabilities.* **Current liabilities** include obligations that are payable within a year, including accounts payable, accrued expenses, and the current portion of long-term debt.

- *Long-term liabilities.* **Long-term liabilities** include notes or loans that are repayable beyond one year, including liabilities associated with purchasing real estate, buildings, and equipment.

- *Owners' equity:* **Owners' equity** is the equity invested in the business by its owners plus the accumulated earnings reported by the business after paying dividends.

Balance sheets, regardless of whether they are actual or projected, are somewhat deceiving. Firms spend money on many things that never show up on their balance sheets. For example, many operating leases, like Prime Adult Fitness's lease of fitness equipment, are "off balance sheet" transactions. Similarly, intellectual property, such as patents, trademarks, and copyrights, receive value on the balance sheet in some cases, and in other cases, they don't. In addition, intangible assets, such as the amount of training a firm has provided to its employees or the value of its brand, are not recognized on its balance sheet. Real estate is valued on a balance sheet at its cost rather than fair market value. Although this stipulation doesn't normally affect pro forma balance sheets, it's another facet of balance sheets that needs to be understood. A firm could buy a piece of land for $250,000 and watch its value increase to $1 million over time but would still value the land at $250,000 on its balance sheet.

As a result of these issues, it's important to understand what a set of pro forma balance sheets potentially accomplish. When evaluating a pro forma balance sheet, the two primary questions are whether a firm will have sufficient short-term assets to cover its short-term debts and whether it is financially sound overall. Two calculations provide the answer to the first question. A the end of 2009, Prime Adult Fitness's projected **working capital,** defined as its current assets minus its current liabilities, is projected to be $53,430. This number represents the amount of liquid assets the firm has available. Its projected **current ratio,** which equals its projected current assets divided by its projected current liabilities, is 1.28, meaning that it is projecting that it will have $1.28 in current assets for every $1.00 in current debt. This is a tight number and may cause you to pause and wonder if the company will have sufficient current assets to meet its current liabilities. The numbers are stronger in future years, as the company's projected earnings help it build cash reserves. Prime Adult Fitness's current ratio is projected to be 3.42, 4.08, and 5.0 at the end of 2010, 2011, and 2012, respectively. This is a healthy trend.

The second question, will a firm be financially sound overall, is assessed by computing a firm's overall debt ratio. A company's **debt ratio** is computed by dividing its total debt by its total assets. Prime Adult Fitness is projecting a debt to asset ratio of 50.50 percent at the end of 2009, which is high. Similar to its current ratio, its debt to asset ratio improves over time as its projected earnings build cash and improve its overall financial situation. Its projected debt to asset ratio is 23.30 percent, 16.45 percent, and 14.81 percent for 2010, 2011, and 2012 respectively. This is obviously a healthy trend. Again, although these numbers are impressive, they hinge on Prime Adult Fitness's management team's ability to execute all phases of its business plan.

The numbers across all of a firm's pro forma financial statements are consistent with one another. Note that the profit of $317,740 Prime Adult Fitness reports on its pro forma 2011 income statement shows up as the difference between its 2011 and 2010 pro forma balance sheets.

The final set of pro forma financial statements that are prepared are the projected cash flows. These statements must be prepared last because they rely on data from their corresponding pro forma income statements and balance sheets to be completed. Prime Adult Fitness's pro forma cash flow statements for 2009, 2010, 2011, and 2012 are shown in Figure 10-5.

CASH FLOW

Many of the readers of your business plan will consider your pro forma cash flows to be the most valuable of your financial statements for the reasons mentioned earlier in the chapter. The **cash flow statements** provide an indication of whether a firm will be able to maintain a sufficient cash balance to get up and running successfully. This issue is critical enough that you should prepare your cash flow on a monthly basis, at least for the first two years of your firm's existence.

Interpreting and analyzing pro forma cash flow statements takes practice. The entries are intuitively obvious but still cause you to pause and think because there are a lot of unusual additions and subtractions involved. The basic idea behind a cash flow statement is to start with a beginning balance, like the amount of cash you have on hand at the beginning of a month; add your projected monthly income (or loss); and then list all the other transactions that either add or subtract from your cash. To capture items in an organized manner, the cash flow statement is divided into three activities: operating activities, investing activities, and finance activities.

- *Operating activities.* **Operating activities** include net income (or loss), depreciation, and changes in current assets and current liabilities other than cash.
- *Investing activities.* **Investing activities** include the purchase, sales, or investment in fixed assets, such as real estate, equipment, and buildings.
- *Financing activities.* **Financing activities** include cash raised during the period by borrowing money, making payments on loans, or paying dividends.

The best way to visualize how a cash flow works is to spend some time looking at the Prime Adult Fitness pro forma cash flow statements, shown in Figure 10-5. On the statements, the uses of cash are recorded as negative figures (which are shown by placing them in parentheses), and the sources of cash are recorded as

FIGURE 10-5   Pro Forma Cash Flow Statements 2009, 2010, 2011, 2012 (Prime Adult Fitness Business Plan)

Pro Forma Cash Flow Statement 2009 (First Year of Business)

	January	February	March	April	May	June
Cash Balance at Beginning of Month	200,000 (Beginning of Year)	133,380	83,790	36,410	8,580	53,700
Cash Flow from Operating Activities						
Net income	(68,770)	(51,740)	(35,530)	(18,480)	(9,030)	3,050
Additions (sources of cash)						
Decrease in accounts receivable						
Decrease in inventory						
Increase in accounts payable	4,000	4,000	5,000	5,000	6,000	6,000
Increase in accrued expenses	2,100	2,100	2,100	2,100	2,100	2,100
Increase in short-term notes payable					50,000	
Decrease in other current assets						
Depreciation	1,500	1,500	1,500	1,500	1,500	1,500
Subtractions (uses of cash)						
Decrease in accounts payable						
Decrease in accrued expenses						
Decrease in short-term notes payable						
Increase in accounts receivable	(4,200)	(4,200)	(4,200)	(4,200)	(4,200)	(4,200)
Increase in other current assets			(5,000)			(2,500)
Increase in inventory	(1,250)	(1,250)	(1,250)	(1,250)	(1,250)	(1,250)
Total Adjustments						
Cash Flow from Investing Activities						
Subtractions (uses of cash)						
Purchase of fitness equipment				(12,500)		
Purchase of vehicles						
Purchase of furniture						
Purchase of office equipment			(10,000)			
Cash Flow from Financing Activities						
Additions (sources of cash)						
Increase in long-term notes payable						
Increase in mortgages payable						
Subtractions (uses of cash)						
Decrease in long-term notes payable						
Decrease in mortgages payable						
Cash Balance at End of Month	133,380	83,790	36,410	8,580	53,700	58,400

FIGURE 10-5 (continued)

	July	August	September	October	November	December	Summary (For Year)
Cash Balance at Beginning of Month	58,400	67,600	81,670	101,140	120,870	135,590	200,000
Cash Flow from Operating Activities							
Net income	3,550	8,420	13,820	19,080	21,570	19,490	(94,570)
Additions (sources of cash)							
Decrease in accounts receivable							
Decrease in inventory							
Increase in accounts payable	7,500	7,500	7,500	7,500	7,500	7,500	75,000
Increase in accrued expenses	2,100	2,100	2,100	2,100	2,100	1,900	25,000
Increase in short-term notes payable							50,000
Decrease in other current assets							
Depreciation	1,500	1,500	1,500	1,500	1,500	1,500	18,000
Subtractions (uses of cash)							
Increase in accounts receivable	(4,200)	(4,200)	(4,200)	(4,200)	(4,200)	(3,800)	(50,000)
Decrease in short-term notes payable						(10,000)	(10,000)
Increase in inventory	(1,250)	(1,250)	(1,250)	(1,250)	(1,250)	(1,250)	(15,000)
Decrease in accounts payable							
Increase in other current assets							(7,500)
Decrease in accrued expenses							
Total Adjustments							
Cash Flow from Investing Activities							
Subtractions (uses of cash)							
Purchase of fitness equipment					(12,500)		(25,000)
Purchase of vehicles							
Purchase of furniture				(5,000)			(5,000)
Purchase of office equipment							(10,000)
Total Adjustments							
Cash Flow from Financing Activities							
Additions (sources of cash)							
Increase in long-term notes payable							
Increase in mortgages payable							

FIGURE 10-5   (continued)

Subtractions (uses of cash)							
Decrease in long-term notes payable						(10,000)	(10,000)
Decrease in mortgages payable							
Cash Balance at End of Month	67,600	81,670	101,140	120,870	135,590	140,930	**140,930** (End of Year)

Pro Forma Cash Flow Statement 2010 (Second Year of Business)

	January	February	March	April	May	June
Cash Balance at Beginning of Month	**140,930** (Beginning of Year)	162,960	185,990	208,520	230,550	259,580
Cash Flow from Operating Activities						
Net income	22,230	23,230	25,230	22,230	29,230	29,230
Additions (sources of cash)						
Decrease in accounts receivable						
Decrease in inventory						
Increase in accounts payable	2,500	2,500	2,500	2,500	2,500	2,500
Increase in accrued expenses						
Increase in short-term notes payable						
Decrease in other current assets						
Depreciation	1,500	1,500	1,500	1,500	1,500	1,500
Subtractions (uses of cash)						
Decrease in accounts payable						
Decrease in accrued expenses						
Decrease in short-term notes payable						
Increase in accounts receivable	(4,200)	(4,200)	(4,200)	(4,200)	(4,200)	(4,200)
Increase in other current assets						
Increase in inventory			(2,500)			(2,500)
Total Adjustments						
Cash Flow from Investing Activities						
Subtractions (uses of cash)						
Purchase of fitness equipment						(25,000)
Purchase of vehicles						
Purchase of furniture						
Purchase of office equipment						
Cash Flow from Financing Activities						
Additions (sources of cash)						
Increase in long-term notes payable						
Increase in mortgages payable						
Subtractions (uses of cash)						
Decrease in long-term notes payable						
Decrease in mortgages payable						
Cash Balance at End of Month	162,960	185,990	208,520	230,550	259,580	261,110

FIGURE 10-5 (continued)

	July	August	September	October	November	December	Summary (For Year)
Cash Balance at Beginning of Month	261,110	291,140	321,170	348,700	378,730	362,260	140,930
Cash Flow from Operating Activities							
Net income	30,230	30,230	30,230	30,230	26,230	19,210	317,740
Additions (sources of cash)							
Decrease in accounts receivable							
Decrease in inventory							
Increase in accounts payable	2,500	2,500	2,500	2,500			25,000
Increase in accrued expenses							
Increase in short-term notes payable							
Decrease in other current assets						17,500	17,500
Depreciation	1,500	1,500	1,500	1,500	1,500	1,500	18,000
Subtractions (uses of cash)							
Increase in accounts receivable	(4,200)	(4,200)	(4,200)	(4,200)	(4,200)	(3,800)	(50,000)
Decrease in short-term notes payable					(40,000)	(40,000)	(80,000)
Increase in inventory			(2,500)			(2,500)	(10,000)
Decrease in accounts payable							
Increase in other current assets							
Decrease in accrued expenses							
Total Adjustments							
Cash Flow from Investing Activities							
Subtractions (uses of cash)							
Purchase of fitness equipment						(25,000)	(50,000)
Purchase of vehicles							
Purchase of furniture							
Purchase of office equipment						(2,000)	(2,000)
Total Adjustments							
Cash Flow from Financing Activities							
Additions (sources of cash)							
Increase in long-term notes payable							
Increase in mortgages payable							

FIGURE 10-5   (continued)

Subtractions (uses of cash)							
Decrease in long-term notes payable						(10,000)	(10,000)
Decrease in mortgages payable							
Cash Balance at End of Month	291,140	321,170	348,700	378,730	362,260	317,170	**317,170** (End of Year)

Pro Forma Cash Flow Statement 2011 (Third Year of Business)

Cash Balance at Beginning of Year	317,170
Cash Flow from Operating Activities	
Net income	269,670
Additions (sources of cash)	
Decrease in accounts receivable	
Decrease in inventory	
Increase in accounts payable	25,000
Increase in accrued expenses	10,000
Increase in short-term notes payable	
Decrease in other current assets	
Depreciation	18,000
Subtractions (uses of cash)	
Increase in accounts receivable	(50,000)
Decrease in short-term notes payable	(10,000)
Increase in inventory	(5,000)
Decrease in accounts payable	
Increase in other current assets	(25,000)
Decrease in accrued expenses	
Total Adjustments	
Cash Flow from Investing Activities	
Additions (sources of cash)	
Sale of fitness equipment	
Sale of vehicles	
Sale of furniture	
Sale of office equipment	
Subtractions (uses of cash)	
Purchase of fitness equipment	(10,000)
Purchase of vehicles	(35,000)
Purchase of furniture	(20,000)
Purchase of office equipment	(28,000)
Total Adjustments	
Cash Flow from Financing Activities	
Additions (sources of cash)	
Increase in long-term notes payable	
Increase in mortgages payable	
Subtractions (uses of cash)	
Decrease in long-term notes payable	(30,000)
Decrease in mortgages payable	
Cash Balance at End of Year	426,840

FIGURE 10-5 (continued)

Pro Forma Cash Flow Statement 2012 (Fourth Year of Business)	
Cash Balance at Beginning of Year	426,840
Cash Flow from Operating Activities	
Net income	309,010
Additions (sources of cash)	
Decrease in accounts receivable	
Decrease in inventory	
Increase in accounts payable	25,000
Increase in accrued expenses	10,000
Increase in short-term notes payable	
Decrease in other current assets	18,000
Depreciation	
Subtractions (uses of cash)	
Increase in accounts receivable	
Decrease in short-term notes payable	
Increase in inventory	
Decrease in accounts payable	
Increase in other current assets	
Decrease in accrued expenses	
Total Adjustments	
Cash Flow from Investing Activities	
Additions (sources of cash)	
Sale of fitness equipment	
Sale of vehicles	
Sale of furniture	
Sale of office equipment	
Subtractions (uses of cash)	
Purchase of fitness equipment	
Purchase of vehicles	(35,000)
Purchase of furniture	(5,000)
Purchase of office equipment	
Total Adjustments	
Cash Flow from Financing Activities	
Additions (sources of cash)	
Increase in long-term notes payable	
Increase in mortgages payable	
Subtractions (uses of cash)	
Decrease in long-term notes payable	
Decrease in mortgages payable	
Cash Balance at End of Month	748,850

positive figures. In regard to operating activities, an item like depreciation is shown as a positive figure because it was deducted from net income on the income statement but was not a cash expenditure. Similarly, an increase in accounts receivable is shown as a negative item because it was added to your net income but wasn't collected as cash. The treatment of investing and financing activities is more straightforward. If you buy a piece of equipment, that subtracts from your cash. If you take out a loan, that adds to your cash. If you make a principle payment on a loan, that subtracts from your cash, and so forth. The closest attention is typically paid to operating activities because it shows how changes in a company's accounts receivable, accounts payable, and inventory levels affect the cash it has available to maintain routine activities.

As stated earlier in the chapter, Prime Adult Fitness's pro forma cash flow shows that it will run low on cash midway during its first year of existence. Anticipating this challenge, the founders arranged for a line-of-credit from a bank, which the company will use to shore up its cash position during this period. If the founders hadn't completed pro forma financial statements and realized that they will run low on cash in May of 2009, they could have found themselves in a very tight cash position. The time to arrange a line of credit isn't when you're running out of cash. Instead, their 2009 pro forma cash flow alerted them to this challenge, which they prepared for by arranging the line of credit.

In summary, it's extremely important that all of a firm's pro forma financial statement be prepared as accurately and realistically as possible. If your business plan does capture the attention of an investor or banker, your financial statements will be gone over very carefully, as part of the "due diligence" process. Incorrect entries, math errors, exaggerated items, and estimates that are simply off the mark (i.e., the average price to rent warehouse space in your community is $12.00 per square foot, and you're projecting you can rent it for $4.00 per square foot) will be picked up and may compromise your ability to get funding or financing if they are serious enough. Conversely, sharp financials that realistically translate a firm's plans into numbers and are error free can make a very positive impression.

Finally, like the business plan itself, going through the process of preparing your pro forma financial projections may be as valuable as the projections themselves. The numbers will invariably change, but the lessons you're bound to learn through preparing the statements are invaluable. Sometimes, entrepreneurs discount the value of financial analysis, thinking that the numbers are just a guess so they're really not important. Still, demonstrating the ability to prepare financial statements and think through the issues behind them is vital. This point is illustrated through a vignette reported by Rich and Gumpert in their book *Business Plans That Work*. The vignette portrays the reaction an investor had when an entrepreneur claimed that financial projections aren't really that important:

> One entrepreneur who was undergoing some intense questioning by panelists about his company's projections finally said, in exasperation, "I really don't take our projections or any projections more than a year out all that seriously. After all, I don't really know how much business is reasonable to expect three, four, and five years into the future." A panelist's response was swift and certain. "We know you can't say for sure what's going to happen," the panelist observed. "But you must go through the thought process. You must consider best-case and worst-case scenarios. You must demonstrate that you can quantify the marketing, production, and other research and testing you've done. We may not agree with your projections, but we want to see that you've thought about where your company might be in five years and quantified your thinking."[3]

BUSINESS PLAN INSIGHT

Break-Even Analysis: A Simple Yet Very Valuable Calculation

Break-even analysis is a calculation that allows a firm to determine the volume of business it must do to "break even" in terms of profit and loss. It's a form of analysis that's often used by startups and by existing firms to discern whether adding a new product to their existing product line makes sense. Technically, the break-even point for a new company or a new product is where the total revenue received equals the total costs associated with the company or product.

The best way to show how a break-even analysis works is to provide an illustration. Say you're interested in opening a smoothie restaurant. You could use a break-even analysis to determine whether opening the restaurant is feasible. The formula for break-even analysis is as follows:

$$\text{Total fixed costs}/(\text{price} - \text{average variable costs})$$

As a result, if the total fixed costs associated with opening the restaurant is $85,000, the average prices of the smoothies you'll sell is $4.50, and the variable cost for each smoothie is $2.10, then the break-point for your restaurant is as follows:

$$\$85,000 \text{ (total fixed costs)}/(\$4.50 - \$2.10) \text{ or } \$2.40 = 35,417 \text{ units}$$

This number means that you'll have to sell 35,417 "units" or smoothie drinks per year to break even. That number breaks down to 98.5 smoothies per day, on average, based on a 360-day year. To determine whether opening the restaurant is feasible and makes good financial sense, that number should be compared to the sales that similar smoothie restaurants experience.

Break-even analysis is also useful in helping entrepreneurs determine whether different business strategies make sense. Assume you're considering moving to a location with more foot traffic to boost your sales. Your rent will be higher, and your total fixed costs will jump from $85,000 per year to $112,000. If your prices and variable costs remain the same, the move will increase your break-even point to the following:

$$\$112,000 \text{ (total fixed costs)}/(\$4.50 - \$2.10) \text{ or } \$2.40 = 46,666 \text{ units.}$$

On a daily basis, the move will increase your break-even point from 98.5 smoothies a day to 130. You'll have to then decide whether moving to the new location will provide you with sufficient increased sales to justify the move.

Another financial instrument that is often used but was not computed for Prime Adult Fitness is the break-even analysis. An explanation of the break-even analysis and how it's used is provided in the Business Plan Insight box.

The next section of this chapter focuses on ratio analysis, which is a standard technique for analyzing pro forma financial statements. This portion of the Prime Adult Fitness business plan is shown in Figure 10-6.

FIGURE 10-6	Ratio Analysis (Prime Adult Fitness Business Plan)

Profitability Ratios

	2009	2010	2011	2012
Return on Assets (ROA)	NA	54%	32%	27%
ROA = net income/average total assets				
Return on Sales (ROS)	NA	13.1%	10.5%	11.3%
ROS = net income/net sales				

Average total assets = beginning total assets + ending total assets/2.
Average shareholders' equity = beginning shareholders' equity + ending shareholders' equity/2.

Liquidity Ratios

	2009	2010	2011	2012
Current ratio	1.28	3.42	4.08	5.00
Current assets/current liabilities				

Overall Financial Stability Ratios

	2009	2010	2011	2012
Debt ratio	50.50%	23.30%	16.45%	14.81%
Total debt/total assets				

RATIO ANALYSIS

The most practical way to interpret or make sense of a firm's historical or pro forma financial statements is through **ratio analysis.**

In general, ratios are computed by taking numbers out of financial statements and forming ratios with them. Each ratio has a particular meaning in regard to the potential of a business. Your readers will instantly recognize the general picture that a particular ratio conveys. For example, as mentioned earlier in the chapter, Prime Adult Fitness's current ratio is projected to be 1.28 at the end of 2009. That ratio will alert a discerning reader to pay attention to whether the firm has a back-up plan (such as a prearranged line of credit) to use if its cash position deteriorates further. It will also alert the reader to look forward to see if the projected cash position improves over time. Another valuable use of ratios is to compare a firm's ratios to industry norms. If a firm's ratios, such as projected ROA and ROS, are consistently better than industry norms, that's probably an indication that the firm's financial projections are too optimistic.

The three most common categories of financial ratios are profitability ratios, liquidity ratios, and overall financial stability ratios. **Profitability ratios** compare the amount of income earned against the resources used to generate it. **Liquidity ratios** measure the relationship between a company's short-term assets and its short-term liabilities. **Overall financial stability ratios** measure the overall financial stability of a firm.

The Prime Adult Fitness projected financial ratios are shown in Figure 10-6. The ROA ratios are high, reflecting in part the company's ability to generate high income in a facility it is leasing, thus the value of the facility doesn't show up on the firm's projected balance sheet. If Prime Adult Fitness was purchasing the building it will occupy for $5 million, its ROA in 2010 would be 7 percent.

Chapter Summary

1. The final section of a business plan presents a firm's pro forma financial projections. Having completed the previous sections of the plan, it's easy to see why the financial projections come last. They take the plans you've developed and express them in financial terms.

2. The source and use of funds statement is a document that lays out specifically how much money a firm needs (if the intention of the business plan is to raise money) and what the money will be used for.

3. An assumptions sheet is an explanation of the most critical assumptions that your financial statements are based on.

4. The pro forma income statement reflects the projected results of the operations for a firm for a given period of time. It records all the projected sales and expenses for the given period and shows whether the firms will be making a profit or experiencing a loss.

5. Pro forma income statements are useful in envisioning a firm's overall earnings potential and prospective changes from year to year. They don't, however, provide an indication of a firm's cash position.

6. Unlike the pro forma income statement, which covers a specific period of time, a pro forma balance sheet is a projection of a firm's assets, liabilities, and owner's equity at a specific point in time.

7. Many of the readers of your business plan will consider your pro forma cash flows to be the most valuable of your financial statements. The statements provide an indication of whether a firm will be able to maintain a sufficient cash balance to get up and running successfully.

8. To capture items in an organized manner, the cash flow statement is divided into three activities: operating activities, investing activities, and finance activities.

9. The most practical way to interpret or make sense of a firm's historical or pro forma financial statements is through ratio analysis.

In general, ratios are computed by taking numbers out of financial statements and forming ratios with them. Each ratio has a particular meaning in regard to the potential of a business.

Review Questions

1. Why is the financial plan typically one of the last chapters in a business plan?
2. What is the purpose of a sources and uses of funds statement?
3. What is the purpose of an assumptions sheet?
4. Briefly describe the three pro forma financial statements that should be included in a business plan.
5. How is it possible for a firm to show a sizable net income on its income statements and still be running out of cash?
6. Describe the term COGS (cost of goods sold).
7. Why would a current ratio of 1.1 raise concerns?
8. Describe why many people feel that the cash flow statement is the most valuable statement of the three financial statements normally included in a business plan.
9. Describe the purpose of ratio analysis.
10. Briefly describe at least one profitability ratio, one liquidity ratio, and one overall financial stability ratio.

Application Questions

1. Suppose a friend of yours showed you the pro forma income statements for his startup and exclaimed excitedly that during its first three years of operation, his firm will make a net income of $200,000 per year, which is just the amount of money, $600,000, that the firm will need to pay off a three-year loan. Explain to your friend why he might not actually have $600,000 in cash, even though his pro forma income statements say that he will earn that amount of money.
2. Suppose a colleague of yours is gearing up to write a business plan for a business she plans to start. She told you she plans to prepare the financial statements first, to get that job out of the way before she tackles the rest of the plan. Explain to your colleague the flaw in her approach.
3. Kate Dodd, a friend of yours, has developed a new wireless application that she feels will revolutionize the communications industry. She has been turned down by several potential investors who seemed to like the idea but insisted on seeing pro forma financial statements as part of a business plan. Kate doesn't think it's a good use of her time to develop pro forma financial statements. She believes, "If the product is good enough, the financials will take care of themselves." Why is Kate's position unwise? In your opinion, how common is the position Kate is taking about financial statements?
4. At a conference you attended recently, you were chatting with a group of people, and the subject came up that you recently completed a business plan, including a full set of pro forma financial projections. One of the people in the conversation asked you, "How in the world do you project income and expenses for a business that doesn't exist?" Write out a brief answer to this question.

5. Refer to the vignette at the end of the chapter (from *Business Plans That Work* by Rich and Gumpert). Imagine you are the entrepreneur in the vignette. How would you have responded to the investor's objection?

Endnotes

1. Dun & Bradstreet, *Industry Norms & Key Business Ratios: Statistics on Over 800 Lines of Business, Desk Top Edition* (New York: Dunn & Bradstreet, 2003).
2. L. Troy, *Almanac of Business and Industrial Financial Ratios* (New York: CCH, Inc., 2007).
3. S. Rich and D. Gumpert, *Business Plans That Work* (New York: Harper & Row, 1985).

CHAPTER 11

PRESENTING THE PLAN WITH CONFIDENCE

INTRODUCTION

If your business plan piques the interest of an investor or banker, or you enter it into a business plan competition, you'll normally be asked to make a verbal presentation of the plan. On these occasions, you'll want to be prepared to present the plan with confidence and poise. If the presentation goes well, it can move you closer to obtaining the funding or financing you need. If it doesn't, it can impede your chances of moving forward and represent a setback in your attempts to get your business off the ground.

This chapter provides a primer on making an effective business plan presentation. Most of us do not routinely make verbal presentations, so careful planning and practice pay off. If you've followed the approach to writing a business plan described in this book, you've put a lot of time and effort into the process. You'll want to cap off your efforts by presenting your plan in a manner that maximizes your chances for success.

This chapter contains two sections. The first section focuses on preparing for and making an effective presentation. Tips and suggestions are provided on steps to take before you make the presentation and how to deliver the presentation effectively. The second section of the chapter focuses on the content of the presentation. This section is augmented by walking you through a 12-slide PowerPoint presentation and making recommendations for what to include on each slide.

PREPARING FOR AND DELIVERING AN EFFECTIVE BUSINESS PLAN PRESENTATION

The first set of issues to think about after you've been asked to make a verbal presentation of your business plan is how to go about preparing for the task and how to deliver an effective presentation. How you present yourself and the manner in which you interact with the people you will be presenting to makes as much difference as the plan itself. As you present your plan, your audience will not only be judging your plan, but also they will be judging you (and your team). The way you carry yourself, your facial expressions, how sharp your PowerPoint slides are, how you handle difficult questions, and similar attributes, are all cues to your audience of how effective a business owner you are likely to be. As a result, it's important that you prepare and deliver the presentation in an effective manner.

This section covers two topics: preparing for the presentation and effective presentation techniques.

PREPARING FOR THE PRESENTATION

The initial task in preparing for a business plan presentation is to find out as much as you can about the people you'll be presenting to. This task may require some legwork but is normally well worth it. All venture capital firms have Web sites that include lists of their portfolio companies and bios of their partners, and it's usually easy to find out the backgrounds of business angels via Web searches and discrete inquiries. If you're involved in a business plan competition, it's not inappropriate to ask about the names and backgrounds of the judges.

Knowing this information is important for two reasons. First, if you can tie the business you're proposing into other activities that the people you're meeting are involved with, they may see more value in supporting your efforts. For example, if you were presenting the business plan for Prime Adult Fitness to a group of angel investors and noticed that one of the investors is a heart surgeon that practices at a local teaching hospital, you might mention during the presentation that Prime Adult Fitness would be open to the possibility of collaborating with the hospital. This comment might prompt the heart surgeon to start thinking about the types of studies he could conduct in your facility relating to exercise and cardiovascular health. If you can establish this type of tie-in with one or more of the panelists during the presentation, it might enhance the value of your business in their mind(s).

The second reason it's important to learn about the people you'll be presenting to is to try to find some type of personal connection with one or more of the individuals involved. Any type of common ground you can find, like having the same college or university affiliation or a similar hobby, helps break the ice and build rapport. You'll have to find an appropriate way of working the connection into your presentation, or bring it up during the informal minutes before or after your presentation. As long as you come across as sincere, people normally consider it a compliment that you went to the trouble of learning about their backgrounds.

The other tasks involved in preparing for a business plan presentation consist of a hodgepodge of activities. Any one of the activities, however, could be problematic if not handled correctly. You should make sure to know how much time you have and plan accordingly. The number one rule in making a presentation is to follow the rules. If an angel group tells you that you'll have 1 hour, but 30 minutes of the hour is reserved for questions and answers, your should carefully time your presentation so it doesn't last for more than 30 minutes—no excuses. You should also dress appropriately. If you're unsure of what to wear, call the receptionist of the firm at which you'll be presenting and ask about attire. If that route isn't practical, it's always better to dress up, by wearing formal business attire, than it is to dress down. The only exception to these rules of thumb is if your business has sharp polo shirts or something similar with your company name and logo on it. In this instance, it might be appropriate for your team members to wear that attire. You should also have business cards, even if you are a very early stage startup. There are many places where you can get generic business cards printed for just a few dollars.

It's also important to practice your presentation. Many experienced entrepreneurs practice their presentations several times in front of colleagues and others to time the presentation and get feedback. It's also a good idea to watch other people present, to get a sense of what works and what doesn't. There are business plan competitions in many areas, and you should sit in on the competitions if possible. There are also places on the Internet where presentations are posted. For example, firms that are planning to launch an IPO are taken on a "road show" by their investment bank. A road show is a whirlwind tour that consists of meetings in key cities where the firm presents its business plan to groups of investors. These presentations are taped and are available at http://www.retailroadshow.com until the IPO is completed. Another option is to view presentations made at the Demo Conference (http://www.demo.com), which is a conference where promising companies (mostly startups) are asked to "demo" their product or service ideas. (Go to the "Video Archives" link on the Demo's Web site.) These pitches are product pitches rather than business plan presentations, but they can still provide useful and interesting examples of effective and ineffective presentation techniques.

Finally, to the extent that you can, you should try to find out as much as you can about the venue you'll be presenting in. If you'll be in a small conference room, then you usually don't have to make any special adjustments. But if you'll be presenting on a stage or to a large audience, which is sometimes the case in the finals of a business plan competition, then you might want to make the fonts on your PowerPoint slides larger, for example, and find innovative ways to project to a larger audience.

DELIVERING AN EFFECTIVE PRESENTATION

Many books have been written about delivering effective presentations, and you may want to visit your library and browse through several of the books. Two particularly good books are *Knockout Presentations*[1] by Diane DiResta and *Presentations for Dummies*[2] by Malcolm Kushner. Both of these books contain numerous tips and pointers for making effective business presentations.

The first thing to consider in making a presentation is who will do the presenting. If you're a sole entrepreneur, you'll obviously be doing the presenting, but if you're part of team, the question always arises regarding how many members of the team should talk during the presentation. This issue is a judgment call, but there is a strong case to be made for involving as many team members as possible. If you tag team your presentation and it goes well, it shows that your team members work well together, and there is no one member of your team who is so dominant that he or she wants all the attention. It also helps keep the listener attentive and alert. It varies the pace of the presentation and allows the listener to learn a little bit about each of the individuals involved.

The second thing to consider is the proper role of the PowerPoint slides you're using and your verbal remarks. This is a place where many presenters, whether alone or as part of a group, miss the mark. Your PowerPoint slides are not meant to tell the story of your business. You (and your team) should tell the story, and the slides should provide an overall context and punctuate your remarks. This is a hard rule to follow because the natural tendency is to try to help the listener by making the slides as complete as possible. But that's usually a mistake. Your PowerPoint slides should be brief and contain only major themes and supporting points. Your audience should spend the majority of their time listening to you rather than reading your slides. The only exception to this rule is if you're sending a set of slides for someone to review instead of making a presentation. In this instance, the slides should be more complete because they'll need to tell the story.

There are many rules of thumb about PowerPoint slides in presentations, and you'll need to use your judgment in making various calls. Some experts recommend a 6-6-6 rule when drafting slides: 6 words per bullet, 6 bullets per page, and no more than 6 text slides in a row before a visual break (a slide that includes graphs, tables, or illustrations). All kinds of colorful metaphors are attached to the dangers of trying to fit too many slides into a presentation or making your slides too dense, including "death by PowerPoint" and "PowerPoint Poisoning" (coined first by Delbert). A maximum of 12 PowerPoint slides in a 20-30 minute business plan presentation and the 6-6-6 rule are good guidelines to follow. In the mock PowerPoint presentation shown later in this chapter, 12 slides are used.

The final and most important advice about delivering an effective presentation is to make it interesting, upbeat, and heartfelt (to the degree appropriate and fitting). No one wants to listen to a plodding, boring presentation, no matter how much potential the venture has. In addition, although it sounds cliché, you need to connect with your audience. The following is a brief list of techniques that presenters use to try to accomplish this objective:

- Tell a personal story or anecdote.
- Use humor.
- Show passion through hand gestures and excitement in your voice.
- Involve the audience by asking for a show of hands on key points.
- Demonstrate a prototype of the product.

This is just a brief list—you can use many other techniques as well. A very telling study conducted by MIT validates the importance of these types of techniques. According to the study, communication happens on three levels: 55 percent visual (body language), 35 percent vocal (tone of voice), and 7 percent verbal (words).[3] There are additional techniques that help a presenter connect with an audience, including building pauses into your presentation to ask if anyone has a question, and varying the pitch of your voice and changing your expressions to help keep the listeners engaged.

It's also important to understand that your overarching goal, during a business plan presentation, is to not only educate your audience about your idea but also to fire them up (to inspire). This goal can be accomplished in both overt and subtle ways. A subtle way is to tell a personal story or anecdote, which indicates why you feel your business is important and why you are fully committed to its success. For example, according to Jeremy Ryan's bio (Jeremy is the CEO and cofounder of Prime Adult Fitness), Jeremy's interest in fitness stems from an incident involving his father. At age 49, Jeremy's father survived a heart attack and restored his health by joining a fitness center and exercising regularly. Jeremy's father is now an active 73-year-old retiree. In his business plan presentation, Jeremy could briefly talk about his father and the impact that joining a fitness center has had on extending his life. This type of heartfelt story, as long as it ties in with the business, usually deeply resonates with an audience.

PREPARING THE CONTENT OF AN EFFECTIVE BUSINESS PLAN PRESENTATION

The second component of putting together an effective business plan presentation is to determine the content to present. As important as the issues are that were just covered, the presentation has little to no chance of succeeding if the content is poorly thought out or important elements are missing.

Obviously, you can't convey everything that's in a 25- to 35-page business plan in a 20- to 30-minute presentation. As a result, you have to focuses on the parts of the plan that are the most important to your audience. The single biggest mistake that people make in putting together a business plan presentation is focusing on the areas that excite them the most, rather than the areas that will help their audience make a decision. As indicated in Chapter 10, whereas you may be very passionate about your product (or service) idea, like starting a fitness center for people 50 years old and older, the people listening to your plan may have other interests. Although they need to know about your product, your market, your management team, and so forth, they usually have very specific information that they're listening for. For venture capitalists, it's usually how quickly you can grow your business and your anticipated rates of return. For bankers, it's normally how predictable your cash flows are and how you plan to minimize risk. For a business angel, it may be another topic. You'll need to anticipate what the "hot-button" issue is for your audience and structure your presentation accordingly.

A number of authors, and business plan experts, have recommended templates for business plan presentations. The templates spell out the number of slides to include, the order in which to include them, and the content to include on each slide. Although slight variations exist across authors, there is general consensus about what should be included in a 20- to 30-minute business plan presentation. The following plan represents a consensus of various approaches. You should tweak and vary the approach to make it fit your plan and to tailor it to the audience you are presenting to.

The plan presented here contains 12 slides. Many experts figure 2 minutes per slide (on average), so this number works fairly well for a 20- to 30-minute presentation. Presumably, the people you will be presenting to will have a copy of your business plan. If you're not confident of that, bring several copies of your plan to the presentation. This is particularly important if you're participating in a business plan competition. There may be members of the audience who are hearing your plan for the first time and may be interested in seeing the entire business plan.

SAMPLE BUSINESS PLAN PRESENTATION

The presentation starts with a title slide, which is normally projected on the screen while your audience is assembling and before you start your formal remarks.

Company Name/Logo

Name of Founder(s)
Contact Information of Founder(s)

Acknowledgement of Whom the
Presentation Is Being Made To

Date

Comments: This slide should be sharp and uncluttered. Make sure to include contact information for at least one of the founders. You should also personalize the presentation by putting the correct date on the cover slide and acknowledging to whom the plan is being presented.

Slide 1: Overview

- Brief explanation of your product or service
- Short explanation of the key points that will be conveyed in the presentation
- Short discussion of the potential positive outcomes (business, societal, financial) that will result from the launching of the business

---

Comments: This slide should give your audience an overview of your business and its potential. It's a good place to include a story, an anecdote, or a statistic that vividly illustrate why the business is important and why you're launching it. It you don't "hook" your listeners here, it's hard to regain their attention. Tailor your remarks specifically to your audience. If one fact about your business is particularly compelling, tell it here.

Slide 2: The Problem

- Explain the problem to be solved
  - What's the pain?
  - Why aren't customers satisfied with current solutions?
  - Will the problem get better or worse over time?
- Validate the problem via research
  - What do your potential customers think?
  - What do the experts say?
- How big is the problem?

Comments: It's always best to first talk about the problem (i.e., no fitness center available that's exclusively for people 50 years old and older), and then present your company (in the next slide) as the solution to the problem. You should validate your assertions via primary and secondary research. Primary research is vital. Prove to your audience that you've talked to potential customers, and they see the problem the same way you do. This is a good place to talk about the results of your feasibility analysis and concept tests. You can also cite industry experts or services such as Mintel and IBISWorld, but nothing is more convincing than your own data. Convey to your audience the size of the problem. The problem normally has to suggest a large market to get the interest of equity investors.

Slide 3: The Solution

- Present your business as the solution to the problem
  - Describe how your solution is distinctly different from others that are addressing the same problem
- Describe the degree to which your solution makes your customers lives richer or more efficient or effective
- Talk about how you'll erect barriers to entry to prevent others from quickly copying your solution

Comments: Present your business as the solution to the problem. Describe how your solution is better than others. For example, in Prime Adult Fitness's case, there are many all-purpose fitness centers that are starting to offer classes for older people, but Prime Adult Fitness will be the only center *exclusively* for older people. Talk about how much difference your business will make in the lives of your customers. Will your solution help your customers as little, a moderate amount, or a lot? You'll also need to address the imitation issue. How will you keep others from immediately duplicating what you're doing? This is where patents or other intellectual property may come into play. You may also benefit by capturing a strong first-mover advantage.

Slide 4: Opportunity and Target Market

- Articulate your specific target market
  - Talk about business and environmental trends that are providing your target market momentum
- Show, graphically if possible, the size of your target market, your projected sales (three years minimum), and your projected market share
  - Explain how you arrived at your sales figures
  - Be prepared to defend your numbers

Comments: Articulates your specific target market. Show graphically, if you think its necessary, how you segmented your market. Demonstrate, through your verbal remarks, that you are fully acquainted with the market and the behavior of its customers. Talk specifically about the trends that are providing your market momentum. Show (in dollars) the size of your target market, your projected sales, and your projected market share for at least three years. Graphs work best and break up the tedium of a primarily text-based presentation. Impress your audience by having a solid rationale to support your projected sales. Be prepared to defend your numbers.

Slide 5: Technology

- Talk about your technology, or unique aspects of your product or service, if appropriate
  - Don't talk in an overly technical manner
  - Make your descriptions easy to understand
- Show pictures or descriptions of your product or your product prototype
  - If applicable, bring a prototype to the presentation
- Talk about any intellectual property issues that are involved

Comments: This slide is optional but is normally included. You should talk about your technology or any unusual aspects of your product or service. Make sure to talk in layman's terms. Show a picture of your product or service (an artist's rendition may be sufficient), or a product prototype if applicable. If a working prototype of your product exists, bring it to the presentation. If you're a service business, like Prime Adult Fitness, a sample brochure or daily schedule of the events that will take place in your center is a form of a prototype. Talk about any intellectual property issues that are involved.

Slide 6: Competition

- Discuss your direct, indirect, and future competitors
- Show your competitive analysis grid
- Use the competitive analysis grid as a way to discuss the advantages you will have over your competitors
  - Talk about why you think your points of competitive advantage are sustainable
  - If your exit strategy is to be bought by one of your larger competitors, this is a good place to introduce the possibility

Comments: Lay out your competitive landscape. Don't diminish your credibility by understating the current or future competition. Display your competitive analysis grid, and use it to visually depict your points of competitive advantage. Talk about why you think your points of competitive advantage are sustainable. If your exit strategy is to be bought by one of your larger competitors, this is a good place to introduce the possibility. Show how your points of competitive advantage would benefit your potential acquirer.

Slide 7: Marketing and Sales

- Describe your overall marketing strategy
- Describe your pricing strategy
- Talk about your sales process
  - Explain what motivates people (companies) in your industry to buy
  - Explain how you'll make your customers aware of your product or service
  - Explain how you'll reach your customers
    - Describe whether you'll field your own sales force or will work through intermediaries

Comments: Begin by describing your overall marketing strategy. Describe your pricing strategy and whether you plan to feature cost-plus pricing or value-based pricing. Describe how your price(s) will compare to your competitors. Talk about your sales process, and walk your audience through how people will become aware of your product or service and how you'll sell it to them. If you plan to field your own sales force, talk about how your salespeople will be compensated. If you've administered a buying intentions survey or conducted other primary research regarding how people feel about your product, report the results here.

Slide 8: Management Team

- Describe your existing management team
  - Describe their backgrounds and expertise
  - Describe how their backgrounds and expertise are key to the success of your venture
  - Describe how the team works together
- Discuss the gaps in the management team and how you plan to fill them
- Briefly discuss your board of directors and/or board of advisors

Comments: As emphasized throughout this book, your audience will see your management team as a key element in the potential success of your new venture. Explain how the team came together and how their backgrounds and expertise are keys to the success of your firm. If you've put together a board of directors or a board of advisors, briefly mention the key individuals who are involved. Show the gaps in your team by displaying a skills profile, and explain how you'll fill the gaps. If, overall, you've been able to put together an impressive team (of employees and advisors), talk briefly about how you've been able to "sell" your vision for the firm to these individuals. If your audience sees that you've been able to get good people to commit to your firm as employees and advisors, they'll believe that you can sell your product to paying customers.

Slide 9: Financial Projections

- Show a summary of your income projections and your cash flow projections for the first three–five years
  - Condense the projections as appropriate to fit them onto a single slide
  - If the font appears to be too small, use an additional slide

Comments: Show a summary of your income projections and cash flow projections for the first three to five years. If the font seems too small, use an additional slide. Make sure to have the actual projections available if anyone wants to see more detail. Know your numbers cold. You shouldn't stumble or hesitate if asked about any number in the projections. Be prepared to explain the assumptions behind your numbers. Describe your projected return on sales in the context of industry norms.

Slide 10: Current Status

- Highlight the milestones achieved to data
- Describe how much money the founders, the management team, and any early investors have put into the firm
  - Describe how the money has been spent
- Describe the current ownership structure of the firm
- Describe the firm's form of business ownership (i.e., LLC, Subchapter S Corporation, C Corporation)

Comments: Describe the current status of your firm in the context of the milestones you've achieved. Describe how much money the founders, the management team, and any early investors have put into the firm. Talk about how the money has been spent. Investors, in particular, want to see evidence that you use money effectively. Don't diminish the value of your accomplishments. Talk about the current ownership structure of your firm (a graph works well for this), and describe your business's form of legal ownership.

Slide 11: Financing Sought

- Show a sources and uses of funds statement that leads you to the financing you seek
  - The sources and uses of funds statement should specify, to the extent possible, specifically how you'll use the funds
- Show the milestones you'll be able to accomplish after you receive the funding you're seeking

Comments: This slide lays out specifically how much financing you're seeking and how you'll use the money. Be prepared to talk about how much of your firm you're willing to give up if you're presenting to equity investors or the type of terms you're looking for if you're trying to obtain a bank loan. Show the milestones you'll be able to accomplish after you receive the funding you're requesting.

Slide 12: Summary

- Summarize the strongest points about your venture
- Summarize the strongest points about your team
- Discuss your exit strategy
- Solicit feedback
  - Set up a follow-up meeting if possible

Comments: Bring the presentation to a close. Summarize the strongest points (two to three maximum) about your venture and your team. Discuss your exit strategy. Solicit feedback if you're presenting to equity investors of bankers. If you're presenting in a business plan competition, thank the judges for their participation. Be ready to answer any questions about your new venture.

Chapter Summary

1. If your business plan piques the interest of an investor or banker, or you enter it into a business plan competition, you'll normally be asked to make a verbal presentation of the plan. On these occasions, you must be prepared to present the plan with confidence and poise.
2. Most of us do not routinely make verbal presentations, so careful planning and practice pay off.
3. The first set of issues to think about after you've been asked to make a verbal presentation of your business plan is how to prepare for the task and how to deliver an effective presentation. How you present yourself and the manner in which you interact with the people you will be presenting to makes as much difference as the plan itself.

4. You should make sure to know how much time you have to make your presentation and plan accordingly. The number one rule in making a presentation is to follow the rules.
5. You should dress appropriately for a presentation. If you're unsure what to wear, call the receptionist of the firm at which you'll be presenting and ask about attire. If that route isn't practical, it's always better to dress up, by wearing formal business attire, than it is to dress down.
6. It's important to practice your presentation. Many experienced entrepreneurs practice their presentations several times in front of colleagues and others to time the presentation and get feedback. It's also a good idea to watch other people present to get a sense of what works and what doesn't work.
7. A strong case can be made for involving as many of the members of your team as possible in a business plan presentation.
8. Your goal, during a business plan presentation, is to not only educate your audience about your idea but also to fire them up (to inspire).
9. An important component of putting together an effective business plan presentation is to determine the content to present. Obviously, you can't convey everything that's in a 25- to 35-page business plan in a 20- to 30-minute presentation. As a result, you have to focuses on the parts of the plan that are the most important to your audience.
10. The 12 slides in the mock business plan presentation in this chapter include overview, the problem, the solution, opportunity and target market, technology, competition, marketing and sales, management team, financial projections, current status, financing sought, and summary.

Review Questions

1. Why is it important to carefully prepare and plan for a business plan presentation?
2. What are the most important issues involved with preparing for a business plan presentation?
3. What is meant by the statement, "as you present your plan, your audience will not only be judging your plan, but they will also be judging you?"
4. Why is it important to know about the people you'll be presenting your business plan to?
5. Why is it important to practice your presentation?
6. What is the proper role of PowerPoint slides in a business plan presentation?
7. What are the positive aspects of involving as many of the members of a management team as possible in a business plan presentation?
8. What is meant by the phrase "death by PowerPoint?"
9. What is a reasonable number of PowerPoint slides to include in a 20- to 30-minute business plan presentation?
10. List the title of the slides included in the mock 12-slide business plan presentation included in this chapter.

Application Questions

1. You recently sat through a business plan presentation and were impressed by the research that founders included in the presentation to validate their points. They included cites from the *Wall Street Journal,* several trade magazines, Standard & Poor's NetAdvantage, Mintel, and the U.S. Census Bureau. As you were driving home, it struck you that although there was a lot of research to back up the business plan's claims, there wasn't a stitch of primary research reported. The founders were relying strictly on secondary research. You're wondering if this aspect of the plan should bother you. Should it?
2. Make a list of 10 mistakes that you could make in a business plan presentation. Next to each mistake, make a brief suggestion for how to avoid the mistake.
3. Sharon Peters, a friend of yours, asked you to sit in on a dry run of her business plan presentation. You know that Sharon is looking for $250,000 to launch her venture. At the end of the presentation, you ask Sharon why she never mentioned how much money she's looking for. She replied, "That's a point of negotiation. I don't want to disclose how much I'm looking for or how much of the company I'm willing to give up, until I know how interested someone is in my venture. Discuss the pluses and minuses of Sharon's approach.
4. You recently sat in on a business plan competition at a local university, and one presentation struck you as odd. It was a good presentation. All five members of the management team were present, but only one person did all the presenting. The other four members of the team never said a word, not even during the question and answer session. Speculate on why you think the presentation struck you as odd and the pluses and minuses of this approach to presenting.
5. A friend of yours showed you the slides she plans to use for her business plan presentation, and you noticed that the slides didn't include any financial information. You asked your friend about this omission, and she said, "financial statements are boring. No one wants to look at a bunch of financial statements in a business plan presentation." How would you respond to your friend's assertion?

Endnotes

1. D. DiResta, *Knockout Presentations* (Worcester, MA: Chandler House, 1998).
2. M. Kushner, *Presentations for Dummies* (Indianapolis, IN: 2004).
3. D. DiResta, *Knockout Presentations* (Worcester, MA: Chandler House, 1998).

Application Questions

NAME INDEX

SUBJECT INDEX